Cartographies of

Culture, politics, subjectivity and identity are highly contested in contemporary debates. This book throws light on these discussions by exploring the inter-relationships of 'race', gender, class, sexuality, ethnicity, generation and nationalism in different discourses, practices and political contexts.

Cartographies of Diaspora maps theoretical and political shifts in approaches to questions of 'difference' and 'diversity' by studying changes in gendered and racialised discourses and state practices over the last half-century. It uses both theoretical material and empirical research to record cultural and political responses. In doing so, it contextualises some of the major post-war debates within feminism, anti-racism and post-structuralism. It asks critical questions about the ways in which identities are constituted and contested.

This book provides an innovative theoretical framework for the study of 'difference', 'diversity' and 'commonalty' which links them to the analyses of 'diaspora', 'border' and 'location'. In relating these questions to contemporary migrations of people, capital and cultures, it offers fresh insights into thinking about late twentieth-century social and cultural formations. It will be essential reading for students of sociology, cultural studies, postcolonial studies, 'race' and ethnic studies, women's studies and anthropology. *Cartographies of Diaspora* will also appeal to teachers, community, youth and social workers.

Avtar Brah teaches at Birkbeck College, University of London.

Cartographies of Diaspora

Contesting identities

Avtar Brah

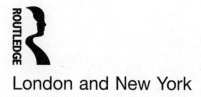

London and New York

First published 1996
by Routledge
11 New Fetter Lane, London EC4P 4EE

Simultaneously published in the USA and Canada
by Routledge
29 West 35th Street, New York, NY 10001

Typeset in Times by Routledge
Printed and bound in Great Britain by Redwood Books,
Trowbridge, Wiltshire

British Library Cataloguing in Publication Data
A catalogue record for this book is available from the British Library

Library of Congress Cataloguing in Publication Data
Brah, A.
Cartographies of diaspora: contesting identities/Avtar Brah.
p. cm. – (Gender, racism, ethnicity series)
Includes bibliographical references and index. 1. Asians–Great Britain–social
conditions. 2. Great Britain–Emigration and immigration. 3. Asia–Emigra-
tion and immigration. 4. Great Britain–Ethnic relations. 5. Group identity–
Great Britain. 6. Great Britain–Race relations. 7. Immigrants–Great Britain.
I. Title. II. Series.
DA125.A84B73   1997   96–2571
305.895'041–dc20   CIP

ISBN 0–415–12125–6 (hbk)
ISBN 0–415–12126–4 (pbk)

Ek Onkar Sat Nam

For my mother, Dhan K. Brah, and in the memory of my father, Bachan S. Brah, and my nephew, Harjinder (Bhola) Grewal

Contents

Acknowledgements

During the summer of 1993, Gail Lewis visited me in California where I was on sabbatical as a Rockefeller Research Fellow in the Center for Cultural Studies, University of California at Santa Cruz. The idea for this book crystallised in our conversations in Santa Cruz cafés. Without her encouragement and that of Catherine Hall, Ruth Frankenberg, Lata Mani, Pervaiz Nazir, Ann Phoenix and Nira Yuval-Davis, this book would never have been completed. I am grateful to them for their love, for critical dialogue, and careful comments on various parts of the text. Among colleagues and friends at Birkbeck College (including those who have now moved elsewhere), thanks are due to Laurel Brake, Josie Charlton, Annie Coombes, Barnor Hesse, Jane Hoy, Nell Keddie, Mary Kennedy, Jasbir Panesar, Marie Sangha, John Solomos and Debra Steinberg. We have shared some very good moments which make work a pleasure.

The last three chapters are the outcome of work started at the Center for Cultural Studies, University of California at Santa Cruz. It was a pleasure to have James Clifford, the then Director of the Center, as a colleague. Our conversations and the fortnightly seminars he organised were a major source of intellectual stimulus. It was invaluable to be part of a reading group on 'Discourse of Race' organised by the Feminist Studies Research Program at UC Santa Cruz. This was a friendly space to take ideas for a walk with Winnie Breiner, Carla Frecero, Helene Moglen, Dana Takagi, Lisa Rofel and Greta Slobin. My thanks also to the members of the reading group on diasporas for their helpful comments on the first draft of Chapter Eight: Gordon Bigelow, James Clifford, Susan Harding, Galen Joseph, Katie Stewart and Anna Tsing. I am grateful to Kum-Kum Bhavnani, Angela Y. Davis, Ruth Frankenberg, Lata Mani, Robert Meister and Ritu Meister for helping to make Santa Cruz feel a little more like home. Veronica Urban was kind enough to take the time to teach me to drive on the right hand side of the road. You have to live in Santa Cruz to appreciate the importance of having wheels! My time there was also a marvellous opportunity to catch up with four friends from my undergraduate days at the University of California at Davis. Thanks to Barbara Cohen, Sandy Larson, John Larson and Wilma Papadogianis for all they did for me.

I would like to thank the following for friendship: Sandra Acker, Madhu Anjali, Caroline Arewa, Reena Bhavnani, Hansa Chowdhama, Helen Crowley, Philomena Essed, Filomena Fernandez, Dorothy Griffiths, Sushila Khoot, Barbara Mayor, Robert Miles, Rehana Minhas, Rafhat Minhas, Rashida Punja, Parminder Vir, Annie Whitehead and Fiona Williams.

I wish to acknowledge a special intellectual debt to Stuart Hall. I have learnt a lot from critical dialogue with his work. Above all, I appreciate his generosity of spirit.

I am grateful to my family for their support over the years. Special thanks to Sareeta and Raj for bringing the sunshine! No words can fully express my debt to my parents. This book is dedicated to them with love and gratitude. It is also dedicated to the memory of my nephew, my sister's son, who, a year and a half ago, left us all too soon.

ACKNOWLEDGEMENT OF SOURCES

Some of the chapters which follow are revisions of material published previously. For permission to reprint, I would like to thank the following: the Open University for Chapter 1 which first appeared as 'The South Asians' in *Minority Experience*, Course E354, Block 3, Units 8–9, Milton Keynes: the Open University Press (1982); The British Sociological Association for Chapter 2 which was published as 'Unemployment and racism: Asian youth on the dole' in S. Allen, A. Waton, K. Purcell and S. Wood (eds) *The Experience of Unemployment*, London: Macmillan (1986); the Open University for Chapter 3 published as 'Women of South Asian origin in Britain' in P. Braham, A. Rattansi and R. Skellington (eds) *Racism and Anti-racism*, London: Sage (1992 [1987]); Jane Aaron and Sylvia Walby for 'Questions of difference and international feminism' in J. Aaron and S. Walby (eds) *Out of the Margins: Women's Studies in the Nineties*, London: The Falmer Press (1991); the Open University for 'Difference, diversity, and differentiation' in J. Donald and A. Rattansi (eds) *'Race', Culture, and Difference*, London: Sage

(1992); *New Community* for ' "Race" and "culture" in the gendering of labour markets: South Asian young Muslim women and the labour market' in *New Community* (1993) 19 (3): 441–58; and the *Feminist Review* for 'Re-framing Europe: en-gendered racisms, ethnicities and nationalisms in contemporary Western Europe' in *Feminist Review* No. 45, Autumn 1993.

Introduction

SITUATED IDENTITIES/DIASPORIC TRANSCRIPTIONS

What does it mean to think about the politics of diaspora in the present historical moment? Reflecting on this question made me acutely aware how my whole life has been marked by diasporic inscriptions. I have had 'homes' in four of the five continents – Asia, Africa, America, and now Europe. When does a place of residence become 'home'? This is something with which those for whom travel constitutes a form of migrancy are inevitably confronted at some stage in their lives. And, it is a question that is almost always enmeshed with politics, in the widest sense of the term.

I was born in the Panjab and I grew up in Uganda. This rather banal statement can also be 'read' as the historical entanglement of a multitude of biographies in the crucible of the British Empire. In this sense my own biography is also a reminder of the collective history of South Asians in what used to be known as 'British East Africa'. This history is underpinned by a series of episodes: indentured labour recruited from India by the British during the nineteenth century to build the railways; the twentieth-century migration of those, such as my parents, who followed in the wake of the folklore that painted Africa as a land of opportunity; the formation in East Africa – via the effects of colonial policy – of the 'colonial sandwich', with Europeans at the top, Asians in the middle, and Africans at the bottom; the restructuring of these hierarchies in complex ways during the period following Uganda's independence from colonial rule; the post-colonial political strife that resulted in the military coup which brought Idi Amin to power; the expulsion of Asians from Uganda by Amin; the devastation of civil war in Uganda; and, in the late

1990s, the emerging policy of Uganda's current president Musevni to encourage Uganda Asians – scattered around the globe – to return to Uganda. Hence, the issue of home, belonging, and identity is one that is perennially contested for people like me. But, as will become clearer in the penultimate chapter, it is no longer a settled issue – if ever it was – even for those who consider themselves secure in their own sense of belonging.

Awareness of the political import of *proclaiming* identity came to me relatively early. During the last year of high school I applied for a scholarship to study in the USA. After a selection process that involved my first encounter with the Scholastic Aptitude Test, a supposed 'ability indicator', I was called for an interview. Candidates were interviewed by an all-male panel that included representatives from various universities in the USA.

'Do you see yourself as African or Indian?' asked an American member of the panel.

He had used the term 'Indian' in the general sense that it was often used in East Africa to refer to all people of South Asian descent. The sub-continent had, of course, long since been partitioned into India and Pakistan – a parting gift of the British Raj.

At first this question struck me as somewhat absurd. Could he not see that I was *both*? Uganda was my home. I held a Ugandan passport. This is where I had spent all but the first five years of my life. The hours spent as a child combing the shamba at Naviwumbi; monitoring with incredible patience every detail of the metamorphosis of a pond of tadpoles into frogs; playing in the warm rain that would begin to beat down in huge bursts, quite out of the blue, and dry up just as suddenly; the aroma of the red soil after the first rain drops, and the sheer pleasure of climbing trees to pick mangoes or jamuns; the gentle murmur of the Nile as it springs out of Lake Victoria; journeys through the lush green forest lining the road from Jinja (my home town) to Kampala; the trials and tribulations, as well as the joys, of adolescence . . . all this and much more was part of my very being. But I had memories, too, of early childhood in the Panjab – the dazzling yellow fields of mustard, playing hide-and-seek in sugar-cane fields, sitting on a charpoy in the evening listening to fairy tales or ghost stories told by a family elder. Memories too of friends and family, including two sisters, left behind in India when we came to Uganda. I remember the childhood pain of displacement during my first years in Africa, mediated by my identification with my mother's acute longing for her daughters and her 'home' in India.

'I am a Ugandan of Indian descent,' I had replied. He seemed satisfied by my answer.

But, of course, he could not *see* that I could be both. The body in front of him was already inscribed within the gendered social relations of the colonial sandwich. I could not just 'be'. I had to *name an identity*, no matter that this naming rendered invisible all the other identities – of gender, caste, religion, linguistic group, generation . . . . The discourse of the interview was not concerned with these. Nor would my interlocutor have asked this question of someone who had 'looked African'. But, dear Goddess, what is an 'African look' or an 'Asian look'? Why could 'my look' not be a signifier of 'African-ness' in Uganda? After all, the white man from the USA was asking me about my identity and, surely, this could not be reduced to 'looks'? Yet I know now and knew then that 'looks' mattered a great deal within the colonial regimes of power. Looks mattered because of the history of the racialisation of 'looks'; they mattered because discourses about the body were crucial to the constitution of racisms. And racialised power operated in and through bodies. Moreover, racialised power configured into hierarchies, not simply between the dominant and subordinate categories of people, but also among them; that is, between the 'Indian' and the 'African' in this instance. In Chapter Five, I argue that such operations of power constitute modes of *differential racialisation*. In East Africa, as I discuss in Chapter One, such hierarchies were lubricated through the economic and political imperatives that shaped the colonial sandwich.

'Why do you wish to study in America, so far from home?' asked another white man?

Ah! So they *do* recognise that Uganda is my home, I thought to myself. But I knew, too, that the 'referent' of 'home' in the two questions was qualitatively different. The first question invokes 'home' in the form of a simultaneously floating and rooted signifier. It is an invocation of narratives of '*the* nation'. In racialised or nationalist discourses this signifier can become the basis of claims – in the proverbial Powellian sense – that a group settled 'in' a place is not necessarily 'of' it. Idi Amin asserted that people of Asian descent could not be 'of' Uganda, irrespective of how long they had lived there. In Britain, racialised discourses of the 'nation' continue to construct people of African descent and Asian descent, as well as certain other groups, as being outside the nation. In the former Yugoslavia such constructions of 'nation' have been the driving force behind the genocide known as 'ethnic cleansing'. In present day

India, the religious Right represents Muslims as being outside the 'nation'.

Implied in the second question, on the other hand, is an image of 'home' as the site of everyday lived experience. It is a discourse of locality, the place where feelings of rootedness ensue from the mundane and the unexpected of daily practice. Home here connotes our networks of family, kin, friends, colleagues and various other 'significant others'. It signifies the social and psychic geography of space that is experienced in terms of a neighbourhood or a home town. That is, a community 'imagined' in most part through daily encounter. This 'home' is a place with which we remain intimate even in moments of intense alienation from it. It is a sense of 'feeling at home'.

'I want to go to America to get qualifications so I can come back and help my country', I had replied, with the youthful patriotic pride of the post-colonial generation.

We believed in the narratives of progress, dreaming that we could make things better. I had not yet learned the downside of patriotism.

There it was! The idealistic me basking in the warm glow of what I saw as love for 'my country'. It is perhaps due to the memory of such moments that I have never found it unduly puzzling why ordinary folk like you and me could, if we did not continually interrogate such politics, get drawn into the nationalist imagination. At some stage in our life most, if not all, of us have had some considerable psychic investment in the idea of belonging to 'a people'. This need not necessarily be a problem in itself. What is at issue is the way in which the construct 'my people' is constituted and mobilised in and through economic, political, and cultural practices. When does the attachment to a community and a place, the sociality of everyday life world, become 'my country right or wrong'? When does the specificity of historical experience of a collectivity become *essentialised* into racism and nationalism? And how does gender figure in these markers of 'difference'? I address these questions explicitly in the last three chapters.

'Also, [I wish to go to America] because higher education is not all that easy to get if you are a girl', I had added.

'So your family is not supportive?' the white male academic from one of the USA universities offered.

'Oh, no! They are supportive. Especially my father. But it is just everything else.'

Terms such as 'patriarchal social relations' were not part of my vocabulary then, but this is what I had meant by 'everything else'. I was already an avid reader of Nanak Singh, a Panjabi novelist, of Amrita Pritam, who writes in Panjabi and Hindi, and of Sahir Ludhianvi, an Urdu poet, all of whom took issue with gender, caste, and class subordination. I was also fascinated by the feminist and anti-cleric perspective of the early eighteenth-century Panjabi Sufi poet Waris Shah, who used the romantic legend of 'Heer Ranjha' to articulate a powerful social critique. Such critique was also embedded in the writings of the Sikh Gurus, and I was strongly influenced by these. But I had found little of their vision in the practices of our local clerics, who often brushed aside my questions about such things with impatience and irritation. Needless to say, I became very uncomfortable with the formal institutions of organised religion. It is not a coincidence, therefore, that my desire to go 'so far away from home' was in part a flight from the restrictions of patriarchal relations as they obtained in Uganda at the time. But, of course, effects of social relations cannot be expunged that easily, for we carry their traces in our psyche. What is the relationship between *affect, psychic modalities, social relations*, and *politics*? This question underpins the whole of this text, but it is explicitly addressed in the last six chapters.

So it was that I went to California, and later to Wisconsin. To be an undergraduate at the University of California in the late sixties and early seventies was to be in the throes of USA student politics, although UC Davis, where I was enrolled, was a lukewarm version of the hotbed that UC Berkeley was. Nevertheless, it was not long before I was involved in demonstrations against the Vietnam war, the grape boycott organised by labour union activists led by Caesar Chavez, and anti-racist politics. The particular forms that such struggles assumed on campuses at this stage were many and varied. This was a period of the Civil Rights Movement, of Black Power, of the Student Non-violent Coordinating Committee, the Black Panther Party... It was the heyday of the Campaign for Nuclear Disarmament, of Flower Power, and the beginnings of 'Second Wave Feminism'.

Among the students who were being called up to join the army, a growing number were beginning to refuse the call to fight in Vietnam. Some of these 'draft dodgers', as they were likely to be called by their detractors, burnt their call-up papers at mass public rallies where anti-war singers such as Joan Baez sang their protest songs. Women were beginning to place the issue of sexual politics firmly on the agenda. It was a time when the slogans of 'Peace' and 'Love' were heard alongside the vibrant language of militancy. While 'hippies' handed out flowers, members of the Black Panther Party were adopting militant tactics against police brutality and other forms of political repression. Organisations such as the Weathermen (which, in fact, included women members) used methods of armed insurgency. I have a distinct memory of being woken up in the early hours of one morning in Madison, Wisconsin, by what seemed to be the first convulsions of an earthquake, and later finding out that one of the science departments on campus had been blown up by a group protesting against research which, in their view, was implicated in the growing might of the armaments industrial complex. There were rallies, demonstrations, marches, teach-ins, and love-ins. There was energy and optimism that the world could be changed for the better, even if many of us were incredibly naive about the inherent complexity and contradictions.

Much of what I learnt about inequality in the USA was not from university courses, which had little to say about the issues which the above social movements were throwing up, although a few individual professors did take up some of the concerns. I became very interested in understanding what the politics of figures such as Martin Luther King, Malcolm X, Angela Davis, the Soledad Brothers and Caesar Chavez were highlighting about American society. A Nigerian friend studying in Georgia introduced me to the history of racism in the Southern states of the USA. Attending UC Berkeley one summer, he found California 'liberal' in comparison to the South. And there was a sense in which he was right, not least because Berkeley then did lend itself to being read as the centre of radical politics. Yet one only had to go to Oakland or San Francisco to see the poverty in which large sections of black Californians lived. Soon, state violence against Black Power activists in California was to match that perpetrated anywhere else in the USA, and it had not been such a long time ago that the Watts district in Los Angeles had witnessed a major uprising of the poor and dispossessed. The sacking of Angela Davis, a young black professor, from her teaching post at the University of California by California's then Governor Ronald Reagan and the Regents of the University, because of her membership of the Communist Party, served to bring the issue of class politics to the fore, although the 'language' of class was not such a central theme in the vocabulary of student politics.

I found the allure of Flower Power also deeply attractive. My fellow students were advocating 'dropping out of the materialist' system, shouting anti-war slogans to the strains of 'We shall overcome', the signatory song of the Civil Rights Movement. I was impressed by their critical, questioning practice. Yet most of these students came from quite affluent backgrounds. There were not many black American students at Davis. Indeed, there were relatively few American 'students of colour', to use present day US terminology. This category was comprised mainly of we 'foreign' students, as we were then called. As I achieved greater familiarity with the issue of poverty in the inner cities of California, the question of 'dropping out' assumed a different meaning. The poor possessed little from which to 'drop out'. The gentle calls for love and peace of the 'flower children' began to sound affected and utopian – the growing-up pangs of a privileged post-war generation – although the idea of 'non-violent' forms of struggle continued to touch a deep chord in me. As a child I had grown up listening to anti-colonial songs from Indian movies of the post-war period. These songs could be heard on Ugandan radio years after the release of a particular movie. The history of the independence movement of India was not on the formal curriculum of our schools, nor indeed was the history of Uganda itself until after independence. Nevertheless, the power of oral history and the media meant that we got to know of the tactics of 'non-violence' used by Gandhi, and the militant strategies of figures such as Bhagat Singh. I had always been quite ambivalent about the relative merits of these strategies of political opposition. Now I was visited by the same ambivalence. I veered between the teachings of Martin Luther King, who, as I later found out, had been influenced by Gandhi, and the arguments against 'turning the other cheek' offered by followers of Malcolm X. It is a dilemma one still faces as one surveys the global conflicts of the 1990s.

My relationship to these political formations in the USA was inextricably entwined with my status as a 'foreign' student who 'looked Indian'. I was not categorised as 'Asian', for this descriptor was then reserved largely for Chinese and Japanese Americans. The highly publicised visits of the pop-band, the Beatles, to India in search of spiritual awakening had made Indian classical music and trans-cendental meditation quite 'chic' in the USA. This might have been one reason why South Asians on USA campuses were constructed as 'non-European others', largely through technologies of exoticism, although of course the USA's own historical relationship with global colonialism and imperialism could hardly be immaterial. As African students we were all constituted as non-Europeans, but students from Africa of South Asian descent were viewed differently from black Africans. The latter were, in turn, differentiated from black Amer-

icans. All this mattered. And not only to white Americans but equally
to black Americans. Once, when I was in Wisconsin, black American
students were planning a protest march. A group of us 'foreign'
students approached them saying that we would like to march with
them. We were told in no uncertain terms that this was their march,
and we could not join them, although we could show solidarity by
marching separately. Here was an important lesson for us. *The politics
of solidarity with another group is one thing, but the self-organising
political mobilisation of the group itself is quite another.* I was to learn
this lesson, from a different positionality, even more convincingly in
Britain.

I came to Britain (or 'Vilayat', as Britain is often called by Panjabi
or Urdu speakers in South Asia) for a short visit on my way back from
the USA to Uganda, and was made a stateless refugee by Idi Amin's
expulsion of South Asians from Uganda. Britain has since been my
country of 'permanent abode', to use the jargon of immigration law. I
was one of the luckier 'Ugandan Asians', in that I was already in
Britain at the time of Idi Amin's edict. This meant that I escaped the
experience of head-on racism which, as I discuss in Chapter One,
greeted this group of Ugandan refugees as they arrived in Britain.

Britain during the 1970s was in the throes of Left politics. There
had been major demonstrations against the Industrial Bill and the
1971 Immigration Act. Edward Heath's Conservative government
was brought down by the striking miners. Margaret Thatcher, the
then Minister of Education, was denounced by the Left in the slogan
'Margaret Thatcher, Milk Snatcher', for abolishing free milk for
children in schools. The Women's Liberation Movement was getting
under way and posing serious challenges to all manner of orthodoxies.
The formation of cartels by the oil producing countries of the Middle
East was beginning to give Western countries a taste of the same
medicine that they had been administering for centuries to the 'Third
World', and it was unleashing anti-Arab and Anti-Iranian racism in
its wake. Some of the major industrial strikes of the period were
mounted by Asian workers and were led by women: at Imperial
Typewriters, at Grunwicks and at Chix. The diminutive figure of Jaya
Ben Patel – erect, defiant, head held high – walking tall in front of a
cordon of towering policemen remains one of the most striking icons
of this 'post-colonial' moment in the heart of the metropolitan.

At the same time, young black people were mounting collective
struggles against racism and police harassment in London, Birmingham, Manchester, Nottingham and Bradford, to name just some of

the geographical locations. Campaigns against such inequities as the practice of 'search under suspicion' – the use by the police of the nineteenth-century 'SUS' law, initially designed to target the white working class but now singling out young blacks; the Prevention of Terrorism Act, directed against Irish people; immigration legislation; the prescribing of the drug Depo-Provera to working-class women, and especially black working-class women, as a means of differentially regulating sexualities; and many other practices of the state, as well as those within the realm of 'civil society', were constituting a variety of new political subjects. These politics were bringing together diverse groups of people in associative solidarity.

I began to look for my own political coordinates in the midst of this political flux. How was I to 'place' myself in Britain? Needless to say, this could not be a simple matter of fiat. Britain's imperial history had already 'situated' me. Within weeks of being in London I had been called a 'Paki'. I was so taken aback the first time I was called a racist name that I was struck silent. I now realised, in quite a different way from when I was expressing my solidarity with black Americans, what it felt like to be called a 'nigger'. I was no longer a 'foreign' student, a visitor on a temporary sojourn. Rather, I was now constituted within the discourse of 'Paki' as a racialised insider/outsider, a post-colonial subject constructed and marked by everyday practices at the heart of the metropolis. The discourse of 'Paki' echoed colonial encounters. But it was not a narrative about the 'natives out there', as it had been during the British Raj, but rather it signified the inferiorised Other right here at the core of the fountain head of 'Britishness'. I had arrived in Britain as a young adult – my sense of myself fairly secure. Yet I had been outraged, mortified and, most importantly, temporarily *silenced* by this racist onslaught. What might the impact of racism be upon young children? I had heard this question asked in the USA, but now my relationship to it had changed. All the children of the world implicated in this question had become part of my genealogy, and I was part of theirs. This is not to suggest that one cannot empathise with those whose experience one does not share. Nor that experience is a guarantor of some essential authenticity. But there is a qualitative difference when this changing fiction we call 'I' or 'Me' is directly *subjected* within specific discursive practices. This *experience* matters.

My use of the technologies of autobiographics in this introduction exposes the contradictions embodied in the production of identity. Throughout, I speak with the authority of 'I' and 'Me' as if 'I' am a pre-given 'reality', when the discussion shows how 'I' and 'me' have been changing all the time. On the other hand, my signature is possible precisely because there is a changing core that I recognise as me. I interrogate my own political biography also because it is so closely tied up with my intellectual labour. I do this especially as a means of highlighting the collective struggles that articulate the social movements of which I have been a part. The autobiographical mode is useful here as a disruptive device that *reveals* my narrative as an *interpretive retelling*, vulnerable to challenge from other interpretations as the vagaries or self-representations of an individual. But the credibility of this narrative of political moments and events is dependent far less upon the scribbling of an 'individual'; the 'individual' narrator does not unfold but is produced in the process of narration. Rather, the deeply invested self that speaks the events relies heavily upon the hope that its version will resonate with the meaning constructed by my various 'imagined communities'. My individual narration is meaningful primarily as collective re-memory.

CARTOGRAPHIES OF INTERSECTIONALITY

This text, then, is in part an inscription of the effects of my involvement with certain political projects. It writes them as much as it is written by them. These projects – feminism, anti-racism, socialist envisioning of democratic politics – have had a critical bearing on the intellectual and political configurations of our times. The chapters that follow explore, elaborate, or re-think the impact of such interventions in fashioning contemporary theoretical and political debate. The first three chapters were written during the 1980s, and the remaining six were written after 1990. They bear the imprint of the alliances as well as contestations between these political currents. Participation in these projects taught me the importance of understanding the intersections between 'race', gender, class, sexuality, ethnicity and so on, precisely because these relationships were rarely addressed together. To be simultaneously concerned about them was to lay oneself open to the charge of being 'divisive', or 'diluting the struggle'. Our attempts to raise these questions within academia were likely to be dismissed with sheer disdain by some of those who saw themselves as doyens of 'high theory'. But these contestations were at times highly productive, as, for example, the feminist debate around racism, analysed in Chapters Four and Five, demonstrates.

I have used the term 'experience' several times above. This book, in many ways, is an attempt to think through the opacity of experience; to understand the relationship between subjectivity and 'collective experience'. I argue, along with many others, that experience does not reflect a pre-given 'reality' but is the discursive effect of processes that construct what we call reality. But then, how do we think about the materiality of that which we call real? The insult and denigration implied in the word 'Paki' felt very real to me. And this is not merely an issue about my individual, personal sensitivities. It felt real, became part of my reality, precisely because its enunciation reiterated an inferiorised *collective* subject through me. That is to say, the power of the discourse was *performed*, was *exercised* through me, and, in other instances, through other 'Asians'. In the process, 'I' and 'We' were relationally articulated and constituted anew, both constructed as changing fictions in this as much as in a psychoanalytic sense. The invention of 'I' and 'We' through embodied living subjects means that these constructions are experienced as 'realities'. In the discursivity of socio-psychic space these fantasmic entities fuse and carry a powerful charge – and *very real* in this sense – as the power of the construct 'my people' testifies.

One aspect of 'experience' that the book analyses is that implicated in the constructions of the 'Asian' in Britain. Elements of this 'experience' are explored in the first three and the sixth chapter of this book. The point is not that every South Asian experienced Britain this way, but rather that these collective trajectories were important constitutive moments in the formation of the 'Asian' subject. I analyse the economic and social conditions marking Asian experience, highlighting the interplay of state policy, political and popular discourse, and a variety of other institutional practices in the construction of 'Asian' as 'post-colonial' other. Simultaneously, I emphasise some of the key moments in the collective struggles of the first three decades after World War II, addressing the specificity of political and cultural processes at different points – as, for instance, when a substantial proportion of Asian families were re-united in Britain, and the population was augmented by the arrival of Asians from East Africa. The issue of cultural identity was now politicised with a resonance different from the early phase of a predominantly male migration.

Levels of unemployment among racialised groups remain high, sometimes twice or three times the rate among the white population. My discussion in Chapter Two of how unemployment was experienced by young Asian men and women during the mid-1980s is a reminder of the enduring nature of this problem. There are several possible reasons which may, in part, account for the high rates of unemployment among specific Asian groups – for example, a high proportion of Asian workers have been employed in the generally contracting manufacturing sector; they are concentrated in industries and levels of skill that have been especially vulnerable to decline, especially in the context of the restructuring of the world economies; and Asian populations are concentrated in regions where unemployment levels have been the highest. However, by themselves, these factors do not provide adequate explanation for the disproportionately high level of Asian unemployment unless the effects of racism and racial discrimination on these populations are fully taken on board.

The study of the encounters of Muslim women of South Asian descent with the labour market in Britain of the 1990s, which forms the subject of Chapter Six, reiterates the intersectionality of racism, gender, generation and class as a *formative* dynamic within processes of the global, national, regional and local *restructuring* of labour markets. Here, I explore an analytic framework which interrogates aspects of my own earlier approach to understanding these relationships. Like many other researchers during the 1980s, I was working with the then commonly held distinctions between 'experience', 'culture' and 'structure', as separate but 'interacting' elements. However, by the time I came to study young Muslim women's narratives of the place of paid work in their life worlds, my thinking on these issues had undergone substantial revision. Not that the embeddedness of these narratives within changing contemporary economic, political and cultural conditions was in question. In this sense at least, Chapters Two and Six attempt to address a similar problem. Rather, it was a question of how best to understand what we mean by categories such as 'experience', 'culture', 'structure' or 'agency', and how best to understand the relationship between them. In Chapter Six I explore these questions through a focus on the construction of young women's labour, but the overall project is revisited in different ways in other chapters.

Asian women's positionality in post-war Britain is an important theme of this text. Historically, Asian women's gender has been the site of colonial debates about 'culture' and 'tradition'. These discursive formations were centrally implicated in mediating the structures of imperialism. Similar processes may be discernible in post-war Britain when racialised discourses of 'Asian family' and 'Asian cultural difference' are played out in the exercise of state power, as well as in popular culture. But, far from the 'passive victims' of racialised imagination, Asian women have been at the forefront of many and varied forms of political intervention, including workplace struggles, immigration campaigns, campaigns against racist attacks, activities around reproductive rights and sexual violence, education and welfare, and contestations around feminist theory and practice. My aim has been continually to deconstruct the idea of 'Asian woman', exposing it as a heterogeneous and contested category even as I analyse the practices of 'Asian women' as historically produced and embodied subjects.

My own politics as an Asian woman in Britain have been inextricably linked with the movement that mobilised around the political subject 'black'. This political subject has a linked, but also a different and distinctive, genealogy from the politics of black in the USA, as I discuss in Chapter Five. The British 'black' political subject emerged as a signifier of the entangled racialised colonial histories of 'black' settlers of African, Asian and Caribbean descent, affirming a politics of solidarity against a racism centred around colour. The silent text of 'non-whiteness' operating as a common thematic within this discourse – despite the differential racialisation of these groups – served to galvanise an otherwise heterogeneous set of people. The condensation of the white/non-white dichotomy constructed certain commonalties of experience as people confronted racist practices in such diverse arenas as employment, education, housing, media, health and social services. Such relations of equivalence created the conditions in which a new politics of solidarity became possible. Although 'black' crystallised around 'white/non-white', it subverted the logic of this binary. Moreover, by addressing a wide range of diasporic experiences in their local and global specificity, the project foregrounded the politics of transnationality.

Black feminism in Britain emerged in conversation with a number of political tendencies. It was partly formed around politics of the 'black', partly within the nexus of global class politics, while simultaneously articulating a constitutive moment within British feminism, and gay and lesbian politics. It interrogated these political formations even as it was a product of the relationality between them. As a heterogeneous and internally differentiated political formation – multiple, contradictory, wedged ambivalently and precariously between diverse sets of subject positions and subjectivities – it marked the possibilities of its own critique. Constituted primarily around the problematic of racialised gender, in the first instance, it later performatively defies confines of the very boundaries of its constitution. It enacts, interrogates, and transgresses the limits of its own heterogeneity. I discuss issues raised by the politics of 'black' and black feminism in Chapter Five. *Inter alia*, I argue that categories such as 'black feminism' and 'white feminism' are best seen as non-essentialist, historically contingent, relational discursive practices, rather than as fixed sets of positionalities. They are both inside and outside each other's field of articulation.

The political history of Britain during the 1970s and 1980s cannot be understood without addressing the significance of 'black' as one of the most enabling, albeit highly contested and contesting, new Left political subjects of the period. Its decline in the late 1980s must form part of any serious assessment of Left politics in the 1990s and beyond. In my view, this eclipse does not herald an end to the type of politics that had initially galvanised the energies of so many of us. Rather, it is an indictment of certain forms of totalising impulses, intolerance, elitism and vanguardisms of various kinds which became a significant tendency within all Left politics. It signifies the limits of politics constituted around the assertion of the 'primacy' of one axis of differentiation over all others as *the* motor force of history. It is a sign of the inability of the Left seriously to engage with what I have described as the 'politics of intersectionality' in the concluding chapters of this book.

Of course, the need to explore the interconnections between different axes of differentiation and social divisions is not a once-for-all-time task. There are those who would find my call for the study of intersectionality as 'old-hat', the recitation of a 'mantra'. I would remind them that mantras are designed for repetition precisely because each repetitive act is expected to construct new meanings. Mantric enunciation is an act of transformation, not ossification. It is my hope that this text will introduce some fresh ways of thinking about these interrelationships.

One of the key organising themes through which such concerns are examined here is that of 'difference'. This is a construct that has underpinned various different arenas of theoretical and political debate: feminism, class analysis, anti-racism, gay and lesbian politics, psychoanalysis, post-structuralism, and so on. What are the processes in and through which ideas about 'difference' acquire meaning and social significance? What is the relationship between the social and the psychic in the play of 'difference'? How do we construct politics which do not reduce everything to the economy of the same and which do not essentialise differences? Engaging with such questions has led me to suggest four ways in which 'difference' might be conceptualised: as experience; as social relation; as subjectivity; and as identity. I had offered these distinctions in a schematic form in an earlier version of the work which constitutes Chapter Five. The present Chapter Five is a revised and extended version, one in which I elaborate how I understand these four dimensions, and the relation between and across them.

How 'difference' is constructed is central to discourses of nation, nationalism, racism, and ethnicity. Chapter Seven analyses these concepts *as gendered phenomena*. This emphasis is important, as much of the literature produced outside of feminist studies treats these categories in gender-neutral terms. In discussing the concept of racism I clarify the grounds on which given phenomena could be distinguished specifically as racism. I argue against positions that conceptualise racism through simple bipolarities of negativity and positivity, superiority and inferiority, or inclusion and exclusion. While acknowledging the processes of exploitation, inferiorisation and exclusion that underlie histories of racism I point to the ways in which racism simultaneously inhabits spaces of deep ambivalence, admiration, envy and desire. The changing forms of a plurality of racisms are analysed with the aid of the concept of *differential racialisation*. This idea is an important component of my conceptual framework, interrogating binarised forms of thinking, and exploring how different racialised groups are positioned differentially *vis-à-vis* one another.

In trying to understand how notions of 'difference' are figured in discourses of 'race' and 'nation', the question of ethnicity is indispensable. The text explores how ethnicity may be mobilised in a given racism or nationalism. But the purchase of the concept of ethnicity is not reducible to its potential cooptation within these phenomena. What is the enabling potential of non-essentialist conceptions of ethnicity? What is the relationship between ethnicity, culture and identity? What is to be learned from the debate on 'new ethnicities'? How do the 'local' and the 'global' figure in the formation of transnational identities? What is the import of the present 'transnational moment'? Such questions led me to address contemporary discourses of diaspora. As I noted at the beginning of this introduction, the biography of persons like myself is centrally marked by diasporic experiences. But what is specific about contemporary diasporas? Is the term 'diaspora' primarily a descriptive category, or can it also be understood as an analytic category?

As a result of such preoccupations, I started to consider the overlap and resonance of the term 'diaspora' with meanings of words such as migrant, immigrant, expatriate, refugee, guest worker and exile. But surely, diaspora cannot replace these categories? Yet it does clearly displace them. But how? I began to think of the concept of diaspora as an interpretive frame for analysing the economic, political and cultural modalities of historically specific forms of migrancy. The concept began to suggest fruitful ways of examining the relationality of these migrancies across fields of social relations, subjectivity and identity. Chapter Eight is the result of these deliberations. Among other things, I suggest that the concept of diaspora offers a critique of discourses of fixed origins while taking account of a homing desire, as distinct from a desire for a 'homeland'. This distinction is important, not least because not all diasporas sustain an ideology of 'return'. The chapter also examines the problematic of the 'indigene' subject position and its precarious relationship to 'nativist' discourses. Inscribed within the idea of diaspora is the notion of border. I conceptualise border as a political construct as well as an analytical category, and explore some of the strengths and limitations of the idea of 'border theory'. The discussion is also allied to the theme of 'location', analysing the contradictions of and between diasporic location and dislocation.

The concepts of *diaspora*, *border*, and *politics of location* are immanent, and together they mark conceptual connections for historicised analyses of contemporary trans/national movements of people, information, cultures, commodities and capital. This site of immanence inaugurates a new concept, namely *diaspora space*. This concept is central to my analytical frame, and is elaborated in the concluding chapters. It is a central argument of this text that 'diaspora space' (as distinct from the concept of diaspora) is 'inhabited' not only by diasporic subjects but equally by those who are constructed and represented as 'indigenous'. As such, the concept of *diaspora space* foregrounds the entanglement of genealogies of dispersion with those of 'staying put'. It is linked to the earlier discussion of 'difference', and, as I explain in Chapter Nine, is underpinned by refiguration of the discourses of 'multi' (in a variety of arenas and forms), 'commonalty' and 'universalism'. This text, then, is about the multiaxiality of power. It is a cartography of the politics of intersectionality.

Chapter 1

Constructions of 'the Asian' in post-war Britain
Culture, politics and identity in the pre-Thatcher years

The presence of Asians and other blacks in this country has added a new dimension to discussions about 'culture', 'politics' and 'identity'. However, before proceeding to examine the specific issues highlighted by the arrival of Britain's ex-colonial subjects, it is worth having a brief look at concepts of 'culture' and 'identity'. This may be done by raising some basic questions. For instance, what do we mean by these terms? What aspects of our social reality do we refer to when we invoke these terms? Within the same society, do all groups have the same 'culture'? What does the phrase 'clash of cultures' signify? What is meant when 'identity' is foregrounded in these discussions? I begin by considering some of these questions with a view to contexualising the shifting debates surrounding culture and identity at the beginning of the 1980s. This chapter is an attempt to identify how, and in what ways, the various debates acquired saliency during the different phases of black settlement in Britain after World War II. It examines how 'the Asian' was constructed in different discourses, policies, and practices; and how these constructions were appropriated or contested by the political agency of Asian subjects. *Inter alia*, I am also concerned in this chapter to map the general parameters of inter- and intra-generational continuity and change.

THE CONCEPTS OF CULTURE AND IDENTITY

If we stop and think about our own 'culture', what type of images come to mind? We will probably find ourselves thinking about the whole spectrum of experiences, modes of thinking, feeling and behaving; about the values, norms, customs and traditions of the social group(s) to which we feel we belong. Thus, if we happen to be, say, working-class Geordies, the images invoked by the above question will be different from those we would have if we were middle class and lived in Surrey.

There is no single 'right' definition of the term 'culture'. For example, Kroeber and Kluckhohn (1952) identified some 164 definitions of 'culture'. In broad terms, culture may be viewed as the symbolic construction of the vast array of a social group's life experiences. Culture is the embodiment, the chronicle of a group's history. Since the group histories of different sections of society differ in important ways, their 'cultures' are correspondingly different. Further, group histories are inextricably linked with the material conditions of society, so that cultures are marked by the social and economic conditions of a group at the various stages of its history. Cultures are never static: they evolve through history. That is why the process of cultural reproduction is, in part, a process of cultural transformation. At any given time a group will inherit certain cultural institutions and traditions, but its acts of reiteration or repudiation, its everyday interactions and its ritual practices will serve to select, modify, and transform these institutions.

On the other hand, while the cultures of different groups in society will differ considerably, it is also the case that, in so far as at a particular point in history all groups are subjected to certain common socio-political and economic forces, they will share some aspects of one another's cultures. For example, in the South Asian sub-continent where the capitalist mode of production coexists with the pre-capitalist mode, power and privilege devolve along the lines of class, caste and gender, with religion underpinning a complex intersection between the three. This context is echoed in the differing social norms, values, customs and lifestyles of the different castes, classes and religious groups. But, at the same time, since these groups also share some aspects of their history, there are some cultural patterns which are common to them all. This common denominator serves to distinguish the South Asian cultural systems from the cultures of those peoples whose historical experience has been significantly different. Similarly, the British social formation may be seen to include four relatively distinct national cultures (namely English, Irish, Scottish and Welsh), each of which is in turn differentiated according to class and gender. Yet there are a number of features which these 'British' cultures have in common.

There is a tendency to regard the social processes which produce cultural differences as being unproblematic. Cultural differences, however, are rarely the outcome of a simple process of differentiation.

Rather, this 'difference' is constituted within the interstices of socio-political and economic relations. Just as social groups with differential access to wealth, power and privilege are ranked in relation to one another, so are their cultures. The esteemed values and modes of behaviour in society are most likely to be those which are associated with the dominant groups in society. For example, when people speak of a person as being 'cultured', they almost invariably seem to refer to certain cultural traits which are supposedly characteristic of persons from high echelons of society. This is not to suggest, however, that the cultures of the subordinate groups become totally subjugated, or that they do not exercise any influence on the dominant cultures. In fact, as Clarke and his co-workers point out:

> [It] does not mean that there is only one set of ideas or cultural forms in a society. There will be more than one tendency at work within the dominant ideas of society. Groups or classes which do not stand at the apex of power, nevertheless find ways of expressing and realising in their culture their subordinate position and experience.... But the structures and meanings which most adequately reflect the position and interests of the most powerful class – however complex it is internally – will stand, in relation to all the others, as a *dominant* social-cultural order. The dominant culture represents itself as *the* culture. It tries to define and contain all other cultures within its inclusive range. Its views of the world, unless challenged, will stand as the most natural, all-embracing, universal culture. Other cultural configurations will not only be subordinate to this dominant order: they will enter into struggle with it, seek to modify, negotiate, resist or even overthrow its reign – its *hegemony*. . . .
>
> The dominant culture of a complex society is never a homo-geneous structure. It is layered, reflecting different interests within the dominant class (e.g. an aristocratic versus a bourgeois out-look), containing different traces from the past (e.g. religious ideas within a largely secular culture), as well as emergent elements in the present. Subordinate cultures will not always be in open conflict with it. They may, for long periods, coexist with it, negotiate the spaces and gaps in it, make inroads into it.
>
> (Clarke *et al.* 1977:12)

Discussions about culture, therefore, must be understood within the context of the power relations among different groups. Accordingly, analyses of South Asian cultural formations in Britain must be informed by an understanding of the colonial history (cf. Dutt 1901; Palme Dutt 1940; Mukherjee 1974 [1955]; Jenks 1963; Ram Gopal 1963; Hutchins 1967; Greenberger 1969; Kiernan 1969; Morris *et al.* 1969; Bagchi 1973; Patnaik 1975; and Nazir 1981), as well as the power hierarchies which currently characterise the British social formation.

The idea of identity, like that of culture, is singularly elusive. We speak of 'this' identity and 'that' identity. We know from our everyday experience that what we call 'me' or 'I' is not the same in every situation; that we are changing from day to day. Yet there is something we 'recognise' in ourselves and in others which we call 'me' and 'you' and 'them'. In other words, we are all constantly changing but this *changing illusion* is precisely what we *see* as real and concrete about ourselves and others. And this *seeing* is both a social and a psychological process. Identity then is an enigma which, by its very nature, defies a precise definition.

Two analyses of the concept to have exercised some considerable influence during the past decade and a half have been provided by Erikson (1968) and Berger and Luckman (1971). Erikson (1968) uses the following phrases to convey its meaning: 'a *subjective sense* of an *invigorating sameness and continuity*' (p. 19); 'a unity of *personal* and *cultural* identity rooted in an ancient people's fate' (p. 20); 'a process "located" *in the core of the individual* and yet also *in the core of his* [*sic*] communal culture, a process which establishes, in fact, the identity of those two identities' (p. 22). For Erikson, the process of identity formation is 'for the most part unconscious except where inner conditions and outer circumstances combine to aggravate a painful, or elated, "identity-consciousness"' (p. 23). He insists that 'identity is never "established" as an "achievement" in the sense of a personality armour, or of anything static and unchangeable' (p. 24).

These themes are echoed in the formulations of Berger and Luckman. The key premise underlying their thesis is that 'reality' is socially constructed. They argue that, during the course of everyday life, a person is conscious of the world as consisting of 'multiple realities', but among them 'there is one that presents itself as the reality *par excellence*. This is the reality of everyday life' (Berger and Luckman 1971: 35). This 'reality' of everyday life is shared with others through common sets of meanings. The world is not experienced by everyone in exactly the same way, however; nor is it experienced by the same person in the same way all the time. But there are connecting threads running through these 'multi-realities', which provides an individual with an on-going sense of self.

Identity, then, is simultaneously subjective and social, and is constituted in and through culture. Indeed, culture and identity are inextricably linked concepts. In the sections which follow I am concerned to identify how, and in what ways: a notion of 'Asian culture and identity' became a major subject of political and cultural debate in Britain; this debate panned out over the different phases of post-war South Asian settlement; South Asian groups appropriated or resisted the meaning of these representations; and the everyday life of Asian people articulated with these discourses. The chapter is divided into three parts, dealing with: the experience of arrival and finding one's bearings during the 1950s and early 1960s; the settlement phase of the 1960s and the early 1970s; and the period of the 1970s and the first two years of the 1980s when young Asians born in Britain started to make their presence felt.

COMING TO 'VILAYAT' (1950s TO EARLY 1960s)

Britain experienced severe labour shortages during the post-World War II period of economic expansion. At the same time, having been systematically exploited during the colonial period, Britain's ex-colonies faced a future of poverty. They had a large labour force, but insufficient means to make this labour productive (Sivanandan 1976). Migration of labour from the ex-colonies to the metropolis during the 1950s was thus largely a direct result of the history of colonialism and imperialism of the previous centuries. If once the colonies had been a source of cheap raw materials, now they became a source of cheap labour.

The South Asians who came during the 1950s were part of this broader movement of labour migrations in Europe. Almost all the jobs available to them were those which the white workers did not want. In the main these were unskilled jobs involving unsociable hours of work, poor working conditions and low wages. Hence, Asian workers came to occupy some of the lowest rungs of the British employment hierarchy. Additionally, as ex-colonial subjects, they belonged to a group whose country was once ruled by Britain. From the beginning, therefore, the encounter between Asians and the white population was circumscribed by colonial precedents. As Zubaida points out:

These cognitive structures (beliefs, stereotype and 'common-sense' knowledge) in terms of which people in Britain experience coloured [sic] minorities must be profoundly imbued with accumulations of colonial experience. The beliefs and stereotypes acquired and disseminated by generations of working-class soldiers and middle-class administrators in the colonies are available to our contemporaries. Many of these cognitions are derogatory, some are patronizing, a few are favourable, but there is one theme underlying all of them: the inferiority and servility of 'native' populations. In this respect, immigrant communities from the ex-colonies are not entirely new to the British people. At times when the economic and political conditions are conducive to increased tensions between the communities, the more negative elements of these cognitions are aroused and modified.

(Zubaida 1970:4)

Partly by virtue of the location of their jobs and partly because they needed cheap housing, the 'immigrants' tended to settle in the rundown parts of working-class areas. Housing shortages, inadequate social services, high levels of unemployment and poor educational facilities were common features of these areas long before the arrival of the 'immigrants'. In the minds of the local residents, however, these problems gradually became associated with the presence of 'immigrants'. The 'immigrant', rather than the social institutions and social policies responsible for the problems of what later came to be described as 'inner-city' areas, became the object of their resentment. This resentment was reflected in the negative constructions of the 'immigrant'. As was the case during the British Raj, it was Asian cultural practices which first came under attack. According to the stereotype, the Asian was an undesirable who 'smelled of curry', was 'dirty', wore 'funny clothes', lived 'packed like sardines in a room', practised 'strange religions', and so forth (Brah 1979).

As the number of Asian and other black children in schools increased, many white parents began to demand that the local schools restrict their intake. In response, a number of local authorities began to introduce quotas for the proportion of black pupils permitted to enrol in a particular school. The excess numbers were 'bussed' to schools outside these areas. For example, in October 1963, white parents in Southall lobbied Sir Edward Boyle, then Minister of Education, during his visit to a local school. Following this meeting, and within the same year, a policy of dispersal was adopted by the

Southall Education Committee, although it did not become the policy of the Department of Education and Science until June 1965 (Ealing International Friendship Council 1968; Department of Education and Science 1965).

At the same time, the Government came under pressure to restrict black immigration. In Parliament the campaign was initiated as early as 1952 by Cyril Osborne, Conservative MP for Louth. In the period 1952–7 his campaign was conducted largely in the House of Commons and the Press and, although for a variety of reasons it met with little success, there are indications that 'many members of the cabinet shared popular concern about coloured immigration and were not in principle opposed to the introduction of controls' (Layton-Henry 1980: 54); see also Moore (1975) and Sivanandan (1976). Black resistance against racial harassment in Nottingham and Notting Hill in 1958 served to bring the issue of 'race' to the forefront. Simultaneously, pressure began to mount from the local authorities to restrict black immigration. After 1955, Cyril Osborne was joined in his campaign by fellow MPs Norman Pannel (Kirkdale) and Martin Lindsey (Solihull). The campaign attracted white support at the grassroots level, and local disaffection and resentment was further fed through active anti-black campaigning by the fascist fringe (Moore 1975). The Government capitulated by introducing the Commonwealth Immigrants Act of 1962. Thus, even during this phase of economic expansion, Asians and other blacks felt less than welcome in their new country of residence.

The liberal opinion of the time (and this included sections of academic, professional and political opinion) also saw the question of 'race relations' primarily in terms of cultural differences. It was likely to subscribe, either implicitly or explicitly, to the general preoccupation of the period with notions such as the 'assimilation of coloured minorities'. The problem tended to be couched primarily in terms of 'helping the immigrant to adjust to the host society', despite the fact that sections of the 'host society' were acting in rather an un-host-like fashion towards the new arrivals. To those who subscribed to the assimilation model, the Asian represented the epitome of the outsider, 'the alien' whose culture constituted an antithesis of the 'British way of life'. The assimilationist was likely to predict that future generations of Asians would abandon what the assimilationist deemed to be their 'archaic cultures' in favour of a 'Western lifestyle'.

During the early phase of migration there was an underrepresentation of women among the Asian population, as the majority of Asian men had come initially without female relatives. They came primarily with the idea of accumulating sufficient savings and then returning home. They were prepared to work long, arduous shifts in order to make up for very low basic wages. Many lived in all-male households. Their busy working schedules left little time for any meaningful participation in the social or political life of the locality in which they lived. In view of the antipathy shown towards them by many of the white residents, it is doubtful if such participation would in any case have been feasible.

A majority of the migrants at this stage had rural origins, and belonged mainly to the peasant proprietor class. Their new role as industrial workers demanded many adjustments and adaptations. For instance, their working schedules were now governed by the clock, which marked the beginning and the end of a particular shift, rather than by the seasons. Overnight, a villager from the sub-continent arriving at Heathrow would be faced with the requirements of an urban, industrial society. The innumerable adjustments which this migrant had to make in day-to-day life often went unnoticed by the media or the white population, who were likely to characterise such a person as 'culturally encapsulated' – as if 'culture' was something entirely separate from lived experience. In general the migrants faced up to their new circumstances with stoicism and a pragmatic attitude. Sikh men, for instance, found that it was easier to find jobs if they took their turbans off, and many did so. Since there was no formal banning of the turban, the Sikhs did not as yet perceive this covert discrimination as an attack on their religious practices. When the direct challenge came in 1959, and a Sikh was banned from wearing a turban at work, the issue became a political one and the Sikhs launched several campaigns in order to retain the right to wear turbans at their places of work (Beetham 1970).

In these early stages, questions of cultural identity as a political issue did not loom large in the minds of the Asians. The early migrants were quite secure in their sense of themselves, rooted as it was in the social milieu from which they originated. Social norms derived from this milieu were the main reference point. But, as their children began to attend local schools, the parents became attuned to the possible influence of 'gore lok' (whites) on their children.

In the main, Asian parents were initially quite favourably disposed towards Western education. During colonialism, acquisition of a Western education had represented an important means of social mobility. In the contemporary world, Western countries continue to play a dominant role in the international social and economic order. Consequently, Western education remains a coveted possession in the 'Third World'. It is not surprising, therefore, that the early Asian immigrants, including those with middle-class backgrounds, held the British education system in great esteem. Educational qualifications acquired in Britain, they assumed, would enable their offspring to get better jobs than those which they had themselves. At this stage, most parents were unfamiliar with the history of the educational disadvantage suffered by the white working classes in the localities where they themselves had now come to settle. The correlation between class and educational inequality was not fully established in their minds. Their disquiet was centred primarily around issues such as the strongly Christian ethos of school assemblies. Some parents were disconcerted by the requirements of the compulsory school uniform which stipulated that girls must wear skirts. Such parents were likely to regard the wearing of skirts as not in keeping with the norms of 'modesty', but, as yet, they rarely translated this discontent into public protest. Nevertheless, a collective concern about the potential undermining of Asian lifestyles under the influence of the British educational system was by now beginning to take shape.

By the early 1960s the anti-immigration campaigns, 'bussing' of Asian children to schools outside the areas in which they lived, discrimination in housing and employment, and the experience of being subjected to racial abuse came to constitute significant facets of the day-to-day social experience of Asians in Britain. Issues of cultural identity now began to assume importance, and strategies designed to foster positive cultural identities amongst the young came to be seriously considered.

A HOME AWAY FROM HOME (1960s TO EARLY 1970s)

When the 'assimilation' model was shown to be generally unacceptable to large sections of the black communities, while at the same time evidence of racial discrimination against them kept mounting (see, for instance, Daniel 1968), liberal rhetoric adopted a new terminology. In a frequently quoted speech delivered in 1966, Roy Jenkins, the then Home Secretary, argued against the notion of 'assimilation' but in favour of 'integration'. He said that the latter should be viewed, not as a 'flattening process of assimilation but as equal opportunity, accompanied by cultural diversity, in an atmosphere of mutual trust' (Jenkins 1966: 4).

On the face of it, this statement seems reasonable and fair, but its underlying assumptions warrant examination. First, this view of integration seems to imply that equality of opportunity for the different segments of British society was already in existence at the time when the migrants first began to arrive, and hence the difficulties facing the newcomers could be overcome quite straightforwardly by the introduction of a social policy which would place the migrant on the same footing as the native. Yet, as is well known, material wealth, power and privilege are differentially distributed among different sections of British society. Second, to speak of 'cultural diversity' in an 'atmosphere of mutual trust', without reference to the socio-economic and political factors which sustain social inequality and give rise to intolerance, is to explain away racism merely in terms of human failing. It is perhaps not surprising, therefore, that while this definition of integration came to be accepted as conventional wisdom by many bodies, welfare agencies and individuals active in the 'race relations' field, racism has continued to grow.

The liberal sentiment paved the way for the emergence of the so-called 'race relations industry' which included the Community Relations Commission (later reconstituted to form the Commission for Racial Equality), the Race Relations Board, locally-based community relations councils, the Institute of Race Relations (which underwent radical change in its structure and political orientation in 1972), the Runnymede Trust, the Research Unit on Ethnic Relations sponsored by the Social Science Research Council, and community relations sections of church and other organisations. The work of these organisations, which contributed to the effort that led to the enactment of anti-discrimination legislation, should be set against the simultaneous entrenchment of racism in stricter immigration controls. The race relations legislation of the 1960s proved to be so ineffective that it had to be replaced by the 1976 Race Relations Act. The 1968 Immigration Act, on the other hand, was far more successful in meeting its primary objective of reducing black immigration. It removed the right of entry of British passport holders unless they had a 'substantial connection' with the UK – i.e. unless at least one parent or grandparent of the applicant was born in Britain. In other words, the overwhelming majority of black people – who, it might be argued, have had quite a substantial connection with this country through the Empire – were now excluded because they could not claim to have grandparents who were born here. The 1971 Immigration Act was even more restrictive.

A non-patrial Commonwealth citizen could no longer enter the UK (other than as a temporary visitor) unless she or he had a work permit for a specific job with a specific employer. Initially the person would be admitted for a year, and permission might be renewed at the discretion of the Home Secretary. Dependants would be admitted for the duration of the work permit only. The Act also extended the power of deportation (Moore 1975).

The Immigration Acts were preceded by extensive anti-immigration lobbying. A highly distorted but pervasive mythology about the presence of black people in this country came into currency: blacks were here to sponge off the state; were running down inner-city areas; were receiving priority in housing and other services; their presence was making Britain over-crowded and, unless controlled, their numbers would increase beyond an acceptable proportion (which was never defined); their children were holding British pupils back in their studies, and so on.

Each one of the above claims has, of course, been contradicted by evidence gathered by some of the most respected data-collecting bodies, but their collective influence has proved difficult to dislodge from the popular imagination. The media's treatment of 'race' issues remained at worst biased and at best ambivalent (cf. Hartman and Husband 1974; Husband 1975). Asian cultural specificities were often represented as wanting against certain unspecified Western standards which, implicitly if not always explicitly, were held up as being superior. Politicians such as Enoch Powell, being fully aware of the potency of cultural symbolism, made speeches which consistently used metaphors that evoked images of the Asian as the archetypal 'alien'. The practice of 'Paki bashing' (an epithet naming the violence perpetrated against South Asians in this period) reached its peak during the late 1960s. The education system and the welfare system were likely to characterise almost any difficulty facing Asians as the result of 'cultural problems'. In other words, during the 1960s the focus shifted away from 'the problems facing the immigrant' and, instead, *Asians and other black people came to be seen as themselves constituting a 'problem'.*

It is against this background that the initial intent to 'return' began to recede as a priority and the Asians started to make emotional and financial investments in a long-term stay in Britain. The 1950s for them had been a period of finding their bearings in a new country. The 1960s was the decade during which a large number of families were reunited. Asian businesses sprang up to meet their special needs in terms of food products, clothing, entertainment, etc. Lifecycle rituals and religious festivals could now be celebrated with greater pomp and ceremony. Older patterns of family life were modified to adjust to the exigencies of the new situation. Neolocal residence, for instance, became fairly typical, partly because not all members of the extended family lived in Britain, but equally because the houses were often too small to accommodate any but the immediate family. Similarly, women who might hitherto have been unfamiliar with wage-labour now started to take up employment on a substantial scale. This became a necessity, due, in large part, to the increasing expense of buying and furnishing houses, meeting the continually rising cost of living, and maintaining the essential obligations towards the extended family. In time, these changes were to initiate important restructuring of the sphere of gender relations.

The 1960s witnessed the first industrial disputes involving a predominantly Asian workforce. When they first arrived, the Asian migrants tended to be unfamiliar with their basic labour rights. They worked under extremely unfavourable conditions, but, for the most part, were unaware that they might try to improve these through the trade union system. As knowledge about the system grew, trade union branches were formed in a number of factories which relied almost entirely on immigrant labour. In 1963, for instance, the Indian Workers Association helped launch a campaign to unionise Asian workers at Woolfe's rubber factory in Southall. An overwhelming majority of the membership of the Indian Workers Association at this stage consisted of manual workers employed in nearby factories. According to Marsh (1967), village-kin and friendship networks were made full use of in an effort to convince Asian workers of the need to join the unions. Meetings would be held in people's homes and sometimes Asian holy books would be brought in to solemnise and underscore the commitment to workers' unity on the shop floor. It is interesting to note the ways in which these cultural resources were mobilised in order to address their new circumstances as industrial workers. Unity as an ethnic group and ties of communal loyalty were as important in this context as the bonds of labour.

Having become organised, these workers went on strike in 1964 and again in 1965. These earliest strikes highlighted not only the nature of the conflict between white management and black workers but also the ambivalent attitude of the unions towards black membership. The complexity of the intersections between 'race' and class was amply demonstrated by these events, as it was in the disputes which later followed in other parts of the country (see, for instance, Marsh 1967; Moore 1975). Asians were now beginning to react against their subordinate position as workers from the ex-colonies. Their activism drew on the political cultures of both their country of origin and Britain. A number of community activists of this period, many of whom were university graduates, were later to leave their factory jobs and set up in businesses, or take up employment in some aspect of the expanding 'race relations industry'.

As we have already seen, by now the notion of 'cultural diversity' had caught the imagination of the liberal segments of British opinion. Community Relations Councils were formed in areas of high 'immigrant' concentrations in order to 'promote friendship and harmony' between blacks and whites. These organisations were predominantly run by middle-class whites. Among other activities, they organised 'cultural evenings' to which everyone in the community would be invited. But the type of Asian who could socialise with ease in these situations was typically one who could speak English. A number of these English-speaking Asians would be coopted as members of the executive committees of these councils. Many of them later became spokespersons for their respective communities and were often referred to as the 'leaders' of these communities.

In contrast, contact between the Asians in manual occupations and the white population was generally limited to the workplace. In so far as Asians were likely to be employed in unskilled jobs which white workers did not now need or wish to do, they would occupy a very low position in the occupational hierarchy. As ex-colonial subjects, Asian workers could be regarded as inferior even by unskilled white workers. There were few opportunities for these groups to engage in meaningful cultural exchange, although workplace cultures did provide an arena where friendly or antagonistic relations could be played out. Many Asians did not speak English but racism was often a bigger barrier than language. This is not to deny, however, that individual Asians and whites might form strong and binding attachments. Indeed, in an earlier piece of work, I gave examples of such individuals and households who seemed able to communicate happily, either through non-verbal signs, forms of creolised English, or through children (Brah 1979).

Asians, on their part, did not necessarily use Western criteria to measure their own status. They might be industrial workers in this country but many came from comparatively well-off, land-owning peasant families. The social hierarchies according to which they were most likely to rank themselves were the ones internal to Asian cultural formations, although, of course, the processes leading to the restructuring of these hierarchies were already under way. The prohibition against certain castes eating together, for example, could not be maintained in British workplace canteens. This is not to suggest that caste became irrelevant in Britain. Indeed, as communal life became more established, caste associations proliferated with the effect that caste became reinscribed in the British context. But the point is that caste in Britain is not an exact replica of caste in India; rather, British-based configurations of caste have their own specific features. In any case, even in India caste is a highly differentiated, heterogeneous, variable and contested institution.

The emergence of the 'East African Asian'

The mid-1960s witnessed the augmentation of South Asian populations in Britain by new arrivals from East Africa. Although South Asian traders and administrators were to be found in East Africa long before the advent of the British in that region, South Asian migration to the area in significantly large numbers resulted largely from the policies of the colonial government in pre-partition India (Ghai and Ghai 1970). As part of this policy, Indians were recruited during the late nineteenth century as 'indentured labour' in order to build the East African railways. The practice of indenturing labour (a system of contract labour which constituted a form of semi-slavery), predominantly using Indian and Chinese workers, was adopted in much of the British Empire, and carried on for a number of years after its formal abolition in 1916 (Tinker 1977). In East Africa, illegal indenture persisted until 1922. When it ended, most Indians returned to India, but some of the labourers stayed on after their contracts expired and took to petty trades because the colonial government would not permit them to buy land. Subsequently, as new opportunities began to open up, 'voluntary' migration from India was set in train. The primary thrust of the colonial policy was to restrict the activities of the Africans to the agricultural economy and those of the Indians to petty trade and commerce, at the same time maintaining both groups subordinate to the white settlers with large plantations or dairy farms, and to the metropolitan bourgeoisie. The substance of this policy is encapsulted in the following comment from Captain Lugard:

Being unaffected by the climate, much cheaper than Europeans, and in closer touch with the daily lives of the natives than it is possible for a white man [sic] to be, they [the Asians] would form an admirable connecting link (under the close supervision of British officers), their status being nearly on par with the natives, while their interests are entirely dependent on the Europeans. As they would establish themselves permanently, with their families, in the country, they would have a personal interest in it.

(Quoted in Mamdani 1976: 71)

This policy was crucial to the processes of class formation in East Africa. With their activities confined largely to retail trade and middle-level clerical and administrative posts in the civil service, South Asians came to constitute the middle layer of the 'colonial sandwich', occupying a position below the white colonist but above black Africans. The South Asian commercial bourgeoisie consisted of a mere handful of families, and it remained subordinate to metropolitan capital. A substantial number of South Asians were employed in enterprises owned by other South Asians, with whom their relationship was mediated through caste and kinship ties. Since the South Asians (and, up until Independence, also the Africans) were excluded from structures of governance, they had no political base in the colonial state and little political clout to deploy in situations of crisis. Political power remained in the hands of the British until its transfer at Independence to the Africans.

To be the middle layer in the colonial sandwich meant that a substantial number of Asian households led a lifestyle that was comparatively more affluent than that of the overwhelming majority of Africans, and substantially less affluent than that of the Europeans. This is not to suggest, however, that the 'middle layer' was a uniform configuration. Indeed, there was considerable differentiation of income and wealth amongst South Asian groups and, given the absence of socialised welfare, it was not uncommon for many Asian households to be living in conditions of considerable hardship and poverty. That is, a significant proportion of the Asians were quite poor and a small section were wealthy. But, since even the richest families had been wealthy for only one or two generations, social distinctions arising from sharply distinctive lifestyles and institutionalised forms of social distance had not yet congealed in rigid forms. Religious, linguistic, regional and caste differences, although retaining their importance in matters of marriage, did not form barriers to social mixing. For example, at the time of Diwali, the Hindu festival, Sikhs and Muslims alike would take part in the non-religious aspects of the celebrations, such as the firework displays. Similarly, the sports tournaments, organised by the mosques or the gurdwaras as part of the events to celebrate Eid and the Gurpurbs respectively, would include participants from the various Asian communities.

Despite the partition of India in 1947 which resulted in the creation of Pakistan, most Asians continued to refer to themselves as 'Indian', save, perhaps, in times of severe political conflict as when India and Pakistan were engaged in war during 1965. A collective identity was maintained *vis-à-vis* the European on the one hand and the African on the other. A number of communal differences and divisions amongst Asians were normally (though not entirely) submerged in this shared identity and, over a period of time, the lifestyles and attitudes of the diverse Asian groups settled in Africa developed common features. Of course, there was a sense in which 'cultural difference' continued to be constructed in terms of the regional differentiations prevailing in South Asia: Panjabi, Gujerati, and so on. But such 'difference' would be cut across by East African-based axes of differentiation. In sports, for example, several identities would simultaneously come into play: one was a Kenyan–Panjabi hockey player, or a Ugandan–Gujerati cricket player, and so on. Religion was construed less as a signifier of 'culture' than one of 'belief'. The construction of this distinction marked an intersubjective space for non-antagonistic identification among different South Asian groups.

Vocabulary drawn from Swahili became an integral component of the South Asian languages spoken in East Africa. Popular culture was another major site for cultural syncretism. Radio, cinema and (from the 1960s onwards) television exercised immense influence in this respect. Many Asian teenagers in Africa idolised Western pop-singers as much as the playback singers or the film stars of Indian movies. The East African musical form 'Hi Life' was another interconnecting strand of cultural fusions. This cultural creolisation was crucial to the constitution of East African Asian identity. It was not without its contradictions, for such creolisation was also one of the crucial sites for the mediation of the social hierarchy *vis-à-vis* Africans and Europeans.

The state institutions, together with the education system, were also critical as primary vehicles of 'Western' influence. It is worth noting that the education system remained segregated until independence from colonial rule. The medium of instruction was mainly English, and both the 'O' and 'A' level examination papers were set and marked in Britain. There was very little about Africa itself in these curricula, although Africa stalked every nook and cranny of the mind. The power and authority of 'the European' seemed distant and aloof to both Asians and Africans. As Captain Lugard had hoped, colonialism did succeed in carving a context in which, 'much cheaper than the Europeans, and in closer touch with the daily lives of the natives', the Asians did indeed 'form an admirable connecting link' (Mamdani 1976). This closer contact meant that the social relationship between Asians and Africans was simultaneously more intimate and passionate in its affect and affection as much as in its antagonistic ramifications. It was not surprising, therefore, that when post-Independence East Africa witnessed intense struggles and shifts in alliances between different segments of the local populations, these conflicts emerged in the idiom of either 'tribalism' – i.e. conflict between different African ethnic groups – or antagonism against the 'wamayindi' (Asians). However, the political management of these conflicts differed in Kenya, Tanganyika, and Uganda.

East African Asians in Britain differ from those from the South Asian sub-continent in several respects. First, they are mainly, though not exclusively, of urban background. Second, in contrast to the sub-continental migrants amongst whom the Panjabis constituted the largest single linguistic group, the East Africans were predominantly Gujeratis. Third, as a group, they had comprised the largest component of the emerging middle classes of East Africa. However, while they might be described as being middle class, they were culturally markedly different from the longer-established middle classes of the South Asian sub-continent. In the main, Asians from East Africa are the descendants of immigrants to East Africa who had rural backgrounds, and most of them continued to maintain relatively close links with their kin in the sub-continent. Thus, Asian cultures constituted in East Africa were characterised by traces of this rural influence, evident especially in lifecycle rituals, in regional dialects, and in cuisine. But, above all, these new cultures were *East African Asian*, constituted in the capillaries and sinews of the economic and social-life world of Asians in East Africa.

When Kenya, Uganda and Tanganyika achieved independence in the early 1960s, South Asians living there were offered the choice of British citizenship, which evidently included the right to enter and settle in the United Kingdom. When this news reached Britain, a strong anti-immigration lobby grew around the issue of the right of entry for South Asians from East Africa, and resulted in the introduction of the Immigration Act of 1968. So effective was the anti-immigration lobby that the Bill passed through the House of Commons and the House of Lords and received Royal Assent in *two days*. The 1968 Act institutionalised racial discrimination in law by removing the right of entry of British passport holders to Britain unless they had at least one parent or grandparent born here. At a stroke, thousands of Asians in East Africa became stateless, and families were torn apart. In 1972, Idi Amin, the then President of Uganda, expelled all Asians from Uganda, irrespective of whether or not they were Ugandan citizens. The Amin edict resulted in a new dispersal of South Asians to various parts of the globe, but most notably to Britain, Canada, and South Asia.

Apart from the tragedy of being uprooted, Ugandan Asians were faced with racism as soon as they set foot in Britain. According to government policy they were to avoid settling in areas of 'high' Asian concentration. In order to disperse them, Britain was divided into 'red' and 'green' zones. The 'red' zones were those where the size of Asian populations was deemed to be already 'too high' and hence they were designated as out of bounds for Ugandan Asian refugees. The green zones, on the other hand, were defined as places where the Asian population was non-existent or so low that a slight rise in their numbers would be 'tolerated'. Thus, many Asian families found themselves flung to remote parts of Britain, without communal channels of support. In Uganda, they were used to a life of daily contact with relatives, neighbours and friends – visiting them in the home; chatting on the streets; congregating in parks and public spaces (in my home town of Jinja, a favourite spot was the pier on Lake Victoria and the banks of the Nile), and in temples, mosques and churches. A large part of daily activity was conducted outdoors. The comparatively regimented life of an advanced capitalist society, with its individualistic ethos of privacy, together with the cold and grey of the proverbial British weather, did not make for a welcoming scenario. At first the refugee response was to withdraw into themselves. The early experience of isolation led to depression and despondency, particularly amongst the older members of households. But the spirit was not broken, and communal networks were soon revived through letters, telephone calls and visits to fellow Ugandans living in other parts of Britain. Once these links were established, the refugees deployed their own initiative and, in defiance of government policy, moved to 'red' zones, which offered greater security and a sense of familiarity and belonging.

The expulsion from Uganda did not make a major impact on the material circumstances of the very rich Ugandan refugees. There is no doubt that they had suffered massive losses in their business activities. But their investments were not confined to Uganda, so the likes of the Madhvanis and the Mehtas simply moved their operations elsewhere. Similarly, the more prosperous sections of the petty bourgeoisie also had some savings transferred abroad. They, too, were able to establish themselves relatively quickly. But the majority of the refugees – the small shopkeepers with all their capital tied up in Uganda, the salaried professionals and the workers – had lost everything and had to start from scratch. Every member of the family of working age had to find employment. Although some women had helped run family enter- prises in Uganda, and others had held professional jobs in fields such as medicine and teaching, the great majority were unused to paid work outside the home. But now, most women who could find a job took one. Living in rented accommodation, and paying high rents for property of poor quality, the refugees gave high priorty to buying their own houses. People worked long hours and saved every penny in order to obtain a mortgage on a house.

With the exception of Asians from Uganda who came to Britain as refugees, a majority of the Asians from Africa were able to transfer their savings and other movable assets to Britain when they left Africa. Those who possessed the necessary entrepreneurial skills and capital set up in business; others sought employment in the professional fields; but a great majority became employed in the factories as semi-skilled or unskilled workers. For this sector of the Asians from Africa, migration involved considerable downward social mobility. Like other labour migrants, they found themselves engaged in low-status, poorly paid jobs. Racial discrimination on the shop floor was fairly common, taking the form of limited opportu- nities for in-service training and promotion, different rates for the same job, the nature of the tasks allocated to them in the production process, and verbal racial abuse. Coming as they did from a comparatively privileged position in Africa, the processes of prole- tarianisation brought the status contradictions between their pre- vious and current social positions into sharp relief. Their discontent was marked by some of the best known industrial disputes involving Asians, such as Mansfield Hosiery, Imperial Typewriters and Grunwicks. Kinship and other communal networks were mobilised in order to provide both moral and financial help. Financial assistance became critical because, in some cases, the local unions

refused to make the strikes official and thereby deprived the workers
of strike pay.

By the early 1970s, Asians from the sub-continent too had come to
accept that their stay in this country was unlikely to be temporary.
Once a family had been reunited, and financial investment made in a
house or a business, the 'myth of return' would become largely
accepted as such, and attention was directed much more towards life
in Britain. The thrift and economy of the earlier years tended to be
replaced by the same consumerism that was prevalent in Britain at
large.

Asian parents were becoming increasingly aware that the ethnocentric nature of the educational curriculum and racialised practices
in schools and other educational institutions could seriously undermine their children's intellectual aspirations and sense of belonging.
The issue of cultural identity now became crucial. Many parents
began to make a conscious effort, albeit an unsystematic one, to teach
their children about their background and history. Temples, mosques
and gurdwaras began to offer classes in religious instruction and
mother-tongue teaching. The notion of self-help, which gained
currency in the 1970s, was born of the efforts made by the black
communities across the country to provide the type of information,
advice, support and education to the members of their communities
which the official agencies were either unable or unwilling to provide.
These initiatives ranged across the social, medical, educational and
welfare fields. With the continuing erosion of even the veneer of
liberalism which had previously accompanied public discussion of
'race relations', Asians were compelled to acknowledge that, in order
to safeguard their interests, they would need to organise against forces
which could potentially undermine their group identity. If they were
being construed and treated as a 'problem', it was incumbent upon
them to challenge this conception. The form in which the new mood
was articulated varied according to whether you were a 'community
leader' accompanying a deputation to the Home Office, an unskilled
worker in a factory, or a young person who had just left school. But, in
all cases, there was an emerging rejection and defiance of the processes
of subordination. The onset of the 1970s thus heralded a new stage in
Asian reaction and response to life in Britain.

HERE TO STAY (MID-1970s TO EARLY 1980s)

During the 1970s, Britain witnessed a deepening of the economic recession on the one hand, and racial conflict on the other. As we have already seen, racial antipathy was not absent even during the period of the economic boom, but the recession helped to create a fertile ground for the rejuvenation of fascist organisations which openly admit to having racist policies. These groups capitalise on the frustrated energies and hopes of the white working class, especially those of the youth. In their recruitment campaigns they consistently make scapegoats of the 'immigrants' or the 'Jews' for the state of the economic crisis. In the style of Enoch Powell and others of his persuasion, these right-wing organisations raise the spectre of the supposed threat to the British way of life posed by 'immigrants with alien cultures' (Nugent and King 1979; Taylor 1979; Troyna 1982).

The 'anti-immigration' and 'alien culture' theme found reverbera-tions in a pre-election speech of Margaret Thatcher. During a television interview in January 1978, she pledged that, if elected, her party would 'finally see an end to immigration'. She plumbed the depths of fear of a defensive identity when she suggested that the British way of life needed special protection, for 'this country might be swamped by people with a different culture'. It is worth noting that these comments were made at a time when, due to the enforcement of the 1971 Immigration Act, primary immigration had virtually ceased. The argument therefore was not about numbers. The speech was calculated to act as a vote-catching device. It is a commentary on the centrality of 'race' in British politics that such a subject should prove an effective means of soliciting votes. It is a device regularly deployed by politicians. When the 'mainstream' politicians resort to using language which has the ring of that of the extreme right-wing groups, the rhetoric and the political position of the latter acquires increasing credibility and respectability.

When elected, the Government kept its promise to do everything in its power further to reduce immigration. However, the only immi-grants who could enter after the enforcement of the 1971 Act (apart from the small proportion who still qualified for a visa on the grounds that their skills were in very short supply) were the dependants or fiancés of those already settled here, and special categories of UK passport holders such as those in Hong Kong. The state dealt with the case of the latter by excluding their entry through the 1981 British Nationality Act, and changes were introduced in the immigration rules which were designed to end the arrival of the apparently small number of people who entered as fiancés. The new Immigration Rules came into effect during 1980, and were mainly directed at South Asians. Their imposition was justified on the grounds that the 'arranged marriage system' supposedly constituted a 'never-ending flow of primary immigration'. The allegation, never substantiated, was that there was a widespread abuse of this cultural practice by Asians. This piece of legislation openly discriminates against groups who subscribe to 'arranged marriage'; in particular it targets young Asian women. It has come under attack from various sources as being both sexist and racist. For instance, David Steele, the leader of the Liberal Party, told Parliament:

> I can understand the air of embarrassment that always surrounds the Minister of State and the Home Secretary when we debate this subject. The reason for that embarrassment is that, while the Minister of State may say that the rules are not racialist in intent, they are certainly racialist in effect. Moreover, some Conservative Back Benchers intend them to be racialist in intent as well. . . . May we be told how many people will be prevented from coming into this country as a result of these miserable regulations? . . . The best estimates that I have been able to get have been between 2,000 and 3,000. We are going through all this paraphernalia of introducing rules which I believe are thoroughly repugnant, and of causing an uncertain degree of suffering to families of those already settled here in respect of their elderly people, their fiancés, their husbands and their children.
>
> (*Hansard*, House of Commons 1979–80, Vol. 980, columns 1032–4)

It is worth noting the way in which the proponents of the rules selected a cultural issue, namely arranged marriage, and exploited it to their own advantage, with the result that Asian women resident in Britain came to be denied the right to settle in Britain with a partner from abroad. The example illustrates how a cultural practice may become racialised and serve as a means of social control. It is also important to note that this legislation is only concerned with heterosexual relationships; the immigration law does not recognise gay and lesbian relations, thereby exercising *de facto* discrimination.

How did Asians experience the decade of the 1970s and the dawn of the 1980s? They witnessed a further entrenchment of institutionalised racism, particularly in the form of immigration laws and the British

Nationality Act. Reports of harassment at the hands of the immigration service were widespread. There were cases of Asian women arriving in Britain being subjected to 'virginity tests', and of Asian children undergoing x-ray examinations in order to establish their age. Asian marriages involving a fiancé from the sub-continent were likely to be subjected to acutely embarrassing forms of surveillance for the first year. A number of factories and other workplaces with an Asian workforce were raided by the police and the immigration service in search of alleged illegal entrants and overstayers. Despite widespread criticism of these raids, which led to a review of these procedures by the Home Secretary in 1980, the practice continues. People suspected of immigration offences were required to prove their innocence, reversing the normal principle which underlies other criminal investigations. In addition, magistrates were empowered to issue 'open' warrants to the police without the names of specific individuals on them (State Research 1981).

A number of well-publicised deportation cases (e.g. that of Nasira Begum, who was served a deportation order when she divorced her husband who held British citizenship) and other types of immigration cases (e.g. that of Anwar Ditta, a British-born Asian woman who was refused permission to bring her children from Pakistan to live with her in Britain until a massive campaign was mounted and a current affairs television programme, using the technique of 'DNA fingerprinting', demonstrated that the children were indeed hers and her spouse's, and not some distant kin that they were trying to pass off as their own for the purpose of 'illegal' entry into Britain) have further highlighted the many and different ways in which the immigration laws operate against Asians settled in Britain.

Discrimination in employment continued. As the recession deepened, Asians' jobs were among the most vulnerable, and the unemployment rates in areas of high Asian concentration rose quite dramatically. Racist attacks remained on the increase, and this period witnessed the murder on the streets of several Asians, including Gurdip Singh Chaggar and Altab Ali. According to a report in the *New Statesman* (24 July 1981), a Home Office minister announced in Parliament that, during 1980, in the Metropolitan Police District alone there had been 2,426 violent attacks on Asians compared with 2,075 in 1979 and 1,865 in 1977.

I pointed out earlier that, during the early phase of settlement, both middle-class and working-class Asian parents showed considerable enthusiasm for the British education system and wanted their children to succeed at school. Educational opinion at that time tended to favour the notion that bilingualism hindered the progress of Asian children, and that one of the primary educational priorities must be to 'integrate' children. Some Asian parents were influenced by this view and tried to use English with their children. This practice was adopted most eagerly by middle-class parents who, in any case, were the group that was best able to speak English. By using English at home, these parents wished also to differentiate themselves from their counterparts from the villages. However, the political scene of the late 1960s and the 1970s soon brought home to these parents that, even if their children were fluent in English and held good educational qualifications, their life-chances in Britain would, most likely, still be shaped by their position as children of black colonial immigrants. Asian communities, together with other black communities, had to confront the possible effects of racism in education on attainment levels, self-image, and the identity of black children. There were two main responses to this situation. First, politically active parents, community activists and some of the 'leaders' formed part of the lobby which was seeking to effect changes in educational and other social policies. Second, the communities undertook to promote initiatives of their own, such as the provision of supplementary education involving the teaching of Asian languages and religious instruction, and the setting up of welfare centres offering advice on a wide variety of topics. This type of provision owes its existence to the combined efforts of religious, political and other community organisations as well as to the hard work of committed individuals. Of course, to the extent that a part of this provision is organised on a religious and communal basis, it tends to perpetuate certain types of cleavage among Asian groups. Nonetheless, this self-help has been a cornerstone of Asian people's sense of self-determination and independence.

'Second-generation' or Asian–British?

The 1970s also witnessed the emergence of the first generation of young Asians with a formal education acquired mainly, if not entirely, in British schools. The media, professional and political opinion and popular imagination all tend to construct Asian youth predominantly as the object of 'culture clash'. It is argued that a young Asian growing up in Britain is exposed to *two cultures*, one at home and the other at school, and, as a result, the young person experiences stress and identity conflicts. This argument is problematic on several counts.

First, to posit a notion of two cultures is to suggest that there is only one 'British' and one 'Asian' culture. Yet, as we have already noted, there are some significant differences in the upper-, middle- and working-class cultures of Britain, with each further differentiated according to region and gender. Similarly, 'Asian cultures' are differentiated according to class, caste, region, religion and gender. Therefore, theoretically at least, there would seem to be as many possibilities of intra-ethnic as of inter-ethnic 'clashes of culture'. To think in terms of a simple bipolar cleavage, then, is quite untenable.

Second, the emphasis on 'culture clash' disavows the possibility of cultural interaction and fusion. There is no *a priori* reason to suppose that cultural encounters will invariably entail conflict. Conflict may or may not ensue and, instead, cultural symbiosis, improvisation, and innovation may emerge as a far more probable scenario. Indeed, even conflict cannot be seen as an absence of these dynamic processes of cultural synthesis and transformation. Moreover, conflict is often a sign of the power relations underpinning cultural hierarchies rather than of 'culture clash' *per se*.

Third, there seems to be an implicit assumption in much of this debate that cultural transmigration is a one-way traffic. Hence, the centuries of cultural contact and mutual influence between 'Asian' and British' cultural forms during the pre-colonial and colonial period, as well as since political independence, is rarely acknowledged. Indeed, India's earliest cultural and commercial links with 'Europe' extend back to the Greek and Roman times when the western hemisphere was not yet known as 'Europe' and Greece and Rome freely acknowledged their indebtedness to the East and to Africa (Hiro 1971). Hence, indirectly Britain has carried the imprint of Asia, Africa, and the Middle East for at least two millennia. In comparison, British colonial rule over India lasted just over a century and a half, until 1947. The point is that inter-cultural travel across the globe is an ancient phenomenon, and Britain is constituted out of these multifarious influences. The more recent, postwar, cultural interactions and reconfigurations within Britain have their own historically specific features, but the influence remains irreducibly multidirectional.

Fourth, the caricature invoked by terms such as 'between two cultures', 'culture clash', and 'identity conflict', which portrays young Asians as disoriented, confused and atomised individuals, is not supported by the evidence. There are many and varied influences that impact differently upon different young Asians, which makes for very heterogeneous and variable outcomes. This is not to deny that *some* young Asians do indeed experience conflicts, and that *some* aspects of this dissonance could well be associated with specific cultural practices. The problem arises when this explanation becomes a central paradigm for addressing young Asian people's experiences. Moreover, while emotional and psychic distress warrants sympathetic attention, the supposed 'cultural conflict' cannot be assumed to be the sole underlying contributory factor. The question of 'identity conflict' is a very complex one which cannot be reduced to any single determinant. Racism, gender, class, the specific trajectory of an individual biography, for instance, are no less relevant to understanding processes of identity formation. In any case, there is no single 'identity' that each and every young Asian avows (Brah 1978, 1979).

Another variation on the theme of 'cultural clash' comes into play when uncertainties of lifecycle transitions are explained primarily by attributing them to the effects of 'inter-generational' conflict. The argument is presented along the lines that young Asians growing up in Britain internalise 'Western' values which are at variance with the 'traditional' world view of their parents; and in the process of emulating 'Western' forms of behaviour, youth comes into conflict with the parental generation. Undoubtedly, the *potential* for conflict may well be there, especially when the early years of parents and their children are separated not only in time but also by country, so that the two age groups are exposed to differing cultural and political influences during their formative years. For instance, I have already shown that the process of migration has involved a major change in social position and this change has been experienced in different ways by the two generations. Nevertheless, inter-generational *difference* should not be conflated with *conflict*. The emergence of conflict cannot be predicted in advance, not least because generational relationship might easily have been negotiated and managed in such a way so as to favour understanding and shared perspectives. The parental age group may not always be as inflexible as is sometimes assumed. The great majority of post-war Asian immigrants were themselves quite young and impressionable when they first migrated to this country. They too have been subjected to new influences. That is to say that they are not always oblivious to the cross-pressures which bear upon their children.

In my own study (Brah 1979), the great majority of Asian parents interviewed expressed sympathy towards the predicament of young Asians growing up in Britain, although certain areas of experience of the young people were sometimes outside the range of experience of their parents. Equally, the young Asians seemed to understand, if not always to agree with, the constraints which were binding upon the parents. There was considerable overlap in the attitudes, norms, and values of the two age groups. Indeed, the incidence of 'conflict' was no higher than amongst white young people (attending the same schools as the Asians) and their parents. There were many similarities between Asians and whites as to the type of issue that was likely to produce agreement or disagreement among members of a household. There can be a variety of intersecting factors which may help generate solidarity rather than conflict between age groups. These include: the subtle cultural meanings we learn to associate from childhood with particular relationships, events, forms of behaviour, and social perspectives; the psychic investments in emotionally charged bonds with family and relations; the security derived from a sense of belonging to a community; and the shared experience by both parents and children of their structural position in society.

At this point it may be helpful to make a distinction between 'age group' and 'generation'. Age group is a category that delineates a vertical relationship between subjects at a specific stage of a lifecycle (e.g. adolescents and their middle-aged parents), whereas 'generation' is a unit of analysis articulating a horizontal relationship between cohorts. As a conceptual category, 'generation' is indexed and calibrated in relation to large units of historical time (Manneheim 1952; Eisenstadt 1971). The discourses examined above operate mainly at the level of age group. When, however, the attention is shifted to generation, it would seem that, while the value systems of Asian age groups may retain many similarities, there may simulta-neously emerge some significant new cultural forms that, *inter alia*, mark generational change.

During the late 1970s, the political activism of Asian young people hit the news headlines as they adopted a highly visible and militant stance against racist oppression. They took to the streets to express their anger at racial attacks and murders. Several youth groups and 'youth movements' were formed during the aftermath of these public demonstrations. The media represented this activism as a new form of youth militancy singularly different from the political behaviour of their more 'docile' parents. But this representation erases the history of militant struggles of the 1950s, 1960s and early 1970s noted earlier. It misreads the criticism levelled by some youth groups at 'community leaders' as a form of protest at 'parental values'.

In addition, the reports focused almost entirely on young men. These male groups came to be constructed as 'youth groups' *par excellence*. Yet some of these groups, such as the Bradford Black, consisting of young people of both Asian and Afro-Caribbean descent, included women. More importantly, young women began to organise in single-sex groups. For example, a 'Young Girls Support Group' formed in 1978 by young Asian community workers based in Southall, West London, was transformed into the feminist group 'Southall Black Sisters' in 1979, and it played a central role in the events considered below. Significantly, young women organised on the basis of their position as women rather than as 'youth', even though the membership of the groups was often almost entirely young. These women's groups addressed patriarchal issues simultaneously with those of class and racism, and in the process found themselves interrogating the gender politics of the male-dominated youth movements and 'Left groups', as much as the ethnocentrism and 'race' politics of white feminist groups. Indeed, these women's groups emerged and operated at the sharp edge of the highly charged politics of the period.

A large-scale police operation on 23 April 1979 involved the arrest of nearly 700 (predominantly Asian) men and women of all age groups, of whom 344 were charged and tried in court. This took place in the heart of one of the oldest established Asian communities, Southall. The arrests were made when the people of Southall began to gather in order to demonstrate against the overtly racist National Front, which was holding a pre-election rally at the local town hall. The National Front had virtually no support in Southall, and they had not fielded a local candidate there since 1970. So their decision to hold a rally there was seen as a calculated act of provocation. Nearly five thousand people had marched to Ealing Town Hall on the previous day to prevail upon the local Council not to let its premises in Southall be used by a fascist group to hold a political rally, but the Council had decided that the meeting should go ahead. So community organisations in Southall drew up plans to hold a peaceful protest, and these plans had been agreed with the local police. But, on the day, people trying to get to the site of the planned demonstration, together with those who were simply trying to return home from work or after collecting young children from school, found themselves trapped between police cordons. As a pamphlet produced by the Campaign against Racism and Fascism/Southall Rights notes:

2,756 police, including Special Patrol Group units, with horses, dogs, vans, riot shields and a helicopter were sent in . . . the evidence of hundreds of eye witnesses shows that . . . police vans were driven straight at crowds of people, and when they scattered and ran, officers charged at them, hitting out at random. . . . A *Daily Telegraph* reporter saw 'several dozen crying, screaming coloured [sic] demonstrators. . . dragged bodily along Park View Road to the police station. . . . Nearly every demonstrator we saw had blood flowing from some sort of injury; some were doubled up in pain. Women and men were crying' . . .

(Campaign against Racism and Fascism/Southall Rights 1981: 2)

A white teacher, Blair Peach, was killed. Later, eleven eye witnesses gave evidence under oath that they had seen Blair Peach hit by one, or in some cases two, police officers attached to the Special Patrol Group. The jury returned a verdict of 'death by misadventure', and the Director of Public Prosecutions decided that there was insufficient evidence to prosecute any police officer. This announcement generated much public controversy and led to the setting up of separate enquiries by three public agencies: the Commission for Racial Equality, the National Council For Civil Liberties and the Runnymede Trust. The depth of concern may be gauged from the following quote from the supplementary report of the NCCL Committee of Enquiry, chaired by Michael Dummett, Professor of Logic at the University of Oxford. Adding to its earlier criticism of the extent of force used by the police in Southall, the Enquiry declared:

We deplore the fact that no police officer has been brought to account for Blair Peach's death. . . . We deplore the fact that neither the Commissioner of Police nor the Home Secretary, as Police Authority, has publicly recognised the failings in the police operation. . . . We are astonished by the failure of both Sir David McNee and William Whitelaw to explain publicly the reasons offered for the presence of unauthorised weapons in SPG lockers. . . We regard the inquest into Blair Peach's death as deficient in conduct and procedure. The evident bias of the coroner, Dr John Burton, combined with his confused and inaccurate direction to the jury, made a fair hearing of the issues impossible.

(NCCL 1980: 50–1)

Clarence Baker, a member of the local band 'Misty in Roots', formed by a group of young Southallians of Afro-Caribbean descent, was wounded and lay unconscious in hospital for some time. He had suffered injury when the police raided the building occupied by the community organisation 'Peoples Unite Education and Creative Arts Centre', of which the musicians' co-op to which 'Misty' belonged was a part. Their music equipment was totally destroyed. On the day of the demonstration, these premises had been converted into a makeshift centre for emergency legal advice and medical treatment. Lawyers and medical staff (black and white, men and women) who were there to provide assistance claimed that they had been roughly handled by the police and forced out of the building amid a barrage of sexist and racist abuse. The events of the day generated a massive political campaign. They represented a watershed in the creation of new youth politics.

In July 1981 Southall witnessed one of the first of a series of 'riots' (or 'uprisings', as these events have been called by the black communities) which swept across the country that year. Asian youth reacted when skinheads arrived in Southall in buses decked with National Front banners and stickers. A group of skinheads attacked an Asian woman in her shop and the news of the incident spread quickly through the various informal communication networks operating among Asians in the area. Large numbers of young Asians came out on the streets and besieged the public house where the skinheads were attending a rock concert. During the pitched battles that followed, between Asian youths and the police, and between Asians and the skinheads, the pub was set ablaze by petrol bombs. The anger triggered off that day was yet another reaction against the growing number of violent attacks on Asians and the alleged lack of police protection against these attacks.

During the same month, in Bradford, twelve young Asian men were arrested and charged with conspiracy; all were community activists and some had been actively involved in the campaigns which grew around immigration cases such as those of Anwar Ditta and Nasira Begum referred to above. For two days after the arrests in July 1981, the young men were not allowed to see their solicitors. They were all held in custody for varying periods, and the majority did not receive bail until 22 October. All of the defendants pleaded not guilty. Their case is seen by many as a deliberate attempt by the police to weaken black resistance against racism, and support groups for the local defence committee have been formed all over Britain. This necessarily brief overview of the realities of Asian life in contemporary Britain does not include the less dramatic episodes, most of which never hit the headlines.

The emergence of the youth groups marks the coming of age of a new form of Asian political and cultural agency. It is not that these groups are more 'progressive' than the parental age group, as they tend to be described in some public discussions. Rather, having grown up in Britain, they articulate a *home-grown British political discourse.* They lay claim to the localities in which they live as their 'home'. And, however much they may be constructed as 'outsiders', they contest these psychological and geographical spaces from the position of 'insiders'. Even when they describe themselves as 'Asian', this is not a reaching back to some 'primordial Asian' identity. What they are speaking of is a modality of 'British Asian-ness'.These homegrown Asian–British identities inaugurate a fundamental *generational* change.

At the beginning of this chapter I noted that identity is not a singular but rather a multifaceted and context-specific construct. In the case of Asians, religion, caste and language, for example, are important features of group identity. The complex interplay of these factors marks intra-Asian relations in Britain. These relations are not a straightforward replay of social relations in the sub-continent. Rather, they are mediated via cultural, political and economic dimensions as these are forged in Britain. The cultural sphere is crucial in affirming or contesting these identities. For instance, sports tournaments with a focus on some specifically South Asian game such as 'Kabadi' may help underwrite an Asian–British Panjabi male identity when Panjabi teams from Birmingham, Coventry and London play against each other. Similarly, the religious ritual dance performed during 'Navratri' as worship of the goddess Durga is an arena for the play of gender and caste-inflected Hindu–Gujerati identities. Caste inequalities may be reinforced, since Navratri congregations meet under the aegis of various caste-based organisa- tions, but these same organisations could well be used by the lower castes as a ground from which to contest these very hierarchies. The ritual fast during Ramadan, the observances during Muharam, or the celebration of Eid, may underscore a Muslim identity at the same time as highlighting the intra-Muslim differentiations such as Sunni and Shia.

In the same way, the performance of 'Mushaira' (Urdu poetry readings) all over Britain inscribe an Asian–British institution against the echoes of a complex South Asian history from the Mughal period onwards. Similarly, the tradition of 'revolutionary' poetry recitation which is marked in Britain at events held to commemorate the political activism of, say, Shahid Bhagat Singh – who was hanged by the British for his part in anti-colonial insurrection – is an instance of the Asian–British form of political culture. Old and new forms of Asian music, dance and theatre groups, drawing upon classical as well as contemporary traditions, are beginning to mushroom all over Britain. Literature produced by Asians living in Britain – in English as well as in various South Asian languages – is fast becoming an established feature of Britain's literary production. These art forms simultaneously interpret, translate and interrogate the subtleties and intricacies of South Asian life worlds in and outside Britain, drawing out their global interconnections as well as what is distinctive about each.

Class differentiation also plays an important part in Asian–British identity formations. There is a small but significant emerging Asian bourgeoisie without, as yet, a fully developed base within the British state. The slightly larger petty bourgeoisie is differentiated into two main constituents: on the one hand, the prosperous owners of more than one enterprise and, on the other hand, the small shopkeepers eking out a living on very narrow profit margins and often labouring under heavy debt. The majority of Asians in Britain are of the working class; many of them are already unemployed or threatened with unemployment.

Asian–British identities are in flux. Racism may have the effect of marginalising them, but they are not marginal identities. The state of the economy, the activities of racist groups, and social policies may generate some feeling of insecurity in British Asians. But there is a growing mood of defiance, and a refusal to allow themselves to be treated as second-class citizens. There is, of course, no single unified strategy which all sections of the Asian communities are equally likely to adopt. For instance, the responses of the professional middle classes may differ from those of the 'nouveau riche'; and the interests of these two categories of Asians are not the same as those of working-class Asians. Asian women may hold a different kind of investment in their lives in Britain from the men; and the children and young people, with their futures ahead of them, will have something quite distinctive at stake compared to their parents. Nevertheless, whatever form these political and cultural identities assume in the late 1980s and beyond, they are interwoven into the British social and cultural fabric.

Chapter 2

Unemployment, gender and racism
Asian youth on the dole

Unemployment has risen dramatically over the last decade.[1] Between 1973 and 1982, while total unemployment in Great Britain increased by 309 per cent, registered unemployment among black people rose by 515 per cent. The proportion of the unemployed in 1973 who were black was 2.7 per cent. In 1982, the figure was 4.1 per cent (Runnymede Trust 1983). A survey carried out by the Policy Studies Institute found unemployment rates of 13 per cent for whites, 25 per cent for people of Afro-Caribbean origin and 20 per cent for those of Asian origin. Asian women were found to have an unemployment rate twice as high as white women, and Afro-Caribbean women a rate one-and-a-half times that of white women (Brown 1984).

The high increase in youth unemployment since 1979 has attracted much publicity. Yet high levels of unemployment have been common among young blacks for a long period of time. There is evidence, too, that British-born young blacks may be especially vulnerable to unemployment (Runnymede Trust 1983; Campbell and Jones 1981). The view that young blacks born and brought up in Britain would face a more optimistic future than the immigrant parental generation has therefore remained unsubstantiated.

In this chapter, my aim is to describe and analyse the experience of one category of unemployed black youth, namely those young people whose family origins are in the South Asian sub-continent.[2] I shall begin with an outline of the broader context of their experience of unemployment.

ASIAN BUSINESS ACTIVITY AND THE YOUNG UNEMPLOYED

Until recently, little attention has been focused on the plight of Asian youth in the labour market. This category of black youth was assumed to be faring well in the competition for jobs. Apparent complacency about the job prospects of young Asians is at least partially related to one popular image of Asians as 'successful entrepreneurs capable of looking after their own'. This image has some basis in so far as the last three decades have witnessed a rapid proliferation of Asian business enterprises (Allen *et al.* 1977; Aldrich *et al.* 1981). Nevertheless, as has been noted:

> Commercial growth is not necessarily to be equated with commercial success and high levels of rewards are confined to a small fraction of the community and won at an extremely high cost...
>
> (Aldrich *et al.* 1981: 188)

Exaggerated claims about the success of Asian business, though frequent, are misleading. According to the available evidence, much of Asian entrepreneurial activity is limited to the level of circulation and distribution, rather than the production of commodities. The large firm operating at a high profit margin and employing a substantial workforce is not typical of Asian enterprises, which are generally small in size and are often dependent on household labour. Despite impressionistic newspaper reports that enterprises owned by Asians are poised to develop into big capital, this is not very likely. The Asian entrepreneurial class constitutes a very small section of the Asian population in Britain, and its ability to provide employment on any appreciable scale to the growing numbers of unemployed, whether Asian or others, is extremely limited. Furthermore, to deduce the future of Asians as a whole from the experience of a small minority would be a gross distortion of reality. Not only are the great majority of employed Asians still to be found in semi-skilled or unskilled manual occupations, but there is growing evidence of substantial levels of poverty among them (Sills *et al.* 1982).

ASIAN YOUTH UNEMPLOYMENT

Evidence from studies carried out during the 1970s shows that unemployment rates among young Asians were generally higher than those among young whites, and that young Asian women were disproportionately unemployed relative to young men (Brooks 1983). The employment prospects for young Asians have deteriorated rapidly since 1979. For instance, Department of Employment statistics for 1980–81 reveal that, among young black people aged 16–24, the rate of increase in unemployment was highest for Bangladeshi young women followed by Indian and Pakistani young men (Runnymede Trust 1983).

A study of employment prospects of young Asians in Bradford found extremely high unemployment levels amongst this group (Campbell and Jones 1981). Twelve months after leaving school in 1980, 41 per cent of the Asians were unemployed and a further 31 per cent were on Youth Opportunities Schemes (YOPS). In comparison, of all 1980 school leavers (the cohort of which the Asians were a part), 19 per cent were unemployed and 14 per cent were on YOP schemes. Therefore, while only 28 per cent of the Asians had obtained jobs, some 67 per cent of the total had done so. The study also shows that a place on a YOP scheme did not necessarily lead to a job for Asians. For every graduate of a YOP scheme who was able to find employment, three were unemployed. A survey carried out in Leicester found that, in all age groups, unemployment was higher among Asian and Afro-Caribbean groups. In the 16–19 age group, for example, the unemployment figure for Asian and white young people was 38.5 per cent and 23.6 per cent respectively (Leicester City and County Councils 1984).

In general, any unemployment figures for young Asians must take account of a marked tendency on the part of this group to stay on in full-time education beyond the minimum statutory school leaving age (Brooks and Singh 1978; Anwar 1982). According to one study, this tendency was greater amongst Asian young women than Asian young men, and amongst Asian young men born in East Africa relative to those born in Asia or in the UK (Lee and Wrench 1983). There is some evidence to suggest that the greater propensity of young Asians to stay on at school longer or go to college is in part a reflection of their realistic assessment of the restricted job opportunities available to them. If this indeed is the case, and a substantial proportion of young Asians are opting to stay on in education because they anticipate problems in gaining employment, then the available unemployment figures for this group may underestimate the size of the problem.

UNEMPLOYMENT, RACISM AND DISCRIMINATION

A number of factors account for the rapidly accelerating rates of unemployment among Asian groups. First, a high proportion of Asian workers are employed in the generally contracting manufacturing sector and, within this sector, are more likely to work in those industries and at those levels of skill which have been especially vulnerable to decline. Second, a greater proportion of Asians live and work in regions where unemployment levels have recently been among the highest. Third, the current high unemployment is in part a consequence of the restructuring of the world economy involving an accelerating trend towards the internationalisation of capital and labour. This development is especially significant for black workers, for they are concentrated in occupations that are vulnerable to technological change and relocation (Sivanandan 1979; Frobel *et al.* 1980).

Important though these factors are, they do not provide an adequate explanation for disproportionately high black unemployment, except perhaps in the case of the textile industry (Smith 1981). And even in relation to textiles, one must be cautious about giving primacy to arguments which attribute high levels of Asian unemployment to the effects of an industry in decline. Asian workers need not have been affected disproportionately by job losses, especially if they had had parity with whites in terms of access to retraining provisions for new work. The issue of racism and discrimination is thus part of the explanation even in textiles.

A considerable body of evidence dating from the late 1960s onwards points to widespread direct and indirect discrimination against black workers in terms of access to employment, promotion, training, etc. (Daniel 1968; Smith 1974; Allen *et al.* 1977; Commission for Racial Equality 1978). The future facing young blacks looking for work is certainly no brighter than the one their parents had to contend with. There is extensive discrimination against them, such that, even when they have equivalent or better qualifications than their white counterparts, their search for jobs is less successful (Brooks and Singh 1978; Hubbuck and Carter 1980; Troyna and Smith 1983; Lee and Wrench 1983).

There is a striking similarity between the employers' perceptions reported by Allen *et al.* (1977) of mainly an adult immigrant generation of Asian workers, and employers' attitudes towards young Asians in Birmingham studied by Lee and Wrench (1983). Both studies found that employers were likely to hold a variety of stereotypic perceptions of the aptitudes and abilities of Asian workers and job seekers, which in turn were used to rationalise discriminatory behaviour towards them. Clearly, this is an important illustration of one of the ways in which the reproduction of labour is mediated through racism. At the same time, racism cannot be seen merely as an ideology affecting individuals (Hall *et al.* 1978). Of greater significance is the way in which racism permeates all the major institutions of British society. It is a structured feature of the social formation rather than a phenomenon of individual prejudice. It needs to be analysed as a set of material practices maintained by relations of power which constitute the conditions of black people's existence – where they live, which schools they attend, how they are skilled or de-skilled for the labour market, what positions in both the labour market and the cultural system they occupy, what treatment they receive at the hands of the various state agencies, and so on. In other words, how they are socially constructed at the economic, political and ideological levels (Hall *et al.* 1978; Centre for Contemporary Cultural Studies 1982). It is in this sense, as we shall see in the following sections, that black unemployment is *experienced* through racism, gender and class.

SWIMMING AGAINST THE TIDE: THE PROBLEM OF LONG-TERM UNEMPLOYMENT

The fastest growth in the number of unemployed in recent years has taken place among the under-25s, and, leaving aside the over-60s, the highest rate of long-term unemployment is also to be found in the 18–24-year-old group. Even so, to find that 70 per cent of the young men and women we interviewed had been unemployed for a period of between one and two years was a matter of serious concern. They reported that they had made a large number of applications – some as many as over a hundred. I was shown files full of copies of written applications and letters of rejection. Despite the disappointment and frustration resulting from this experience, there was no indication that these young people had given up looking for work. Indeed, the perseverance and tenacity shown was quite remarkable.

In the early stages of unemployment, the local newspaper, the Job Centre and informal channels were cited as the most frequently used sources of information. Whenever it was appropriate, direct applications were also made. With the passage of time, however, the attraction of the Job Centre tended to decline sharply, so that local press advertising and direct application were the most favoured methods of job search among the long-term unemployed. These two methods of recruitment are reported to be the most popular with employers in Leicester (Ashton and Maguire 1982). Where employers recruit through 'word of mouth', young Asians are at a disadvantage, because this excludes them from firms with a predominantly white workforce. I found that the young men and women had explored all the available channels of information about jobs, and their lack of success in the labour market could not be attributed to inadequate job search methods.

THE LOSS OF AN INCOME

The loss of, or serious reduction in, income is of course one of the most difficult aspects of being unemployed. Research by the Policy Studies Institute demonstrates that Asian households are particularly badly hit by the loss of wage-earners through unemployment (Brown 1984). This can be due to a number of factors, including the higher rates of unemployment affecting Asian families, the comparatively high ratio of dependants to earners, and the responsibility many of them have for supporting dependants outside the immediate household, sometimes overseas. On the one hand, immigration law prevents these families from being able to live together, and on the other, social security law penalises them financially for living apart, since persons with dependants in the country of origin can no longer claim benefit for them. The poverty associated with unemployment has particular features in the case of Asians through institutionalised discriminatory legislation as well as the other factors.

Most of the interviewees were long-term unemployed. Those who had been in work had consequently exhausted their eligibility to unemployment benefit and were now, like those who had never had a job, dependent on supplementary benefit. It is not surprising, therefore, that financial difficulty was at the core of the problems faced by the young people and their families. With the exception of a very small minority of young men, the interviewees lived with their families, which were often a variant of the extended family. Loss of an income was experienced not merely as an individualised personal deprivation but as a reduction in the family's total budget. The level of material deprivation in a family varied according to the number of unemployed to employed members (and whether those latter were low-waged), and the number of dependants to earners and unemployed.

Of the thirty-one unmarried interviewees, eight were members of a family where parents and sometimes sisters and brothers were in employment. For these young men and women, unemployment was associated much more in the short term with frustration arising from boredom than with financial problems, though it did mean foregoing some forms of recreation and consumer goods. In such cases, the family seemed temporarily to cushion young people against the full material and ideological impact of unemployment, but it was clear that the working-class Asian family was in a weak position to sustain this role over a long period of time because even the pooled wages of employed members were rarely adequate to withstand the financial pressures of the long-term maintenance of unemployed family members.

In contrast to the above minority, most of the respondents were faced with acute financial problems. In some families there was not a single employed person, and in others the mother was the sole breadwinner, earning – like most female workers – a low wage. Unable financially to set up independent households, a large proportion of married young couples lived with their parents and siblings in overcrowded conditions. Those with a mortgage had great difficulty maintaining mortgage repayments. Some of those living in rented accommodation were in arrears with their rent.

The emotional upset caused by unemployment manifested itself through boredom, depression, anxiety and anger. The young people felt that their future was bleak.

> There is no future for me. I try not to think about my future. It is so depressing, you know. What future have I got? I become very depressed. You beat somebody just to let off pressure.
>
> (Single male)

Arguments, conflict and tension at home were all too common, and this was especially the case when several members in a single family were unemployed. While the hardships resulting from unemployment were borne by the family as a collective entity (Bradley 1986), it was clear that the experience was differentiated by gender.

Predicament of 'masculinity' and 'femininity' on the dole

Somewhat ironically, though by no means surprisingly, the ideology of the male as the 'breadwinner' – constituting as it does a key element in the structuration and legitimation of male dominance – was central to many of the social and psychological pressures which the male respondents described as underpinning their experience of unemployment. In analysing the experience of unemployed young white males, Paul Willis has described this aspect as the 'male gender crisis' (Willis 1984). In the case of the Asian male, the obligation to 'provide' extends beyond spouse and children to include a range of designated kin in the extended family. Consequently, both married and single men, particularly if they are eldest sons, feel under pressure to shoulder this responsibility. Hence, many male respondents spoke of feeling a sense of failure at not being able to contribute to the family income. One single male, living with his widowed mother and a younger brother, had been unemployed for two years. His younger brother worked as a packer and brought home a wage of £50 a week. His own weekly supplementary benefit of £21.15 did not last beyond the Monday or Tuesday of the following week. As the eldest son, without a father, he experienced considerable guilt and unhappiness because he was a non-earning member of the family

> I can't live off my mother and younger brother. I am supposed to look after them and not the other way around. My mother thinks I am not trying hard enough to find a job. If I don't go to the Job Centre for just a couple of days she thinks I am not really interested in finding a job. Then we get arguments. I keep telling her there are so many people unemployed. It's not her fault. It's embarrassing for her that I don't have a job.

Another young man from a family of six younger brothers and sisters had also been unemployed for two years. No one in his family had a job. While all members of the family who were of working age were under pressure to find a job, he felt that the responsibility weighed more heavily on his shoulders because he was male. He expressed his anger and frustration thus:

> The worst is when your mother can't even buy shoes for the little ones. You feel so awful because you can't do anything about it. What future have I got? There are times you just want to kill yourself. Sometimes you get so angry you feel like going out and shooting everyone else.

Thus, unemployment brings into sharp focus the centrality of the wage as an affirmation of masculinity. While the current high levels of unemployment should mean that the unlikelihood of this being readily attributed to personal deficiency should lessen the stigma, it does not entirely disappear. One young man had virtually stopped going to any family or community gatherings because people were bound to ask what kind of work he did.

For those single young men contemplating marriage, the lack of a job can mean reduced opportunities for, or a delay in, securing a suitable match. For the married male wishing to set up an independent household, unemployment poses other kinds of problems. While a married Asian young man will not be under the same pressure to leave the parental home as his white counterpart, for, according to custom, a married male and his family is normally expected to continue living with his parents, lack of suitable accommodation makes this difficult in Leicester, where the need for separate accommodation has become very acute indeed. The majority of Asian households live in small terraced houses. Compared to the housing conditions of white families, Asians are much more poorly housed (Leicester City and County Councils 1984).

Due to the sexual division of labour in the household, which frees men from domestic work, it is largely the unemployed men rather than the women who can claim to have considerable 'free time' at their disposal. The young men spent this time engaged in a variety of activities, such as watching television; going to a pub, youth club or a disco; walking the streets with friends or just hanging around the local park or the city centre; participating in community-based political activities; or attending activities sponsored by religious and cultural organisations. It was normally while on the streets that the young men came face-to-face with racial violence from their white counterparts, and a number of the respondents had themselves been attacked. There was a general feeling that the police provided inadequate protection against racial harassment. Both male and female respondents expressed sympathy with Afro-Caribbean youth, whom they saw as facing the brunt of 'heavy policing'. The experience of youth from the two communities, they said, was becoming increasingly similar.

The pressures on young women are different as well as more acute. The burden of keeping the family together under dire financial circumstances bore especially hard on women in the family, particularly those who were married. It was they who had to decide what economies to make in order to make ends meet. A 23-year-old woman in a household which included not only her husband, herself and two young children, but also her husband's younger brother and his elderly parents, explained:

> There is so much tension with my husband being out of work too. Money is a big problem. Lack of money creates a lot of tension, lot of bickering, lot of conflict. The wife suffers most. It's really depressing. You get pressurised from all directions – needs of children, family, other people in the house. Our house is not big enough for the whole family but we can't afford to have a home of our own. You can't go out for a meal or something. Children's needs cannot be fully met. You have to economise on everything – gas, electricity. House repairs – well you have no choice but to leave the house as it is or you end up borrowing money from relatives.

Divorced young women with children to support faced even greater hardships. One 21-year-old divorced woman with a six-month-old baby had to meet all her expenses from the £32 that she received as her weekly benefit. She was on the council's waiting list for accommodation and, in the meantime, had no option but to live with her family in overcrowded conditions and at a time when three other members of the family were also unemployed. Women like her were extremely unhappy about the renewed dependence on the natal family which the lack of a wage imposed upon them. Understandably, they did not wish to be a financial burden on their families who, as often as not, were themselves not all that well off. Equally, however, they were concerned about the stigma of divorce which faced not only themselves but also their families. Economic reliance on the family meant that a woman would be under greater pressure to comply with the wishes and demands of the family. Indeed, the importance of paid work for women was a theme that was echoed throughout the interviews with the young women. Most of the single women said they would wish to work after marriage, and the married women shared this view. There was in fact strong consensus about the desirability of paid employment, because this was thought to give women a measure of independence.

> Having a job means independence. You don't have to rely on the husband for money. I want a job. I hate staying at home. I want to be able to earn some money – buy clothes I want to, and not be a burden on my parents.

Of course, the women knew that paid employment did not by itself lead to equality with men. Either through their own previous experience of paid work, or the experience of their mothers and of other female relatives, the young women were fully aware of the 'double burden' of combining work outside the home with domestic duties. They knew, too, that they would earn less than the men, and that there were domains of the labour market from which they, as women, were excluded. Thus, these young women were not unfamiliar with the inequality embedded in the sexual division of labour at work and in the home. But they recognised that a wage did allow women to have a degree of autonomy and control; that it did prevent women from being totally dependent on a male wage. The women saw these as very real gains which they felt were being seriously threatened by their own unemployment.

The young women argued that, in most Asian families, a woman's wage was a very necessary part of the family's income: that it was not possible to keep up with the cost of living on male income alone, so that women's paid work was a pressing economic necessity. Of course, for low-income families generally, the female wage has become a vital part of the household income. The number of households with income below supplementary benefit level would treble if it were not for this second source of income. But the concentration of Asian workers in low-paid work renders Asian women's wages that much more central to the household budget.

Unemployment also meant one less contribution to the family savings intended for the 'dowry' of some of the single women. In the absence of a job, the fantasy of marriage seemed to hold out the promise of relief from the sheer boredom of life on the dole. Other young single women felt robbed of the opportunity to embark on a career which they said they might or might not have wished to combine with marriage. For them, unemployment meant a closing of options.

Work outside the home was regarded by the women as important also because it provides social contact beyond family networks. A number of studies of women's employment have analysed female cultures in the workplace (cf. Pollert 1981; Cavendish 1982; Westwood; 1984). These cultures are shown to be deeply contradictory – shot through with divisions of gender, 'race' and ethnicity, and encapsulating the potential for resistance at the same time as they confirm racist patriarchal relations in contemporary Britain. Whatever their limitations, these cultures nevertheless enable women to forge an identity outside the confines of the home. The workplace offers women the opportunity to socialise with a wider range of people, to break out of their isolation and to be able to share their concerns with other women. As one young married woman put it:

> At work you are a different person. You are mixing with all kinds of people. You find out about their ways, they find out about yours. It's more fun than just being in one room, sitting around with children and just the husband.

Compared with men, the young women spent more of their time at home. As is the case among white families, there are important differences in the way the daily lives of young women, including their 'leisure' pursuits, are structured (cf. Deem 1983). While young men wishing to 'let off steam' could take part in a variety of outdoor activities, there were greater constraints on the women. This is not to say that young women were confined to their homes by 'authoritarian families', as the stereotype seems to suggest. In general, visiting friends and relatives and entertaining them in their own homes was common. Young women went shopping with friends, and some attended youth clubs, but they refrained from 'hanging around' on the streets without purpose. This was due as much to the inhibiting influence of ideologies of femininity and the concrete demands of domestic responsibilities as to the lack of suitable provision for young Asian women. Fear of racial attack was also cited as a factor affecting women's participation in activities outside the home, particularly in the evenings.

Contrary to the common ideological social construction of Asian cultures and family life as the cause of problems faced by young Asians in Britain, most young people said that their families were their major source of financial and emotional support, and that their Asian cultural life provided a strength that was not available to them outside their communities (see previous chapter; also Brah and Minhas 1985).

It is evident that, for both male and female respondents, the social and economic pressures of unemployment were accentuated by the surrounding culture of racism. In addition to racial attacks, immigration and nationality laws were identified as being particularly significant features of contemporary racism:

> Many Asian people died for the British in the World Wars. My father used to be in the army. But now British people are trying to throw us out. They don't say direct but through laws like the immigration laws and the new one, the Nationality one.

What I want to know is – and I get angry indeed – when people talk about immigrants they talk about Africans. Asians and West Indians. What about all those Australians, Canadians, Americans, Germans – are they not immigrants? No, because they are white! When they talk about immigrants they talk about us. Disgraceful! Not a lot of people know that more people leave this country than come in. They never tell you that in the papers.

Unemployment seemed to have heightened the young people's sense of group identity as blacks. Since leaving school their contacts with white people in other than official capacities had been minimal. With the closing of the school gates behind them, and without work, most came to recognise the tenuous nature of relationships they had developed with white peers.

I tried to mix with white people for a few years. But no matter how much you tried to mix with them, at the back of their minds they always have this thing that you're black and they are white – that you're not the same. So taken in that sense you have to stick to your own. You could be born here but our colour doesn't change.

I see myself very much as an Asian. Of course you can go round flashing your British passport but you still get kicked over the head by the fascists 'cos you're black. It doesn't matter where you are born – it doesn't matter how many 'O' levels you have got. It doesn't matter, because your skin is black. I am very proud to say I am black.

Thus, lack of social 'contact' between them and white people was not due to 'cultural encapsulation' on the part of the respondents, as the popular view has it, but rather it was a consequence of racial divisions in society exacerbated by unemployment. These young people were not 'between two cultures'. Their cultural identity was secure and firmly based in the lived experience of Asians in Britain. Though interconnected with the cultures of the sub-continent, these new cultural configurations are indelibly marked by the British context in which high levels of unemployment increasingly play a major part.

EDUCATION AND TRAINING FOR WHAT?

The great majority of the young men and women who took part in the research had left school with few or no qualifications. They argued, however, that their lack of qualifications was a reflection of the inadequacies of the education system, rather than of their own abilities and attitudes. They felt that the education system had failed them, claiming that, while few teachers were overtly racist, the overall ethos of the schools conveyed the message that they were regarded by their teachers as somewhat inferior.

> No one ever actually said this but you were made to feel that you were not meant to be more intelligent than your average British person. If you were bright the teachers saw it as some kind of genetic fault in you.

> They couldn't understand our problems, feelings and our ambitions. They kept pushing us towards factory jobs, almost as if we were not good enough for anything else.

Some felt that problems they had faced at school were also shared in part by white working-class pupils:

> I think schools in Highfields suffer from the fact that it is a working-class area. Teachers tend to think that pupils from this area are not clever enough, so they don't bother to train them. If you work very hard yourself you may do well.

> Working-class kids – black and white – face these problems more, because middle-class teachers like middle-class kids – they have more in common. I know no working-class teachers around here.

It is clear from above that the part played by low teacher expectations and 'labelling' in the reproduction of black labour was not obscured from these young men and women, and the class nature of education was also seemingly transparent to some.

The school curriculum came under severe criticism for perpetuating a Eurocentric world view that was seen to neglect the history and cultures of black groups and the issue of racism. Discontent was also expressed at the underrepresentation of Asian and other black teachers in the schools, and the relative absence of black people from positions of authority and power. These experiences of marginalisation tended to elicit broadly two types of reaction from the young people. Both sets of responses represent oppositional strategies directed at structures and processes which they felt stigmatised them as fit only for low-level manual work.

The first of these was to reject the school values as embodied in the perceived characteristics of a 'good pupil'.

We felt, why should we go through this humiliation just for a few qualifications. [We reacted] by not doing any work.

The second response entailed quite the opposite, in that the interviewees became determined to try and achieve against all odds. As one young man stated:

> When I first came to this country my English was not very good. They put me in the bottom class. We were non-exam pupils. They didn't bother teaching us. There were other Asian kids in the class. They also had a problem with English. We felt we didn't belong in that class. We were not stupid. We used to get angry or mess about. In the third year I started fighting for my education. At the end of the year, we Indians got together and told the teacher we wanted to take Mock Exams. I didn't pass my English but I passed Maths, Physics, Biology, Chemistry and Metalwork. My careers teacher said I was stupid not looking for work. But I went to college to do 'O' and 'A' levels, and later got a degree.

He was one of three men and two women graduates among the respondents. Only one of these was a recent graduate, the remaining four having been unemployed for a period of between one and two-and-a-half years, a reminder that the possession of educational qualifications does not guarantee jobs. Such cases and the collective experience of Asian communities in the labour market, together with the difficulties the respondents themselves had encountered during the course of their search for work, had made them recognise discrimination as a key constraint circumscribing the job opportunities available to them.

> You have to be ten times, even a hundred times better than a white applicant.

> An Asian goes for a job and they say there's no vacancy, and a white person goes and they say you can start from Monday.

> What kind of person do you think employers tend to look for? I think somebody white.

Despite this, however, those with paper qualifications were determined to resist deskilling, and to repudiate the relatively low social expectations of them. They held on to a residual optimism that educational credentials would be an asset in the long term, if not in the short term.

The respondents also expressed grave concerns about the amount and quality of careers advice available to them, both in school and from the Careers Service. Such advice, they claimed, was offered infrequently, and was not very helpful – a view that finds support in a study of local careers provision (Sherridan 1981). One of the major complaints made was that the careers teachers and careers officers were prone to underestimate the abilities of Asians and to discourage them from pursuing careers in higher education and the professions. As one young woman put it:

> The careers teacher made you feel that you were at the bottom of the ladder, and no matter how hard you tried you couldn't get to the top.

A similar tendency was identified among some of the staff at the Job Centre. The young people said that the jobs for which they expressed a preference would tend to be considered by the Job Centre staff as unsuitable for them. The issue of 'suitability' is a crucial one, and it is implicated in subjective judgements which may reinforce racialised forms of gender inequality.

The young people's attitudes towards the MSC (Manpower Services Commission) schemes for the unemployed were both critical and pragmatic. Since the interviews were conducted before the new Youth Training Initiative became operative, their comments reported below refer to schemes which preceded the YTS. On the whole, these schemes were seen as a poor substitute, indeed no substitute, for 'proper' training and 'proper' jobs. The following types of observation were typical:

> They are not proper training schemes. Not like apprenticeships and that. They are just there to keep people off the street; keep the unemployment figures down. I have never met someone who came off a scheme and was successful in getting a job. I don't know what good they are doing.

> You get £22.50 on the dole and 25 quid on a scheme. For a 40 hour week you get a paltry £25. It's cheap labour they are getting.

> An average worker gets £75 a week. They stick an unemployed person on to a scheme for £25 and save £50. They don't train you,

and when you leave 5 months later they stick in another one. They are using you.

There was an overall consensus that the employers did not value skills gained on these schemes.

Employers think these schemes are for 'dunces'.

These schemes are seen to be for people who can't get jobs when they come out of school. They dump them on the schemes what they don't want on the dole. Employers think these people are second best.

Despite this overall disaffection with the schemes, there was recognition that schemes varied greatly in the quality of training and work experience provided. One of the local schemes was remembered with considerable pleasure by some of its former trainees. These young women said they had appreciated the friendly atmosphere of this scheme and had enjoyed being on it, even though they had not managed to get a job since leaving it. For some respondents, the schemes provided an escape from the boredom of staying at home:

It's better than being on the dole. At least you have somewhere to go every day and you might even learn something useful.

The views of the young people find resonance in a number of recent critiques of MSC schemes for the unemployed, which stress that the schemes are not about training for jobs. These initiatives have been variously described as establishing the necessary conditions to depress wages and wage expectations; being an attempt to shift labour market control and resources away from working people; and as seeking to redefine the cultural outlook of new generations (Green 1983; Finn 1984; Goldstein 1984).

Clearly, the young Asians interviewed possess quite a sophisticated analysis of the 'hidden curriculum' of schools and other agencies that affects the unemployed. Their comments expose the hollowness of the ideology of equal opportunity, and reveal some of the ways in which these institutions and agencies are implicated in reproducing Asian labour at the lower rungs of the socio-economic formation. But it is equally apparent that they are not passive victims of structural determinations. They question, resist, challenge and repudiate the social and cultural mechanisms which underpin their subordination. Their political consciousness is marked by their first-hand experience of the processes of exclusion/inferiorisation, and their responses are embedded within ideologies developed and elaborated in dialogue with a variety of political discourses, Asian peer groups and, increasingly, in discourse with young Afro-Caribbean blacks and anti-racist young whites.

NOTES

1 Figures on unemployed black people were collected from employment offices and Job Centres from 1963 to 1983, and were published quarterly in the *Employment' Gazette*. The table was discontinued at the end of 1982.
2 This chapter is based on research undertaken during 1983. In-depth personal interviews were carried out with fifty young men and women (twenty-seven male, twenty-three female) in the age range 16–25 living in an inner-city area of Leicester. Of these, twenty-four were Hindus, sixteen Muslims and ten Sikhs. While twenty-four were born in the South Asian sub-continent, nineteen in Africa and seven in Britain, nevertheless half the respondents came to Britain under the age of eleven. The majority (thirty-one) were single. These interview data were augmented by four full-length group discussions with groups of between ten and fifteen young men. Thus, altogether 100 young people participated.

Chapter 3

Gendered spaces
Women of South Asian descent in 1980s Britain

The social reality of Asian women's lives in Britain is constituted around a complex articulation of the economic, political, and cultural modalities which mark the interrelationship between 'race', class, ethnicity, and gender. To understand fully the life experiences of Asian women in Britain, it is necessary to analyse the socio-cultural processes of colonialism and imperialism, the historical basis of the international division of labour, and the position of women in the global economy. It is also important to address issues of politics and identity. These are linked processes – some complementary, others contradictory. The question is *not*, as it is often posed, whether patriarchal relations pre-date capitalism, for they patently do, but rather how gender relations are constituted in articulation with class, racism, ethnicity or sexuality in the construction of capitalist, imperialist, or indeed any other form of social relation, and what type of identities are inscribed in the process. The point is that concepts such as capitalism, patriarchy or imperialism do *not* signal *independent*, albeit interlocking *systems*. Rather, these concepts signify contingent relations of power, so that, for instance, capitalist relations are themselves patriarchal, taking varying forms in different contexts.

When we speak of South Asian women in Britain we are referring to a very heterogeneous category of people. South Asian women have come to Britain from different parts of the world, most notably from India, Pakistan, Bangladesh, Uganda, Kenya and Tanzania. While women who have migrated from the Asian sub-continent are predominantly from the independent proprietor class of peasants, those from East Africa are overwhelmingly from an urban, middle-class background. Asian women are also differentiated according to religion, linguistic group, caste and sect. There are three main religions – Islam, Hinduism and Sikhism – and five major languages – Panjabi, Gujerati, Bengali, Urdu and Hindi – represented among Asians in Britain. There are also smaller groups of Buddhists and Zoroastrians; and further complexities in terms of language – for instance, 'Bengali' speakers are in effect Sylhetti speakers, South Asians from Azad Kashmir use Kashmiri, and the asylum seekers from Sri Lanka are predominantly Tamils. Each religious and linguistic group is in turn differentiated along various castes and sects. The cultures that these groups inhabit and the gendered social relations of which they are a part are correspondingly different.

Apart from the case of Asians who arrived together as families after being evicted from Uganda by Idi Amin, Asian women generally migrated later than the men. Various factors have influenced the timing of female immigration, e.g. the variation in the timing of the principal period of migration of men from India, Pakistan and Bangladesh, and the series of legal and administrative measures introduced by successive British governments to reduce black immigration. On the whole, migration of women from India has preceded that of women from Pakistan and Bangladesh. Indeed, the relatively high ratio of men to women among these latter groups suggests that a substantial proportion of Bangladeshi and Pakistani families are still waiting to be reunited.

Because of the variation in timing of migration, some of the issues and concerns facing different categories of Asian women are correspondingly different, even though their structural position as black women will expose them to many common experiences. For example, many Sikh women from India have been resident in Britain for over two decades, whereas a significant number of Bangladeshi women are newcomers to the country. A high proportion of the Sikh women are engaged in paid work. They have been involved in a number of industrial struggles. In the current recession many have lost their jobs or are faced with the prospect of losing their jobs. A key area of concern for these women is the issue of unemployment. Many of the recently arrived Bangladeshi women, on the other hand, are facing exclusion from the labour market even before they have had the opportunity to seek paid employment. Similarly, the housing problems of the long-established Sikh families living in owner-occupied properties are qualitatively different from those of Bangladeshi families in East London, who have been housed in poor quality council flats on estates where racial violence is a common feature of daily existence.

Bangladeshi women on these estates lead a life of acute isolation and fear of racial attacks.

It is not possible to do justice to the complexity of Asian women's experience in a short general piece of this kind. My intention here is to sketch an overview by analysing their position within the labour market, household, and education. I examine how patriarchal racism underpins Asian women's experience within each of these sites, and how it articulates with racialised discourses, policies and practices of the state such as those centred around immigration controls. I argue against European orientalist ideologies which construct Asian women as 'passive'. Instead, my aim is to address the many and different ways in which women of Asian origin in Britain are actively setting their own agendas, challenging their specific oppressions in their own ways, and marking new cultural and political trajectories.

ASIAN WOMEN AND PAID WORK

The use of Asian women's labour in the heart of the metropolis is not simply a post-World War II phenomenon. As early as the beginning of the eighteenth century, British employees of the East India Company would import Asian women to Britain as domestic servants. These 'ayahs' were required to minister to the whims and needs of the white adults and children during the long and arduous journey back to Britain. Some were kept on by these families as domestics, while others were discharged upon arrival without a return passage to India and left to fend for themselves. Many lived in squalid lodging houses, faced racism and were grossly exploited (Visram 1986).

As we saw earlier, the post-war Asian migration to Britain was part of the wider labour flow from the European periphery and the Third World to advanced Western Europe. Asian workers were recruited to Britain in response to the chronic labour shortages that accompanied the post-war economic expansion. The economic boom made it comparatively easy for white workers to secure better-paid jobs or to obtain places on skill apprenticeships and training schemes. This led to the most pronounced labour shortages occurring in those sectors of the economy where working conditions were poor and the work was low-paid. It was mainly for this work that immigrant labour was recruited. Thus, Asian workers in Britain came to be disproportionately represented in textiles, clothing and footwear, metal manufacture, transport and communications and the distributive trades.

Within these mainly manual occupations, Asian workers tend to be concentrated in unskilled and semi-skilled jobs.

The great majority of Asian women came in order to join kin already here, although, of course, there were some women – students, widows, single professional women, etc. – whose migration did not conform to the above pattern. The concentration of Asian men in low-paid occupations soon had the effect of drawing Asian women into the labour market. Their income has been an essential requirement for the payment of mortgages and rents and for meeting the continually rising cost of living. However, Asian women's involvement in the labour market is uneven. A recent survey has shown economic activity in the 25–34 age group of Hindu and Sikh women to be higher than amongst white women (Brown 1984). In the case of the Muslim sample, however, less than a fifth of those eligible for work were in employment. It is worth stressing that this figure is probably an underestimate, since a substantial proportion of Muslim women are involved in home-working – a form of paid work that tends to fall outside the net of statistics. A reason most commonly put forward for the lower economic activity rates for Muslim women is that Muslim families do not permit female members to work outside the home. Such exclusively *culturalist* explanations are, however, inadequate, for they do not take into account factors such as: the later migration of Muslim women from Pakistan and Bangladesh compared with Hindu and Sikh women from India; the differences in the economic activity levels of Muslim women from Africa as compared with Muslim women from the sub-continent; the regional variation between the levels of Muslim women engaged in wage labour in the south-east and south-west of England compared with Yorkshire and the West Midlands; the socio-economic position of the women prior to migration and the different time period in which these women entered the 'modern' job market in their countries of origin; and the structure of the local labour markets in the areas of Muslim settlement in Britain. Moreover, research on young Asian women fails to show any marked difference in the job aspirations of young Muslim women compared with non-Muslims, thus bringing into focus the significance of generational issues (see Chapter Two, and Parmar 1982). When all such factors are taken into account, the influence of religion and family ceases to acquire the overarching determinacy often ascribed to it in Western discourses about Asian women.

But this is not to underplay the effects of the ideology of domesticity and femininity in structuring the labour market situation of both black and white women. The expectation that household duties and child care are primarily the women's responsibility, and ideas about the appropriateness of particular types of work for women outside the home are important players in circumscribing the kind of paid work women do, whether they do it full-time or part-time, whether or not their work is recognised as skilled or unskilled (for the definition of skill is itself socially constructed), and the level of remuneration awarded for the paid work that women do. Thus, for instance, a higher proportion of women than men in Britain are engaged in part-time work; women are concentrated in service industries; within particular occupations women tend to be employed at lower grades; women are concentrated in low-paid work and this work is often defined as unskilled, even when it involves complex competencies (Beechey and Whitelegg 1986). Asian women's position in the labour market is affected, not only by gender ideologies, but also by their structural location as black workers. On average, Asian men earn substantially less than white men. This has in part meant that a comparatively higher proportion of Asian women than white women have had to take up full-time employment from sheer economic necessity rather than choice. Even in industries where female labour predominates, Asian women are concentrated in the lowest-level jobs. In contrast to the overall pattern of women's concentration in the service industries, Asian women are more commonly found in low-paid, semi-skilled and unskilled work in the manufacturing sector, particularly in the clothing and textile industries which have recently been in decline (Beechey and Whitelegg 1986).

As we saw in the last chapter, the employment profile of Asian women and men has changed relatively little over the last three decades, with much evidence which highlights discrimination against these workers in terms of access to employment, promotion and training. Young Asian women, born and brought up in Britain, are no less subject to racism than their parents have been; and their search for jobs is likely to be less successful even when they have equivalent or better qualifications than their white counterparts. Asian unemployment has risen dramatically over the last decade. The rate of unemployment among Asians is substantially higher than among whites, with a figure twice as high for Asian women compared with white women. In the previous chapter we saw that there are several reasons for this, including the concentration of Asian women in industries and skill levels which have been on the decline, the restructuring of the world economy involving technological change and relocation of jobs, and discrimination due to racism. At the same time there has been a growth in the 'sweatshop' economy which enables some of the multi-national corporations to have access to cheap and disposable labour from the unemployed and underemployed. Many Asian women work in this economy, especially as home-workers, a sector which has been characterised as one of the most exploited groups of workers (Mitter 1986).

On a number of occasions since the early 1960s, Asian workers have had to take industrial action in order to improve their work conditions. Low wages, different rates for the same job paid to Asian and white workers, allocation of worse tasks to Asians in the production process, and racial as well as sexual harassment, were some of the key issues around which the major industrial struggles of the period were initiated by Asian workers (see Chapter One). Asian women have played a central role in all of these struggles. The Imperial Typewriters strike of 1974 in Leicester, and the Grunwick strike of 1977 in London, were mainly led by women, while all the strikers at the Chix sweet factory in Slough and at Fritters in north London were women. Women have also been the backbone of other industrial struggles through their activities to mobilise support among the Asian communities. When Asian men at the Woolfe's rubber factory went on strike in the mid-1960s, for instance, Asian women were the mainstay of community solidarity which proved to be as crucially important as the bonds of labour. These struggles highlighted endemic racism, both among white fellow-workers and in the trade union movement.

PATRIARCHAL RACISM, CULTURE AND 'FAMILY'

This section is divided into two parts. In the first part my aim is to show that the legitimation of state racism in post-war Britain has been secured in an important way through particular ideological constructions of Asian cultural practices. I exemplify this point with specific reference to the introduction and implementation of immigration controls. I also consider, albeit briefly, the effects of immigration policy on Asian communities, particularly on women. Furthermore, I suggest that there is considerable overlap between the colonial and contemporary racialised discourses on Asian women's position within gender relations. In other words, the first part is concerned with inscriptions of 'the Asian family' via the institutionalised practices of the British state. The second part of the section offers a focus on 'family' as a lived experience.

Asian 'family' and state racism

The trajectory of Britain's anti-black racism is closely bound up with the history of the development of capitalism and its relationship to colonialism and imperialism. Ideologies of 'race' have featured centrally in the historical constitution and contemporary elaboration and reorganisation of the international division of labour, and they have been pivotal in the reproduction of a racially divided British working class (Hall *et al.* 1978). The British Raj was legitimated by the discourse of the 'civilising mission' which, at best, was patronising. India was recognised as *'having had* a civilisation'; i.e. a polity with a past rather than a present, one that had lost its way and descended into chaotic stupor from which it needed 'awakening'. How precisely it ought to be 'awakened' varied, depending upon the economic, political and religious interests of the particular category of 'civiliser' in question. The merchants of the East India Company and, later, the different segments of industrial, commercial, and finance capital, the administrators of the colonial government, the missionaries, etc.; all had a partially overlapping, but frequently conflicting, stake in India. The different political tendencies in Britain – Tory, Whig, Utilitarian, Labour, Suffragette, Communist and so on – found their avid exponents in India. Indeed, the colonial governance of India was a battleground for these ideologies, each vying for hegemony as 'the solution' to India's slide into its current 'decline'. But they were not solutions, so much as constitutive factors in that to which they were represented as a solution. Colonial representations offered reified and contradictory readings of Indian cultures, constructing 'them' variously as: lofty and spiritual but too other-worldly and steeped in superstition; subtle and sensuous yet simultaneously licentious and barbaric; grand but ostentatious; replete with ancient 'scientific' wisdom yet encapsulating unbridled emotionality in contradiction to 'Western' rationality (Hutchins 1967; Greenberger 1969). These discourses were often elaborated around the notions of 'the family' as the bearer of these cultures, and around the imagery of Indian women as ruthlessly oppressed creatures who must be saved from their degradation. The British claimed they were a liberalising force in the colonies, especially for women, yet as Liddle and Joshi (1985) show, colonial policy on issues concerning the position of women was shot through with contradictions. While they liberalised the law on some issues, on others their policies had the effect of either reinforcing existing gender inequality or creating a new form which was as oppressive to women, if not more. Liddle and Joshi argue that the British were not interested in women's position for its own sake, but in the way that gender divisions mediated the structure of imperialism.

There would seem to be a remarkable continuity between the imperial discourses about Asian women and those which construct Asian women's experience in post-World War II Britain. Many of the contemporary academic, political and popular discourses on Asian women also present them as 'docile' and 'passive' victims, both of archaic 'traditional' customs and practices, and of domineering Asian men. These discourses pathologise the Asian family, presenting it, rather than the effects of racial, sexual or class inequalities, as the main site of problems faced by Asian women. To posit a continuity between imperial discourses and contemporary ones is not necessarily to suggest an identity between the two. As Stuart Hall has argued, present-day racism is the racism of a declining social formation and not of the 'high imperial noon'. It is embedded within the economic, political and cultural crisis experienced at the heart of the metropolis; and it has its own specificity (Hall 1978). The new discourses draw upon the old but connect with new repertoires within changed social and cultural conditions.

Ideological constructions of Asian marriage and family norms (which, in fact, vary significantly across different categories of Asians) as a 'problem for British society' have been critical in the legitimation of post-war immigration control. Over the last twenty years successive British governments have introduced increasingly restrictive immigration legislation designed to reduce black – in particular Asian – immigration. The Immigration Acts together with the Nationality Act of 1981 divide the world into patrials (mainly white) with rights normally associated with citizenship, and non-patrials (mainly blacks) who are subject to immigration control, deportation and restrictions on taking employment. The history of immigration control is a testament to how common-sense racism has been appropriated into the mainstream of British parliamentary politics with the result that patriarchal racism is now institutionalised within the state apparatus. Notions of 'race' and 'culture' were central themes in the parliamentary debate that ushered in the immigration and nationality legislation. Racist images of 'tidal waves' of potential immigrants from the sub-continent were invoked to justify these controls.

Immigration law defined men as prospective workers who posed a threat to the indigenous labour market, but the women and children were regarded as 'dependants'. The so-called 'Asian arranged-marriage system' was singled out as a mechanism potentially to be used by the Asians to circumvent immigration restrictions. Hence, every single Asian woman settled in Britain was regarded as a prospective sponsor of a fiancé from the subcontinent. The Immigration Rules governing the entry of foreign husbands and fiancés were changed five times between 1969 and 1983, with the primary aim of preventing black and immigrant women from having their partners join them in Britain while allowing white women the right to do so. In 1985, the European Commission of Human Rights ruled that the British Immigration Rules discriminated on the grounds of sex. The British government responded by amending its rules to give women equality, but by making it equally difficult for a man to sponsor his wife or fiancée.

This background to British immigration controls means that every Asian arriving in British ports of entry can expect to be treated with suspicion. Asian marriages involving a partner from the sub-continent are subject to the 'primary purpose' clause, which requires that the couple must 'prove' that their marriage is 'genuine'. Such couples may be made to submit themselves to acutely embarrassing forms of surveillance. Reports of harassment at the hands of the immigration service are widespread. Although it is claimed that the practice has been discontinued, there have been cases of Asian women being subjected to 'virginity tests', and Asian children to x-ray examinations in order to establish their age. As we saw earlier, workplaces with an Asian workforce have been raided by the police and the immigration service in search of alleged illegal entrants or overstayers. As a result of the immigration and nationality legislation, many Asian families are separated. Some wives and children have been waiting in countries such as Bangladesh for several years to be reunited with their husbands and/or parents. There have been instances when Asian women with children, legally settled in Britain for many years, have became liable to deportation when a marriage broke down or a husband died, because the wife was considered legally the husband's dependant. Such cases have resulted in a number of successful anti-deportation campaigns led by Asian women. South Asian and other women victims of immigration control have now become more formally organised into the Immigration Widows' Campaign Group. There is also an invidious link between immigration controls and social security benefits, which results in discrimination against black claimants (Gordon 1986).

The Asian 'family' as lived experience

Feminists have argued that the institution of the family constitutes one of the key sites where the subordination of women is secured. Patriarchal ideology constructs 'home' as the 'rightful' place for women. Marriage constitutes a pivotal mechanism in the regulation and control of female sexuality. 'Family' is also where the appropriation of women's caring work masquerades as 'labour of love'. Not that love or other 'structures of feeling', to use Raymond Williams's evocative phrase, are not important. Indeed, they are. The psychic investment in relationships with family mark the person even as she may challenge patriarchal discourses and practices. Given the power of the emotional bond – say, between parents and children – *and* the power of social sanction, it is perhaps not surprising that 'family' remains an area of acute ambivalence for women. Moreover, the desire for intimacy and a sense of belonging, as well as the lack of many viable alternatives for the majority of women, means that 'family' remains an important unit of social organisation. For Asian women, family support may also become necessary in the struggles against the onslaughts of racism. But it needs to be borne in mind that families are composed of many different types of households across Britain, and the 'nuclear household' is no longer overwhelmingly the predominant form.

Women may often stress the importance of 'family' but, by doing this, they do not necessarily accept as legitimate the hierarchical organisation of the household, or the exercise of male power. In a study of Asian and white fifteen-year-old girls and boys and their parents, I found the influence exercised by the ideology of housework and child-care as primarily a 'woman's job' to be significant among Asians and whites alike (Brah 1979). Those who believed in this seemed to accept that the man should shoulder some responsibility for domestic work, but the discussion was likely to be couched in terms of 'helping' the woman with 'her' housework, and household tasks were divided into male and female ones. The boys said that they would expect their own responsibility generally limited to occasional washing-up and vacuum-cleaning, periodic gardening, washing the car, and minding the children for short periods. The majority of the mothers and many girls colluded with this ideology of domesticity, with one white girl saying, 'I like a man to be a man – wouldn't like him to be running around with a duster'. But at the same time they did not completely acquiesce, deploying a variety of strategies to avoid doing all the work themselves.

The strongest opposition to the sexual division of labour in the household came from Asian girls, with half of those interviewed rejecting the notion of nominal help from men and insisting that housework should be shared on an equal basis. Clearly, both Asian and white girls' views embody elements of collusion, resistance and opposition. In comparison with the white mothers, a greater proportion of Asian mothers were in full-time paid work. Not surprisingly they complained about the 'double-shift'; in the words of one woman, 'It's a dog's life. There are bills after bills to be paid. You wear yourself to the bone with work.' Many Asian women lamented the absence of support in Britain of other women from an extended household. Where extended households did exist, domestic work was indeed shared amongst the women, but it was no less onerous, since there were now more members of the household to cater for.

Statistics show that marriage remains popular in Britain despite the high rate of divorce (Leonard and Speakman 1986). This orientation was reflected among both white and Asian adolescents whom I interviewed. Yet, while they did not reject marriage, the girls in particular wanted their own marriages to be established on a more egalitarian basis, with both partners having an equal say in the decision-making. The great majority of the Asian adolescents expected their marriages to be arranged – a prospect most of them seemed to accept with either equanimity, ambivalence, as a *fait accompli*, or with fear and trepidation. Contrary to the media portrayal, of bullying Asian parents ramming arranged marriages down the throats of their children, many adolescents said they were confident that they would not be forced into a marriage that they did not want. This confidence did not seem to be misplaced, as most parents told me that they would not countenance forcing their children into a marriage against the latter's wishes. A significant majority of the parents saw the whole process as a joint undertaking between the parents and the young person. This is not to suggest that there were no intransigent parents determined to impose their authority, or adolescents who did not have a major disagreement with the adults in the family, but rather that in most households there was scope for negotiation between the generations. When an un-bridgeable chasm did occur, both the adolescent and the parents experienced considerable distress. Most young people had strong emotional and psychological attachment to their close relatives and felt that they could not 'let the family down'. The Asian girls argued that the little they had seen of the process which led to white girls marrying did not convince them that the latter had 'more freedom' than themselves. In saying this, the girls highlighted the problematic nature of marriage for all women. And, as Parita Trivedi has argued, Asian women want to make their own choices as to how and why they challenge their own marriage norms, rather than accept a racist definition of such marriages (Trivedi 1984).

In her book on adolescent girls in British schools, Sue Lees highlights the importance of the concept of 'reputation' in structuring women's sexuality. She shows how the term 'slag' and its equivalents are used by both boys and girls to cast doubts on a girl's reputation. She argues that:

> While everyone apparently knows a slag and stereotypically depicts her as someone who sleeps around this stereotype bears no relation to the girls to whom the term is applied. . . . What is important is the existence of the category rather than the identification of certain girls. . . . All unattached girls have to be constantly aware that the category slag may be applied to them. There is no hard and fast distinction between the categories since the status is always disputable, the gossip often unreliable, the criteria obscure. If a girl does get the reputation of being a slag, all the girls interviewed agreed that the one thing she could do about it to redeem herself would be to get a steady boyfriend.
>
> (Lees 1986)

Lees's last sentence is problematic when applied to Asian girls because, in their case, having a boyfriend would in itself constitute a transgression from certain norms of 'respectability'. The strategies they may use in the school context could well produce considerable dissonance in the wider context of Asian life world. Nevertheless, the importance of Lees's study lies in illustrating how, even in the 1980s when women were supposed to have made considerable gains towards sexual equality, notions of respectability could have the power to control female sexuality through sheer innuendo. It is important to stress that notions of female sexuality in Britain are racialised concepts. Asian women's sexuality is categorised broadly in three ways. First, there is the image of the exotic oriental woman – sensuous, seductive, full of Eastern promise. Her sexuality is projected as suitably controlled but vulnerable. This image is most explicitly available in the portrayal of airline 'hostesses' in advertisements.

The second type of representation is almost an antithesis of the first. Here, Asian women are characterised as 'ugly', 'smelly', 'oily-haired', etc. This image plays a vital role in the substantial exclusion of black women from 'glamorous jobs' where women's femininity is required to be visible. In the third construction, Asian women's sexuality is portrayed as licentious. All three elements are captured in the following quotation from a *Guardian* article of 5 September 1985, in which a nineteen-year-old Asian girl, Sunjita, describes her experience:

> If I'm with a white boy, say just on the way home from college, they shout in the street, 'What's it like to fuck a Paki?', or if I'm on my own with other girls it's, 'Here comes the Paki whore, come and fuck us Paki whores, we've heard you're really horny'. Or maybe they'll put it the other way round, saying that I am dirty, that no one could possibly want to go to bed with a Paki. . . . I don't think any white person can possibly identify with what it's like.

Such racialised discourses 'privilege' white women over black women, even as they subordinate both categories and at the same time render lesbian sexuality largely invisible. Of course, these definitions are repudiated by Asian women in a variety of ways, and, in any case, white people do not always constitute the primary 'significant others' in the formation of Asian women's sexual identity. Nevertheless, such dominant definitions have powerful effects when translated into social policy or when they become the 'professional common sense' of teachers, social workers, health visitors and others working within agencies of social welfare. The actual lived experience of the family often bears little resemblance to the stereotypic notions which structure professional values and perspectives.

SCHOOLING AND ASIAN GIRLS

The consequences of sexism in schooling are now well known. Attention has been drawn to the underrepresentation of girls in key science subjects, the invisibility of women in key content areas of the curriculum, the tendency on the part of teachers to pay more attention to boys, the role of education in contributing to a gender-divided occupational structure, and the pressure on girls to see their lives primarily in terms of marriage and the family (Deem 1980; Spender 1982). In the case of Asian girls, these effects are further compounded by racism. Racism in schools operates in a variety of complex ways. It may be direct or indirect, conscious or subconscious. It can operate through implicit stereotyped assumptions made by teachers or other educationists about Asian girls and boys, or it may be institutional-ised in the routine structures and practices of the school, as, for example, when the school curriculum neglects, negates or misrepre-sents the history and cultures of Asian and other black groups.

There is a tendency among teachers to see most problems encountered by Asian girls as being the result of 'intergenerational conflict'. Yet there is no evidence to support the implied assertion that conflict levels are higher amongst Asian families than among white families. Asian parents tend to be portrayed as 'authoritarian', 'conservative' and supposedly 'opposed to the liberating influence of schools'. But there is as much variation among Asian parents on issues concerning the education of their children as can be expected in any other group of parents. There are many problems with 'culturalist explanations', not least that they can have the effect of blaming the subordinate group as well as providing legitimacy to the ideology which claims the superiority of Western cultural practices over non-Western ones.

If girls in general tend to receive less attention from teachers than do boys, Asian girls may find themselves at an even greater disadvantage. The 'passive' stereotype can lead some teachers to pay an even lesser degree of attention to this category of girls. There are other ways, too, in which cultural stereotyping can work against the interests of Asian girls. For instance, teachers who may assume Asian parents to be opposed to their daughters going into further or higher education, may discourage these girls from studying subjects at 'O' and 'A' levels, and from pursuing academic careers. Yet many Asian parents are very keen for their daughters to gain higher-level qualifications. There is evidence that Asian girls who may require additional support in English can find themselves presented with a restricted curriculum as if they were remedial learners. Asian girls in schools can also experience ridicule from white pupils if they wear Asian styles of dress (Parmar and Mirza 1983; Brah and Minhas 1985).

Of course, educational disadvantage also accrues if, as is common, the formal and hidden curriculum of the school is Eurocentric and the cultures and identities of Asian children are devalued; if there are very few Asian teachers in the schools and even fewer Asian people in the power hierarchy of the education system; if the ideology that 'black people are problems for white society' is not challenged; and generally if no connection is made between the educational process and the broader social context to the arrival and settlement of Asian and other black groups in post-war Britain.

ASIAN WOMEN ORGANISING

Despite the Western stereotype of the abjectly submissive Asian woman, we have a long history of resistance and struggle, both in the sub-continent and in Britain. A significant number of South Asian organisations existed in Britain even during the colonial phase, and many female and male activists made an important contribution to Britain's intellectual and political life. Women such as Renu Chakraverty and N. C. Sen were prominent activists of the time (Liddle and Joshi 1985; Nazir 1986a).

Since World War II, Asian women have continued this tradition of resistance and struggle, although their responses may not always take a form which is familiar to a Western observer or be crystallised around issues defined as relevant from a Western frame of reference. As we have already seen, Asian women have been at the forefront of several major industrial struggles and have been the principal protagonists in a number of well-publicised immigration campaigns. Asian women have also played a crucial role in a variety of defence campaigns launched in support of people arrested while defending communities against fascist attacks. Over the years, racist attacks have become a common feature of life in several parts of Britain. These attacks have included arson and murder, yet few attackers have been convicted. On the other hand, Asians taking measures to protect themselves and their communities have been subjected to the heavy hand of the criminal justice system. It is only after extensive campaigning that many of the defendants in some of the well-known cases have been acquitted.

Asian women have also been actively engaged in placing the question of reproductive rights firmly on to the political agenda. There have been campaigns against the use of the contraceptive drug Depo-Provera for black and Third World women, and for working-class women in general. This intervention challenged the narrow focus of the National Abortion Campaign upon abortion rights, when certain categories of women were subjected to forced sterilisation. Racist ideologies about the reproductive capacities of Asian women abound within the whole spectrum of the agencies of the welfare state, ranging from the social services and the National Health Service to education welfare. Both as clients and staff, Asian women are increasingly uniting to fight back against the oppressive practices of these institutions.

A major priority for women has been the need to fight male violence in its variety of manifestations, which include rape, incest and domestic violence. These issues are a focus of activity for several Asian women's groups across the country. Separate refuges have been set up for Asian women so as to enable these victims of violence to work out their futures in the supportive environment of other Asian women facing similar problems. Protest demonstrations have been held, conferences organised and campaigns mounted to highlight the issues. A range of political opinion is represented among the Asian women whose efforts have led to the growing emergence of an organised revolt.

At home, Asian women combine with other female kin and friends to create a dynamic and lively social and cultural life. These female cultures are not devoid of contradictions, tensions, rivalry or inter-generational differences that may spill over into conflict, but they are constitutive of structures of support and space within which gender-specific activities, including leisure, may be constructed and performed. They are a means of negotiating and/or combating hierarchies of power in the household and in the wider community. These cultures are the arena where diverse and heterogeneous women's identities are played out.

The organising activities of Asian women take a variety of forms. A directory listing Asian women's groups in London has recently been published. The groups range from religious organisations to collectives of feminists. Whatever their political perspective, these groups seek to develop support networks for one another, organise social and cultural activities, provide information and advice (for example, on immigration, law and social welfare) and offer space to women to organise and campaign on issues they see as relevant. These self-help groups speak to the shared experience of Asian women and address issues of common concern in an atmosphere of trust and self-respect. It is not easy to categorise these groups along some conventional notion of a political continuum from the 'Right' to the 'Left'. The multi-faceted nature of our oppression demands resistance at so many different levels that such labels become quite problematic. Organisations whose *raison d'être* is religious or caste exclusivity, for example, will actively support and/or join in with members of other religions and castes in a range of anti-racist activities. Similarly, major workplace struggles involving Asians have relied on support from diverse sections of the Asian communities.

While it is important to acknowledge the broad base of support among Asian women for tackling the multiple manifestations of their specific forms of subordination, there is equally a need to distinguish between those forms of mobilisation which are primarily concerned with specific, largely single issues, and others which derive from a wider-ranging feminist analysis of the condition of being Asian and female in Britain. The two, of course, are not mutually exclusive, but nor are they identical. Asian feminism is one of the most creative and vigorous forces within contemporary black politics in Britain. It draws upon the political traditions of women and men in the sub-continent, but its identity is indelibly composed within the British social and political dynamic. Asian feminists have had to address issues surrounding the ways in which factors such as caste, class and religion configure in the British situation. We have placed great emphasis on the need for unity between women of different castes, religions and regional backgrounds in the sub-continent, while recognising the specificity of each experience. A number of Asian feminist groups were jointly formed with black women of Afro-Caribbean origin as an expression of solidarity against the shared experience of anti-black racism. This combined black feminism has posed a major challenge to the theory and practice of the whole feminist and socialist movement. Black feminists have sought to gain priority for issues which underpin our particular oppression in the context of the international dimension of race, class and imperialism. The aim has been not to assert the primacy of one form of oppression over the other, but to examine how they articulate. On this, black activists in general have had continuing skirmishes with those sections of the white Left which continue to assert the primacy of class over race and gender.

Chapter 4

Questions of 'difference' and global feminisms

> Why do we have to be concerned with the question of Third World women? After all, it is only one issue among many others. Delete 'Third World' and the sentence immediately unveils its value-loaded clichés.
>
> (Trinh T. Minh-ha 1989: 85)

For several hundred years now a global economic system has been in the making. It evolved out of the transatlantic trade in human beings, it flourished during the Industrial Revolution, it has been nurtured by colonialism and imperialism, and now it has achieved a new vitality in this age of microchip technology and multinational corporations. It is a system that has created lasting inequalities, both within nations and between nations.

All our fates are linked within this system, but our precise position depends on a multiplicity of factors, such as gender, class, colour, ethnicity, caste, whether we practise a dominant or subordinate sexuality, and whether we live in a rich, industrially advanced society or a poor country of the Third World. Given the global nature of this system, it is axiomatic that questions of feminism cannot be framed without reference to this international context. This point may seem self-evident. But the ongoing debate surrounding questions of Eurocentricism, racism and feminism shows that these issues are far from settled.

The feminist slogan 'sisterhood is global' that was commonly used by the women's movement in the 1970s signalled the centrality of an international dimension to feminist practice, but, as many critics have since pointed out, the slogan failed to acknowledge the heterogeneity of the condition of being a woman. What does it mean to be a Native American or Native Australian woman whose land rights have been appropriated and whose cultures have been systematically denigrated by the state as well as by the dominant ideologies and practices within civil society? What precise meaning do questions of 'domestic labour' hold for peasant women in the poorest areas of Kenya, who not only are responsible for caring work at home but also have to undertake long hours of strenuous work on the land as well as carry water and firewood for long distances to ensure daily survival? What are the realities facing low-paid women workers employed by multinational companies in countries such as the Philippines, Hong Kong and Sri Lanka? What are the similarities and the differences between their life chances and those of women doing similar work in Britain and other 'overdeveloped countries'? How do patriarchal ideologies articulate with international relations of power in the formation of sex-tourism as a growing industry? What are the points of convergence and divergence in the lives of black and white women in Britain? Such questions point to major differences in the social circumstances of different groups of women, and this will mean that their interests may often be contradictory. How will feminism in the 1990s address the contradictions underlying these different womanhoods?

How can we ensure that – as we grapple with the construction of strategies which would give women greater economic independence and political control; which would alleviate the burden of child care and domestic work; rid society of patriarchal violence; and allow women to have control over our sexuality and freedom of choice over childbearing – these strategies do not reiterate and reinforce inequalities? I do not believe that we can begin to develop these strategies unless they are grounded in an understanding of the ways in which issues of class, racism, gender and sexuality are interconnected and inscribed within the global social order.

Of course, these questions are not new. But they take on new meanings in the context of major changes, both in the global economy and in the political and cultural map of the world. This period of momentous events in Eastern Europe, the Soviet Union, South Africa, Central and South America and the Persian Gulf – to mention a few examples – calls for an urgent assessment of the implications of these changes and new alignments within the global social order for different groups of women, men and children the world over. What implications will the predicted 'triumph of the market' have on vulnerable social groups in Eastern Europe? How will women's lives be affected by the resurgence in ethnic conflict and racism? Will consolidation of a new European identity strengthen the racisms through which Europe and its diasporas have constructed the non-European 'others'?

The present crisis in the Gulf illustrates both the strength and the inherent instability of the emerging new configuration of world alliances.[1] It is interesting to note how vested economic interests have converted those who have previously been strongly opposed to economic sanctions in South Africa into staunch supporters of an economic blockade in the Gulf. Governments and peoples who have consistently ignored the decades of struggle for self-determination of the Palestinian people are now vehemently in support of Kuwait's right to exist as a sovereign state. This is not to suggest that the invasion of Kuwait is justified but to point out the double standards that characterise particular political positions on the Gulf crisis.

The role of labour migration in lubricating the world economic order is graphically illustrated by the events in the Gulf, as we watch television pictures of thousands of Asian workers, both women and men, stranded in the desert with little food or water. Their plight had been all but ignored in the early stages of the crisis when only the Western citizens in the Gulf were a focus of concern. It is also worth noting how Western residents in the Gulf have been constructed as heroic and valiant bearers of a 'civilised sensibility' against an 'oriental despot', bent on using Western women and children as a 'human shield'. On the other hand, when the world's attention did ultimately shift to the appalling living conditions of Asian workers, this collectivity came to be seen not so much as subjects with human rights than as the object of Western charity. Racism, class and gender divisions are all combined in the unfolding of these global events.

The Western response to the Gulf crisis highlights commonalty as well as conflict of interest between the superpowers. The crisis also places into relief the rivalries among the nations of the Middle East and internal class contradictions in these societies. The massive military build-up, costing billions every day, reiterates the scandal of the growing militarisation of a world in which millions still do not have enough to eat. Women may not be as visible as the men on the centre stage of world politics, but political processes are indelibly marked by *constructions* of female gender. Women's labour, both inside and outside the household, is a constitutive element of the global economy. The signification of woman in nationalistic discourses as carrier of the 'race', of male honour, and as the dependant of man has the effect of 'producing' women (and children) as ideological fodder in competing nationalisms. Equally, women's own political practices – in terms of whether we collude with, accept, resist, or challenge international hierarchies of power – are also thoroughly implicated in all these processes.

Global relations take complex forms, but this need not imply that we are not able to develop strategies for concrete political intervention. We may use abstract concepts such as gender, racism, or class to address political phenomena, but these abstractions have very 'real' effects, albeit of varying types, upon different groups of women. The plight of Asian and white women stranded in the Gulf region during the present crisis provides a clear illustration of this point. The difference in their accommodation and general treatment during the process of evacuation has been striking. While waiting to be flown out to safety, white women have been kept in high quality hotels, whereas Asian women have been shunted off into makeshift tents. Television interviews with white 'expatriate' women have shown them describing the loss felt when leaving their overseas homes and all their material belongings behind. The Asian women, too, are leaving empty-handed. But the consequences for the two groups will be rather different.

The majority of the Asian women have been employed in the Gulf doing low-paid, menial jobs as domestic workers with very few political or social rights. Their wages have been a major, if not the sole, source of income for their extended families in Asia. Their loss of livelihood is likely to result in considerable hardship and poverty since they are faced with the prospect of almost certain unemployment upon their return. The Western women have been in the Gulf region either as the wives of diplomats, of military personnel, professionals, technicians or businessmen, or, to a lesser extent, they have themselves been engaged in these well-paid occupations. While their return to Western countries with established welfare systems may in some cases result in a drop in their standard of living, it is nonetheless unlikely to lead to impoverishment.

Of course, we will wish to sympathise with the personal losses suffered by all women. But we need feminist perspectives which enable us to develop understandings of why, for instance, the rich and the poor countries of the world supply different types of labour to the Middle East, and why this present crisis is expected to have a far more devastating impact on the economies of South Asia than on those of richer countries because of such factors as the loss of migrant workers' remittances, which constitute an important source of foreign exchange with which to service the foreign debt, higher oil prices, and the cost of sanctions and repatriation of workers. We need accounts of why certain sectors of the world economy become feminised, why certain categories of women perform particular kinds of paid work, and how these different groups of women are differently represented within different political, religious, academic and common-sense discourses (cf. Mitter 1986; Mohanty 1988; Enloe 1989).

We can find equally pertinent examples in Britain. As is now well known, it is not a matter of coincidence but rather a result of the history of colonialism and imperialism that the post-war labour shortages in Britain were met via the recruitment of workers from the former colonies in Asia and the Caribbean. Research evidence shows that, although the employment profiles of women of Afro-Caribbean and South Asian descent are not identical (and there are differences between different categories of South Asian women), nonetheless these women are predominantly concentrated at the lowest rungs of the gender-segregated labour market (see Chapter Three, and cf. Brown 1984; Bruegel 1989).

Black women's experiences of racism in the labour market, the education system, the Health Service, the media and in consequence of a variety of state policies such as those on immigration, policing and social welfare, mean that, even when black and white women share a broadly similar class position, they constitute distinctive fractions within that specific class location.[2] Their everyday life experiences will therefore be characterised by certain commonalties, but also by crucial differences. But all this begs the question of how 'difference' is to be conceptualised. I believe that discussions around 'differences' may be conducted at cross purposes unless we attempt to clarify how the notion of 'difference' is used under particular circumstances.

How may 'difference' be conceptualised? For heuristic purposes, 'difference' may be understood as comprising several conceptually distinct modalities, each constitutive of and embedded within the other. At the most general level, 'difference' may be construed as a *social relation* constructed within systems of power underlying structures of class, racism, gender and sexuality, and so on. At this level of abstraction we are concerned with the ways in which our social position is circumscribed by the broad parameters set by the economic, political and cultural structures of a given society. Some of the examples I have so far given refer to women's positioning in such simultaneously local and global structural terms. It is extremely important to address the modality of social relation, as it has a crucial bearing on shaping our life chances. 'Difference' may also be conceptualised as *experiential diversity*. Here, the focus is on the many and different ways in which ideological and institutional practices mark our everyday life. These everyday practices are the matrices enmeshed within which our personal and group histories are made and remade. But we need to make a distinction between 'difference' as the marker of the *distinctiveness of our collective histories* and 'difference' as *personal experience*, codified in an individual's biography. Although mutually interdependent, the two modalities cannot be 'read off' from each other. Our personal experiences arise out of mediated relationships. How we perceive and understand our experience may vary enormously. For example, we may experience subordination without necessarily recognising it as such. The same social practice may be associated with somewhat different meanings in a different cultural context. There may be psychic and emotional disjunction between how we feel about something and how we believe we ought to feel from the standpoint of our analytical and political perspectives. The group histories that chronicle our shared experience will also contain their own measure of contradictions, but the point is that there is no simple one-to-one correspondence between collective experience and personal biography. To state the obvious, collective experience does not represent the sum total of individual experiences any more than individual experiences can be taken to be a direct expression of the collective (see Chapter Five for a fuller discussion of 'difference').

Hence we need to make distinctions between, for example, 'black' and 'white' women in British discourse as historically contingent analytical or 'common-sense' categories marked by specific historical processes of slavery, indentured labour, colonialism, imperialism and anti-black racism, *and* black and white women as individuals. While the former describes a social division, the latter draws our attention to the person as a complex and continually changing subject who is the site of multiple contradictions, and whose everyday practices are associated with effects that may reinforce or undermine social divisions.

It is now widely accepted that 'woman' is not a unitary category. The question remains whether it can be a unifying category. I believe that it is possible to develop a feminist politics that is simultaneously local and global. But it demands ongoing commitment, together with sustained and painstaking effort. It calls for the development of political practice which appreciates how and why the lives of different categories of women are differentially shaped by articulating relations of power; and how under a given set of circumstances we ourselves are 'situated' in these power relations *vis-à-vis* other categories of women and men. For example, as an Asian woman living in Britain I am subjected to racism, but as a member of a dominant caste within the specific community from which I 'originate' I also occupy a position of power in relation to lower-caste women. From my standpoint, a feminist politics would demand of me a commitment to opposing racism as much as casteism, although I am positioned differently within these social hierarchies, and the strategies required of me in dealing with them may be different.

Similarly, we may take the example of Irish and black women in Britain. Both black and Irish people have a history of being colonised, both occupy predominantly working-class positions within the British class structure, and both have been subjected to racism. But anti-Irish racism and anti-black racism have different histories. As white Europeans, Irish women are constructed as a dominant group *vis-à-vis* black women in and through the discourses of anti-black racism, even when they themselves are in turn subordinated within anti-Irish racism. Alliances that would empower both groups must not only take into account the similarities in their material circumstances but must also involve commitment to combating the differing racisms to which the two groups are subjected. Black and Irish women would need to examine the ways in which their 'womanhoods' are both similarly and differently constructed within patriarchal, racial and class relations of power.

As a consequence of the major restructuring of the world economy, the acceleration in the growth of multinational capital, the impact of the new communications revolution, and the profound political upheavals of recent times, we are witnessing global tendencies that are simultaneously complementary and contradictory. On the one hand, the ever increasing globalisation of cultural industries is leading to the homogenisation of cultural consumption across transnational boundaries. On the other hand, we are faced with the parallel tendency towards greater fragmentation; the resurgence of local aesthetic, political and ethnic tradition; and the assertion of 'difference'. Under such circumstances it is important to identify when 'difference' is organised hierarchically rather than laterally. We need to distinguish instances when 'difference' is asserted as a mode of contestation against oppression and exploitation, from those where 'difference' becomes the vehicle for the legitimation of dominance. In practice this exercise is not clear cut. For instance, nationalistic discourses may be employed by liberation movements as well as by racist and chauvinistic groups and organisations. Moreover, both sets of discourses may be constituted around, and/or be constitutive of, representations of women which reinforce rather than undermine women's subordination. In these instances feminist practice would require that we pay careful attention to the historical and social circumstances which underpin a given nationalism, and its consequences for different economic groups and for different groups of women.

A distinction between 'difference' as a process of differentiation referring to the particularities of the social experience of a group, from that whereby 'difference' itself becomes the modality in which domination articulates, is crucial for several reasons. First, it draws our attention to the fact that 'difference' need not invariably lead to divisions among different groups of women. Second, it reminds us that our experiences are not constituted solely within 'oppressions'. Our lives encompass such an immense range of variability – geographical, environmental, physical, emotional, psychological, psychic and social, all imploding into one another – that meaning constantly eludes compartmentalisation and totalisation. In this sense, *cultural diversity* is the refusal of 'fixity of meaning', as articulated, for example, in art, music, literature, architecture, religious practices, science and technology, forms of economic organisation, political traditions, and changing modalities of subjectivity. Cultural diversity may be affirmed and celebrated while bearing in mind that the notion of 'cultural difference' is vulnerable to appropriation within political tendencies marking essentialist and impervious boundaries between groups. Contemporary racism in Britain provides an instance of such appropriation of 'cultural difference'.

Symbols of 'cultural difference' may also be mobilised by subordinated peoples as a means of consolidating a political challenge. Such a political assertion of cultural identity could potentially constitute a progressive force, although it too cannot be assumed to be invariably unproblematic, simply because it is a form of struggle by a subordinate group. Politics of cultural pride may prove contradictory, as, for instance, if cultural practices are treated as reified symbols of an essentialist historic past. Hence, the meaning of 'cultural difference' is contingent not only on social and political circumstances but also upon the extent to which the concept of culture is posited in essentialist or non-essentialist terms.

The issue of essentialism seems to call for conceptual clarification between:

1 essentialism as referring to a notion of ultimate essence that transcends historical and cultural boundaries;
2 'universalism' as a commonalty derived from historically variable experience and as such remaining subject to historical change; and
3 the historical specificity of a particular cultural formation.

It should be possible to recognise cultural difference in the sense of (3), and to acknowledge commonalties that acquire a 'universal' status through the accumulation of similar (but not identical) experiences in different contexts as in (2), without resorting to essentialism. It is evident that, as women, we can identify many commonalties of experience across cultures which nonetheless retain their particularity. In other words, historical specificity and 'universalism' need not be counterposed against each other. My own use of the term 'universal' in the way described above is something of a departure from the general usage of the term. I am arguing the case for a non-essentialist 'universalism'; that is, for a concept of 'universalism' as a historical 'product'. But, in the light of the complicity of the discourse of 'universalism' with hegemonic projects of imperialism, it might be helpful to substitute 'universalism' with the idea of 'trans-cultural' identifications.

We would be in a better position to have mutual respect for 'cultural difference' without recourse to essentialism if cultures were to be conceived less in terms of reified artefacts and rather more as processes. This may also circumvent the issue of 'cultural relativism'. If cultures are understood as processes instead of fixed products, it would be possible to challenge a particular cultural practice from a feminist perspective without constructing a whole cultural group as being inherently 'such and such'. For example, we may condemn the practice of 'suttee' without being positioned within those colonial and post-colonial discourses (such as the novel and its televised film *The Far Pavilions*) which represent such practices as symbols of the inherent barbarism of Indian cultures. This would demand that racialised discourses and practices are challenged equally vehemently and persistently. Similarly, we could condemn racist practices in Britain without assuming that British cultures are inherently racist, and instead acknowledge racism as a historically specific product.

It follows that human subjects are not fixed embodiments of cultures. Since all cultures are internally differentiated and never static, though the pace of change may be variable, our subjectivities are formed within heterogeneous discursive practices. A variety of subject positions will emerge within a single cultural context offering the possibility of political change: from a non-feminist to a feminist position, for example. But shifts in subject position are far from smooth transitions. There could be considerable emotional and psychic ambivalence or distress which must be confronted and addressed if feminist visions are to make a lasting impact. Understanding the dynamics of power which produce and sustain specific forms of subjectivity is crucial if we are to challenge the hegemony of, say, racism or heterosexism; that is, analysis of the nature of power marking white subjectivity or heterosexual subjectivity becomes essential if 'non-white' people are subjected to racism, or if lesbian and gay sexuality is subjugated. Such enquiries should highlight (and help us address and deal with) the personal implications of adopting anti-racist or anti-heterosexist political positions.

The constitution of subjectivity within heterogeneous discursive practices means that we inhabit articulating and changing identities interweaving across relations of race, gender, class or sexuality. How we work with and across our 'differences' would depend upon the political and conceptual frameworks which inform our understanding of these 'differences'. It is our political perspectives and commitments that determine the basis for effective coalition building. I believe that coalitions are possible through a politics of identification, as opposed to a 'politics of identity'. We develop our first sense of community within a neighbourhood, but we soon learn to see ourselves as part of many other 'imagined communities' – imagined in so far as we may never actually meet those people face to face. But we learn to identify with these groups, their experiences, their struggles. These processes of political identification – of the formation of 'communities in struggle' – do not erase the diversity of human experience; rather, they enable us to appreciate the 'particular' within the 'universal', and the 'universal' within the 'particular'. However, this politics of identification is only meaningful – indeed, only possible – if it is based on understandings of the material and ideological basis of all oppressions in their global manifestations; of the interconnectedness as well as the specificity of each oppression. And it is only meaningful if we develop a practice to challenge and combat them all. We can work locally in our own groups, organisations, workplaces and communities, but we need to make connections with wider national and global struggles and movements.

NOTES

1 This chapter was first written as a talk presented at the annual conference of the Women's Studies Network (UK) in July 1990. It was revised for publication during September 1990, so that any reference to the situation in the Persian Gulf is applicable only to the events as they had unfolded by the end of that month.
2 The concept of class fraction is the subject of considerable debate in the literature on 'race' and ethnicity. See, for instance, Phizacklea and Miles (1980); Miles (1982); Sivanandan (1982); Rex and Mason (1986).

Chapter 5

Difference, diversity, differentiation

Difference, diversity, pluralism, hybridity – these are some of the most debated and contested terms of our time. Questions of difference are at the heart of many discussions within contemporary feminisms. In the field of education in Britain, questions of identity and community continue to dominate debates surrounding 'multiculturalism' and 'anti-racism'. In this chapter, I consider how these themes might help us to understand the racialisation of gender. No matter how often the concept is exposed as vacuous, 'race' still acts as an apparently ineradicable marker of social difference. What makes it possible for the category to act in this way? What is the nature of social and cultural differences and what gives them their force? How does 'racial' difference, then, connect to difference and antagonisms organised around other markers like 'gender' or 'class'? Such questions are important because they can help to explain people's tenacious investment in notions of identity, community and tradition.

One recurrent problem in this area is that of essentialism: that is, a notion of ultimate essence that transcends historical and cultural boundaries. Here, I argue against an essentialist concept of difference while simultaneously problematising the issue of 'essentialism'. At what point, and in what ways, for example, does the specificity of a particular social experience become a sign of essentialism? In reviewing feminist debates, I suggest that black and white feminism should not be seen as essentially fixed, oppositional categories, but rather as historically contingent fields of contestation within discursive and material practices. In similar vein, I shall be arguing that analysis of the interconnections between racism, class, gender, sexuality or any other marker of 'difference' must take account of the positionality of different racisms with respect to one another. Overall, I underline the importance of a macro-analysis that studies

the interrelationships between various forms of social differentiation, empirically and historically, but without necessarily deriving
them all from a single determining instance. In other words, I shall
also be trying to avoid the danger of 'reductionism'. Simultaneously,
I draw attention to the centrality of analysing the problematic of
subjectivity and identity in understanding the power dynamics of
social differentiation.

The chapter is divided into three parts. In the first, I address the
various notions of 'difference' that have emerged in the recent
controversy about the category 'black' as a common sign for the
experience of African-Caribbean and South Asian groups in post-war
Britain. My aim here is to signal how 'black' has operated as a
contingent sign under different political circumstances. The issue is
not whether the term 'black' should have been mobilised in the way
that it was. Rather, my interest lies in analysing the type of political
subject that the British black movement inaugurated. The second
section is concerned with the ways in which issues of 'difference' were
framed within feminist theory and practice during the 1970s and
1980s. My primary focus here is on the British debate. I conclude with
a brief examination of some conceptual categories used in the
theorisation of 'difference', and suggest a new framework for analysis
which I hope will help to clarify issues in the development of political
strategies for social justice.

WHAT'S IN A NAME? WHAT'S IN A COLOUR?

Over the past few years the usage of the term 'black' to refer to people
of African-Caribbean and South Asian descent in Britain has been the
subject of considerable controversy. It is important to address some of
these arguments, as they often centre around notions of 'difference'.

The African-Caribbean and South Asian people who migrated to
Britain in the post-war period found themselves occupying a broadly
similar structural position as workers performing predominantly
unskilled or semi-skilled jobs on the lowest rungs of the economy.
They were then commonly described in popular, political, and
academic discourses as 'coloured people'. This was not a simple
descriptive term. It had been the colonial code for a relationship of
domination and subordination between the coloniser and the colonised. Now the code was re-worked and re-constituted in and through a
variety of political, cultural and economic processes in post-war
Britain. In other words, the African-Caribbean and Asian groups

experienced the racialisation of their gendered class positioning through a racism which foregrounded their 'non-whiteness' as a common thematic within the discourse of 'coloured people'. Although the precise ways in which these heterogeneous sets of people were racialised were not identical, the condensation of the binary white/non-white in this discourse constructed equivalence and similarity of experience, as they faced racist practices of stigmatisation, inferiorisation, exclusion, and/or discrimination in arenas such as employment, education, housing, media, the criminal justice system, immigration apparatus, and the health services. These relations of equivalence created the conditions under which a new politics of solidarity became possible.

The concept of 'black' now emerges as a specifically political term embracing African-Caribbean and South Asian peoples. It constitutes a political subject inscribing politics of resistance against colour-centred racisms. The term was adopted by the emerging coalitions amongst African-Caribbean and South Asian organisations and activists in the late 1960s and 1970s. They were influenced by the way that the Black Power movement in the USA, which had turned the concept of 'black' on its head, divested it of its pejorative connotations in racialised discourses, and transformed it into a confident expression of an assertive group identity. The Black Power movement urged black Americans to construe the 'black community' not as a matter of geography but rather in terms of the global African diaspora. Eschewing 'chromatism' – the basis of differentiation amongst blacks according to lighter or darker tone of skin – 'black' became a political colour to be claimed with pride against colour-based racisms. The African-Caribbean and South Asian activists in Britain borrowed the term from the Black Power movement to foster a rejection of chromatism amongst those defined as 'coloured people' in Britain.

Class was an important constitutive element in the emergence of the concept of 'black' as a political colour. The project is best understood as part of the British New Left. A number of organisations active in this political movement defined themselves as workers' organisations; for instance, the Indian Workers Association and the Black Peoples Alliance. Major political publications of the period, such as *Race Today* and *Race and Class*, addressed the articulation between racism and class relations. The journal *Race and Class* is still going strong in the 1990s as a leading journal committed to challenging global racisms and class inequities. The new political subject produced by the politics of 'black' transformed class politics by interrogating political discourses which asserted the primacy of class.

The politics of solidarity between African-Caribbean and South Asian activists of the period were also influenced by the memory of recent anti-colonial struggles and decolonisation in Africa, Asia and the Caribbean. Some were also involved in the agitation against the war in Vietnam, the Campaign for Nuclear Disarmament, and other similar protest movements. The discourse of 'Afro-Asian' unity in Britain resonated with the call of anti-colonial liberation movements for unity among the colonised. Moreover, as Mercer (1994) argues, the sign 'black' was mobilised also as a displacement for the categories 'immigrant' and 'ethnic minority' which, throughout the 1960s and 1970s, had come to denote racialised re-definitions of belonging and subjecthood. The fusion of these various influences in the formation of a project concerned to address the social condition of post-colonial experience in the heart of the British metropolis meant that the concept of 'black' has been associated with rather distinctive and somewhat different meanings in Britain as compared with the USA.

British usage of the term 'black' has been criticised by commentators like Hazareesingh (1986) and Modood (1988). They argue that the 'black' in Black Power ideology referred specifically to the historical experience of people of sub-Saharan African descent, and was designed to create a positive political and cultural identity among black Americans. When used in relation to South Asians the concept is *de facto* emptied of those specific cultural meanings associated with phrases such as 'black music'. The concept can incorporate South Asians in a political sense only, and they therefore conclude that it denies Asian cultural identity. Clearly there is some force in this argument. It is certainly the case, as we have already noted, that the Black Power movement's mobilisation of the term 'black' was an attempt to reclaim an African heritage that had been denied to black Americans by racism. But, as a historically specific political project located in the socio-political and economic dynamics in the USA, the Black Power ideology did not simply reclaim a pre-given ancestral past. In that very process, it also constructed a particular version of this heritage.

Given that cultural processes are dynamic, and the process of claiming is itself mediated, the term 'black' does not have to be construed in essentialist terms. It can have different political and cultural meanings in different contexts. Its specific meaning in post-war Britain cannot be taken to have denied cultural differences between African, Caribbean and South Asian people when cultural difference was not the organising principle within this discourse or political practice. The concrete political struggles in which the new meaning was grounded acknowledged cultural differences but sought to accomplish political unity against racism. In any case, the issue of cultural difference cannot be posed purely in terms of differences between South Asian and African-Caribbean cultures. There are, for example, many differences between African and Caribbean cultures (which also include the cultures of people of South Asian descent). Cultures in the diasporas always have their own specificity. In other words, even when the use of the term 'black' is restricted to sub-Saharan Africa and its diasporas, it can be said, within the parameters of the terms set by the critics, to deny the cultural specificities of these diverse groups.

A second criticism of the ways in which 'black' has been employed in Britain has been that the concept is meaningless, since many South Asians do not define themselves as black, and many African-Caribbeans do not recognise them as such. This assertion hinges partly on the criterion of numbers, but without providing supporting numerical evidence. In my own research I have found that South Asians will frequently describe themselves as 'kale' (black) when discussing issues of racism. But since the whole social being of South Asian and African-Caribbean peoples is not constituted only by the experience of racism, they have many other identifications based on, for example, religion, language and political affiliation. Moreover, as many demonstrations and campaigns show, the concept of black was mobilised as part of a set of constitutive ideas and principles to promote collective action. As a social movement, black activism has aimed to generate solidarity; it has not necessarily *assumed* that all members of the diverse black communities inevitably identify with the concept in its British usage.

Another topic of contention has centred on the distribution of resources by the state to different categories of consumers. It is argued that the term 'black' serves to conceal the cultural needs of groups other than those of African-Caribbean origin. This particular critique is often steeped in 'ethnicism'. Ethnicism, I would suggest, defines the experience of racialised groups primarily in *'culturalist'* terms: that is, it posits 'ethnic difference' as the primary modality around which social life is constituted and experienced. Cultural needs are defined largely as independent of other social experiences centred around class, gender, racism or sexuality. This means that a group identified as culturally different is assumed to be internally homogeneous, when this is patently not the case. The 'housing needs' of a working-class Asian living in overcrowded conditions on a housing estate, for instance, cannot be the same as those of a middle-class Asian living in a semi-detached house in suburbia. In other words, ethnicist discourses seek to impose stereotypic notions of 'common cultural need' upon heterogeneous groups with diverse social aspirations and interests. They often fail to address the relationship between 'difference' and the social relations of power in which it may be inscribed. It is clearly important that the state should be sensitive to the plurality of needs among its citizens. But we need to be attentive to the ways in which 'needs' are socially constructed and represented in various discourses.

There is another limitation to the ethnicist critique of the use of the term 'black' by the local state. Ethnicism does not seem to differentiate between 'black' as a term adopted by subordinate groups to symbolise resistance against oppression and the appropriation of the same term by some local authorities as a basis for formulating policies for the allocation of resources (Sivanandan 1990; Gilroy 1987; Cain and Yuval-Davis 1990). The term has different meanings in the two contexts and signifies potentially different social and political outcomes, but ethnicism seems to conflate these different meanings. Furthermore, certain politicians may mobilise the discourse of 'ethnic difference' as a means to create their own power base rather than to empower those whose 'needs' are supposed to be better met by jettisoning the term 'black'. The point is that the replacement of 'black' by some other politically neutral descriptor will not secure more equitable distribution of resources. Arguably, it was a mark of the success of the politics of 'black' as a political colour that the sign was appropriated into state discourse. Once that happened, 'black' assumed new meanings. While previously it had served to generate solidarity between groups of African-Caribbean and South Asian descent around specific political isssues such as immigration or policing, it now became a site of dissent and conflict as members of these groups competed for jobs in the state sector, and for grants, services, and other resources. Black self-help projects which had been the showpiece of early post-war black politics (see Chapter One) now became dependent upon the state sector. During the 1980s, as Thatcherism in Britain began to exercise a major impact upon local government budgets, many community projects lost funding. Towards the end of the 1980s, as the Left movements generally began to break up and fragment, so did the project constituted around 'black' as a political colour.

What kind of a terminology has been proposed to replace 'black'? Writing from somewhat different political perspectives Hazareesingh (1986) and Modood (1988) come to rather similar conclusions. Hazareesingh suggests that the use of 'black' should be confined to people of African descent and that people from the South Asian subcontinent should all be subsumed under the concept of 'Indian', on the grounds of a shared 'culture in a historical sense'. But there is an immense diversity of cultures in the subcontinent which have emerged and been transformed under varying material and political circumstances. Furthermore, these cultures are underpinned by class, caste, religious, regional and linguistic differences and divisions. So in what sense can one speak of a common Indian culture? Hazareesingh's construction of this commonalty in terms of a shared experience of imperialism and racism is vulnerable to the same criticism he directs against those who support 'black' as a political colour. He, too, privileges historical and contemporary processes of domination, and the role of the state in mediating these, as centrally important in structuring people's experiences. His view of a common Indian culture could also be seen by many South Asians as 'an attempt to straitjacket their experience'. Given the position of the modern state of India *vis-à-vis* other countries of the Asian sub-continent, Hazareesingh's concept of 'Indian' might be construed by some as reinforcing a hegemonic project in that region. How will Pakistanis or Bangladeshis recognise themselves in this definition, given the recent history of partition?

Unlike Hazareesingh, Modood employs the term 'Asian' instead of 'black', which, he claims, 'sells short the majority of the people it identifies as black', and instead of 'South Asian', which he dismisses as an academic term. Leaving aside the fact that Asia covers a much larger part of the globe than the sub-continent of South Asia, it is his definition of 'Asian' which is particularly problematic: 'what I mean by an "Asian" identity', he states, 'is some share in the heritage of the civilisations of old Hindustan prior to British conquest' (Modood 1988: 97). First, the term Hindustan as used by the Mughals referred largely to the northern states of latter-day India. More importantly, Modood seems to attribute a unified identity to pre-colonial India which, by implication, was destroyed by the British Raj. Historical evidence shows, however, that pre-colonial India was a heterogeneous entity, and that people were much more likely to define themselves in terms of their regional, linguistic or religious affiliation than as Hindustanis. Indeed, it may be possible to argue that 'Indian identity' as a set of identifications with a nation-state was the outcome of resistance and struggle against colonialism rather than something that existed prior to this period.

[The point I wish to stress through this foray into the debate surrounding the use of the term 'black' in Britain is how 'difference' is constructed differently within these competing discourses.]That is, the usage of 'black', 'Indian' or 'Asian' is determined not so much by the nature of its referent as by its semiotic function within different discourses. These various meanings signal differing political strategies and outcomes./ They mobilise different sets of cultural or political identities, and set limits to where the boundaries of a 'community' are established,]This debate has to an extent been echoed within feminism. And it is against this general background that I turn to issues of 'difference' within feminism.

IS SISTERHOOD GLOBAL?

In 1985, I attended the International Women's Conference in Nairobi. There, over 10,000 women from more than 150 countries gathered to address questions of our 'universal' subordination as a 'second sex', yet the most striking aspect of this conference was the heterogeneity of our social condition. The issues raised by the different groups of women present at the conference, especially those from the Third World, served to underline the fact that issues affecting women cannot be analysed in isolation from the national and international context of inequality (Brah 1988; Mohanty 1988).

Our gender is constituted and represented differently according to our differential location within the global relations of power. Our insertion into these global relations of power is realised through a myriad of economic, political and ideological processes. Within these structures of social relations we do not exist simply as women but as differentiated categories, such as 'working-class women', 'peasant women' or 'migrant women'. Each description references a specificity of social condition. Real lives are forged out of a complex articulation of these dimensions. It is now axiomatic in feminist theory and practice that 'woman' is not a unitary category. Yet, this does not mean that the category itself is meaningless. The sign 'woman' has its own specificity constituted within and through historically specific configurations of gender relations. Its semiotic flux assumes specific meanings in discourses of different 'womanhoods' where it comes to symbolise particular historical trajectories, material circumstances and cultural experiences. Difference in this sense is a difference of social condition. Here, the analytical focus is on the social construction of different categories of women within the broader structural and ideological processes. No claims are made that an individual category is internally homogeneous. Working-class women, for instance, comprise very diverse groups of people both within and between different social formations. Class position signals certain commonalties of social outcomes, but class articulates with other axes of differentiation such as racism, heterosexism or caste in delineating the variable forms of life chances for specific categories of women.

The primary objective of feminism has been to change the social relations of power embedded within gender. Since gender inequalities pervade all spheres of life, feminist strategies have involved a challenge to women's subordinated position within both state institutions and civil society. The driving force behind feminist theory and practice in the post-war period has been its commitment to eradicate inequalities arising from a notion of sexual difference inherent in biologically deterministic theories, which explain women's social position as a result of innate differences. Despite evidence that 'sex differences' in cognitive behaviour among infants are slight and the psychological similarity between men and women is very high, research to establish innate differences continues unabated (Rose *et al.* 1984; Segal 1990). Feminists do not, of course, ignore women's biology, but they challenge ideologies which construct and represent women's subordination as resulting from their biological capacities.

The ways in which questions of biology are addressed varies within different feminisms. It is problematic to construct clear-cut boundaries between feminisms, not least because there is agreement in so many of the key areas. The following 'textbook typology', therefore, is intended merely to highlight certain broader 'differences' which remain the subject of contestation. According to such typologies, 'radical' feminist accounts may tend to identify women's biologically based subordination as the fundamental basis of gender inequality. The relations of power between men and women are seen as the primary dynamic of women's oppression, almost to the exclusion, sometimes, of other determinants such as class and racism. 'Radical' feminist perspectives are seen to represent women's procreative abilities as an indicator of certain psychological qualities which are uniquely and universally female. These qualities are assumed to have been undermined through patriarchal domination and thus need to be rediscovered and reclaimed. As a consequence there may be a celebration of 'sexual difference' in the form of presumed unique female attributes and qualities. It has been argued that, while repudiating biological determinism embedded within patriarchal discourses, some versions of 'radical' feminism, in turn, construct a transhistorical notion of essential femaleness in need of rescue and recapture beyond patriarchal relations (Segal 1987; Weedon 1987; Spelman 1988).

A central premise of 'socialist' feminism, on the other hand, is taken to be that human nature is not essential but is socially produced. The meaning of what it is to be a woman – biologically, socially, culturally and psychically – is considered to be historically variable. 'Socialist' feminism mounted a powerful critique of those materialist perspectives which prioritise class, neglect the social consequences of the sexual division of labour, privilege heterosexualities and pay scant attention to the social mechanisms which prevent women from attaining economic, political and social equality. This strand of feminism distances itself from the presumed 'radical' feminist emphasis on power relations between the sexes as the almost exclusive determinant of women's subordination.

In the 1990s, the debate has shifted quite radically, and these 'typologies' now assume a somewhat 'historical' interest. Since the demise of 'state socialism' in the former Soviet Union and Eastern Europe, 'socialism' has come to signify authoritarian and anti-democratic politics. The Forum of European Socialist Feminists, for example, has been re-named 'The European Forum of Left Feminists'. This change in nomenclature came about not because the political issues which used to be debated under the sign of 'socialism' became irrelevant. Rather, 'socialism' now became associated in Eastern Europe and the member states of the former Soviet Union with the discredited practices of the previous regimes, and women from these parts of Europe argued that they would no longer be able to mobilise support using 'socialism' in the title. It is important to stress that the change does not signal a mere pragmatic approach so much as a *strategic* response to new political circumstances. What long-term political shifts such changes imply are as yet difficult to predict.

It is worth remembering that, until recently, Western feminist perspectives, on the whole, paid little attention to the processes of racialisation of gender, class or sexuality. Processes of racialisation are, of course, historically specific, and different groups have been racialised differently under varying circumstances, and on the basis of different signifiers of 'difference'. Each racism has a particular history. It arose in the context of a particular set of economic, political and cultural circumstances, was produced and reproduced through specific mechanisms, and has assumed different forms in different situations. Anti-black racism, anti-Irish racism, anti-Jewish racism, anti-Arab racism, different varieties of Orientalisms: all have their distinctive features. I have already shown in Chapter Four how the specific histories of these various racisms place them in particular relationship to each other. I explored there some aspects of the differential racialisation of Irish and black groups in Britain. A second example, of African-Caribbean and South Asian groups, may clarify this point further.

These communities have developed different responses to racism because their experiences of it, though similar in many ways, have not been identical (Brah and Deem 1986). State policies have impacted differently on these communities. African-Caribbean communities have mobilised far more around their collective experience of the criminal justice system, particularly the police and the courts, whereas Asian groups have been much more actively involved in defending communities against violent racial attacks, racial harassment on housing estates, and in organising campaigns against deportations and other issues arising from the effects of immigration laws. The stereotypic representations of African-Caribbean and South Asian communities have also been substantially different. The gendered discourses of the 'nigger' and the 'Paki' in post-war Britain represent distinctive ideologies. Yet they are two strands of a common racism structured around colour/phenotype/culture as signifiers of superiority and inferiority in post-colonial Britain. This means that African-Caribbean, South Asian and white groups are relationally positioned within these structures of representation.

There is a tendency in Britain to see racism as 'something to do with the presence of black people'. But it is important to stress that both black and white people experience their gender, class and sexuality through 'race'. Racialisation of white subjectivity is often not manifestly apparent to white groups because 'white' is a signifier of dominance, but this renders the racialisation process no less significant. It is necessary, therefore, to analyse the processes which construct us as, say, 'white female' or 'black female', as 'white male' or 'black male'. Such deconstruction is necessary if we are to decipher how and why the meanings of these words change from plain descriptions to hierarchically organised categories under given economic, political and cultural circumstances.

Black feminism, white feminism?

During the 1970s there was little serious and sustained mainstream academic engagement with issues such as the gendered exploitation of post-colonial labour in the British metropolis, racism within state policies and cultural practices, the radicalisation of black and white subjectivity in the specific context of a period following the loss of Empire, and the particularities of black women's oppression within feminist theory and practice. This played an important part in the formation of black feminist organisations as distinct from the 'white' Women's Liberation Movement. These organisations emerged against the background of a deepening economic and political crisis and an increasing entrenchment of racism. The 1970s was a period when the Powellism of the 1960s came to suffuse the social fabric, and was gradually consolidated and transmuted into the Thatcherism of the 1980s. Black communities were involved in a wide variety of political activities throughout the decade. There were major industrial strikes, several led by women. The Black Trade Union Solidarity Movement was formed to deal with racism in employment and trade unions. There were massive campaigns against immigration control, fascist violence, racist attacks on person and property, modes of policing that resulted in the harassment of black people, and against the criminalisation of black communities. There were many self-help projects concerned with educational, welfare and cultural activities. Black women were involved in all these activities, but the formation of autonomous black women's groups in the late 1970s injected a new dimension into the political scene.

The specific priorities of local black women's organisations, a number of which combined to form a national body – the Organiza-tion of Women of Asian and African Descent (OWAAD) – varied to an extent according to the exigencies of the local context. But the overall aim was to challenge the specific forms of oppression faced by the different categories of black women. The commitment to forging unity between African, Caribbean and Asian women demanded sustained attempts to analyse, understand and work with common-alties as well as heterogeneity of experience. It called for an interrogation of the role of colonialism and imperialism and that of contemporary economic, political and ideological processes in sustaining particular social divisions within these groups. It required black women to be sensitive to one another's cultural specificities while constructing common political strategies to confront patriarchal practices, racism and class inequality. This was no easy task and it is a testimony to the political commitment and vision of the women involved that this project thrived for many years, and some of the local groups have survived the divisive impact of ethnicism and remain active today (Brixton Black Women's Group 1984; Bryan *et al*. 1985).

The demise of OWAAD as a national organisation in the early 1980s was precipitated by a number of factors. Many of these divisive tendencies have been paralleled in the women's movement as a whole. The organisations affiliated to OWAAD shared its broad aims, but there were political differences among women on various issues. There was general agreement that racism was crucial in structuring our oppression in Britain, but we differed in our analysis of racism and its links with class and other modes of inequality. For some women, racism was an autonomous structure of oppression and had to be tackled as such; for others it was inextricably connected with class and other axes of social division. There were also differences in perspectives between feminists and non-feminists in OWAAD. For the latter, an emphasis on sexism was a diversion from the struggle against racism. The devaluation of black cultures by the onslaughts of racism meant that for some women the priority was to 'reclaim' these cultural sites and to situate themselves 'as women' within them. While this was an important project, there was, at times, more than a hint of idealising a lost past. Other women argued that, while affirmation of cultural identity was indeed crucial, it was equally important to address cultural practices in their oppressive forms. The problem of male violence against women and children, the unequal sexual division of labour in the household, questions of dowry and forced marriages, clitoridectomy, heterosexism and the suppression of lesbian sexualities: all these were issues demanding immediate attention. Although most women in OWAAD recognised the importance of these issues, there were nonetheless major differences about priorities and political strategies to deal with them.

Alongside these tendencies there was an emerging emphasis within the women's movement as a whole on identity politics. Instead of embarking on the complex but necessary task of identifying the specificities of particular oppressions, understanding their interconnections with other oppressions, and building a politics of solidarity, some women were beginning to differentiate these specificities into hierarchies of oppression. The mere act of naming oneself as a member of an oppressed group was assumed to vest one with moral authority. Multiple oppressions came to be regarded not in terms of their patterns of articulation but rather as separate elements that could be added in a linear fashion, so that the more oppressions a woman could list the greater her claims to occupy a higher moral ground. Assertions about authenticity of personal experience could be presented as if they were an unproblematic guide to an understanding of processes of subordination and domination. Declarations concerning self-righteous political correctness sometimes came to substitute for careful political analysis (Ardill and O'Sullivan 1986; Adams 1989).

Despite the fragmentation of the women's movement, black women in Britain have continued to raise critical questions about feminist theory and practice. As a result of our location within diasporas formed by the history of slavery, colonialism and imperialism, black feminists have consistently argued against parochialism and stressed the need for a feminism sensitive to the international social relations of power (Carby 1982; Parmar 1982; *Feminist Review* 1984; Brah and Minhas 1985; Brah 1987; Phoenix 1987; Grewal *et al.* 1988; Mama 1989; Lewis 1990). Hazel Carby's article 'White women listen', for instance, presents a critique of such key feminist concepts as 'patriarchy', 'the family' and 'reproduction'. She criticises feminist perspectives which use notions of 'feudal residues' and 'traditionalism' to create sliding scales of 'civilised liberties', with the 'Third World' seen at one end of the scale and the supposedly progressive 'First World' at the other. She provides several illustrations of how a certain type of Western feminism can serve to reproduce rather than challenge the categories through which 'the West' constructs and represents itself as superior to its 'others'.

These critiques generated some critical self-reflection on the part of white feminist writers. In an attempt to re-assess their earlier work, Barrett and McIntosh (1985), for example, acknowledged the limitations of the concept of patriarchy as unambiguous and invariable male dominance undifferentiated by class or racism. They opted for the use of 'patriarchal' as signifying how 'particular social relations combine a public dimension of power, exploitation or status with a dimension of personal servility' (Barrett and McIntosh 1985: 39). But they failed to specify how and why the concept of 'patriarchal' should prove to have greater analytical edge over that of 'patriarchy' in studying the interconnections between gender, class and racism. The mere substitution of the concept of patriarchy by patriarchal relations cannot in itself address the charges of ahistoricism, universalism or essentialism that have been levelled at the former, although, as Walby (1990) argues, it is possible to provide historicised accounts of patriarchy. As a response to such reconceptualisations of patriarchy, Joan Acker suggests that it might be more appropriate to shift 'the theoretical object from patriarchy to gender, which we can define briefly as structural, relational, and symbolic differentiations between women and men' (Acker 1989: 238). She remains cautious about this shift, however, as 'gender', according to her, lacks the critical political sharpness of 'patriarchy' and could much more easily be coopted and neutralised within 'mainstream' theory. It is as well to remember that this whole debate was generally located within the parameters of the binary male/female and does not address the indeterminacy of 'sex' as a category (Butler 1990).

I prefer retaining the concept of 'patriarchal' without necessarily subscribing to the concept of 'patriarchy' – whether historicised or not. Patriarchal relations are a specific form of gender relation in which women inhabit a subordinated position. In theory, at least, it should be possible to envisage a social context in which gender relations are not associated with inequality. In addition, I hold serious reservations about the analytic or political utility of maintaining system boundaries between 'patriarchy' and the particular socio-economic and political formation (for example, capitalism or state socialism) in which it is embedded. It would be far more useful to understand how patriarchal relations articulate with other forms of social relation in a determinate historical context. Structures of class, racism, gender and sexuality cannot be treated as 'independent variables' because the oppression of each is inscribed within the other – is constituted by and is constitutive of the other.

Acknowledging the black feminist critique, Barrett and McIntosh (1985) stress the need to analyse the ideological construction of white femininity through racism. This, in my view, is essential, since there is still a tendency to address questions of inequality through a focus on the victims of inequality. Discussions about feminism and racism often centre around the oppression of black women rather than exploring how both black and white women's gender is constructed through class and racism. This means that white women's 'privileged position' within racialised discourses (even when they may share a class position with black women) fails to be adequately theorised, and processes of domination remain invisible. The representation of white women as 'the moral guardians of a superior race', for instance, serves to homogenise white women's sexuality at the same time as it fractures it across class, in that the white working-class woman, although also presented as 'carrier of the race', is simultaneously constructed as prone to 'degeneracy' because of her class background. Here we see how class contradictions may be worked through and 'resolved' ideologically within the racialised structuration of gender.

Barrett and McIntosh's (1985) article generated considerable debate (see contributions by Ramazanoglu, Kazi, Lees and Safia-Mirza: *Feminist Review* 1986; Bhavnani and Coulson 1986). While acknowledging the importance of the reassessment of a part of their work by two prominent white feminists, the critics argued that their methods of re-examination failed to provide the possibility of radical transformation of previous analysis, thus leaving the ways in which 'race' features within social reproduction largely untheorised. This feminist exchange contributed to the wider debate as to whether the social divisions associated with ethnicity and racism should be seen as absolutely autonomous of social class, as reducible to social class, or as having historical origins but articulating now with the divisions of class in capitalist society.

I would argue that racism is neither reducible to social class or gender nor wholly autonomous. Racisms have variable historical origins but they articulate with patriarchal class structures in specific ways under given historical conditions. Racisms may have independent effectivity, but to suggest this is not the same as saying, as Caroline Ramazanoglu (1989) does, that racism is an 'independent form of domination'. The concept of articulation suggests relations of linkages and effectivity whereby, as Hall says: 'things are related as much by their differences as through their similarities' (Hall 1980: 328). In similar vein, Laclau and Mouffe (1985) note that articulation is a practice and not the name of a given relational complex; that is, articulation is not a simple joining of two or more discrete entities. Rather, it is a transformative move of relational configurations. The search for grand theories specifying the interconnections between racism, gender and class has been less than productive. They are best construed as historically contingent and context-specific relationships. Hence, we can focus on a given context and differentiate between the demarcation of a category as an object of social discourse, as an analytical category, and as a subject of political mobilisation, without making assumptions about their permanence or stability across time and space. This means that 'white' feminism or 'black' feminism in Britain are not essentialist categories but rather that they are fields of contestation inscribed within discursive and material processes and practices in a post-colonial terrain. They represent struggles over political frameworks for analysis; the meanings of theoretical concepts; the relationship between theory, practice and subjective experiences, and over political priorities and modes of mobilisations. But they should not, in my view, be understood as constructing 'white' and 'black' women as 'essentially' fixed oppositional categories.

More recent contributions to the debate make somewhat different points, and their object of critique is also different in that they interrogate black and/or anti-racist feminism. One argument has been that, far from facilitating political mobilisation, black/anti-racist feminist discourses of the late 1970s and 1980s actually impeded political activism. Knowles and Mercer (1992), for example, contend that Carby's and Bourne's emphasis on the inscription of racism and gender inequality within processes of capitalism, colonialism and patriarchal social systems produced functionalist arguments – that sexism and racism were inherent within these systems and served the needs of these systems to perpetuate themselves. They believe that this approach demanded nothing short of an all-embracing struggle against these 'isms', and thereby undermined more localised, small-scale political responses. Yet, we know that the 1970s and the 1980s witnessed a wide variety of political activity at both local and national levels. Their own method of dealing with what they presume are the shortcomings of an emphasis on macroanalysis is to suggest that racism and sexism be 'viewed as a series of effects which do not have a single cause' (Knowles and Mercer 1992: 110). I would accept the arguments that the level of abstraction at which categories such as 'capitalism' or 'patriarchal relations' are delineated does not provide straightforward guidelines for concrete strategy and action, and also that racism and sexism are not monocausal phenomena. Nonetheless, I am not sure how treating racism and sexism as a 'series of effects' provides any clearer guidelines for political response. The same 'effect' may be interpreted from a variety of political positions, and lead to quite different strategies for action. Taking up a specific political position means that one is making certain assumptions about the nature of the various processes that underline a social phenomenon, of which a particular event may be an effect. A focus only on 'effects' may render invisible the workings of such ideological and material processes, thereby hindering our understanding of the complex basis of inequalities. Although crucial in mobilising specific constituencies, the single-issue struggles as ends in themselves may delimit wider-ranging challenges to social inequalities. The language of 'effects', in any case, does not get away from an implicit subtext of 'causes'.

I share Knowles and Mercer's (1992) reservation about analytical and political perspectives in which social inequality comes to be personified in the bodies of the dominant social groups – white people, men, or heterosexual individuals in relation to racism, sexism or heterosexism – but we cannot ignore the social relations of power that inscribe such differentiations. Members of dominant groups do occupy 'privileged' positions within political and material practices that attend these social divisions, although the precise interplay of this power in specific institutions or in interpersonal relations cannot be stipulated in advance, may be contradictory, and can be challenged.

A slightly different critique of black feminism challenges its validity as representing anything more than the interests of black women (Tang Main 1990). By implication, black feminism is cast as sectarian in comparison with radical or socialist feminism. This comparison is problematic, since it constructs black feminism as being outside radical or socialist feminism. In practice, the category 'black feminism' in Britain is only meaningful *vis-à-vis* the category 'white feminism'. If, as I have argued earlier, these two categories are contingent rather than essentialist, then one cannot ask the question, as Tang Main does, whether 'black feminism' is open to all women, without simultaneously asking the same question of 'white feminism'. Tang Main's characterisation of radical or socialist feminism as 'open to all women' flies in the face of massive evidence which shows that, in Britain and the USA at least, these feminisms have failed to take adequate account of racism and the experience of racialised groups of women. The ideology of 'open to all' can in fact legitimise all kinds of *de facto* exclusion. Socialist feminism, for example, cannot really include women who are subjected to racism unless it is a non-racist socialist feminism, or lesbian women unless it is simultaneously non-heterosexist, or lower-caste women unless it is also non-casteist. But these issues cannot be realised in the abstract, nor can they be settled once and for all, but through ongoing political struggles.

For similar reasons, Floya Anthias and Nira Yuval-Davis's (1982) critique of the category 'black' on the grounds that it failed to address diversity of ethnic exclusions and subordinations seems misplaced. The boundaries of a political constituency formed around specific concerns are dependent upon the nature of the concerns and their salience and significance in the lives of the people so affected. Black feminism constructed a constituency in terms of the gendered experience of anti-black racism. White ethnic groups who were not subjected to this particular form of racism could not, therefore, be part of this constituency. This does not mean that their experiences of, say, anti-semitism are any the less important. Rather, anti-black racism and anti-semitism cannot be subsumed under each other. This becomes patently clear if we compare the experience of a white Jewish woman and a black Jewish woman. The black woman is simultaneously positioned within two racialised discourses. Anthias and Yuval-Davis make some incisive points about ethnicity as a category of social differentiation, but their contention that 'black feminism can be too wide or too narrow a category for specific feminist struggles' (1982: 63) remains problematic, since the emergence of the black women's movement as a historically specific response is a testament that organisation around the category 'black women' is possible.

It bears repetition that black feminism was constituted in articulation with a number of political movements: the project of 'African-Asian Unity' around the sign 'black'; class politics; anti-colonial movements; global feminist movements; and gay and lesbian politics. This multi-locationality marked the formation of new diasporic subjectivities and identities; and it produced a powerful new political subject. Like most political subjects, this one, too, embodied its own contradiction – in/of multplicity. As we saw earlier, its seeming coherence was disrupted by internal debate and contestation. But it was one of the most enabling and empowering political subjects of the period. Black feminism's figuration of 'black' – as was the case generally with the politics of 'black' – dislodged this signifier from possible essentialist connotations and subverted the very logic of its racial codings. At the same time, it undermined gender-neutral discourses of 'black' by asserting the specificities of black women's experiences. In so far as black women comprised a highly differentiated category in terms of class, ethnicity, and religion, and included women who had migrated from Africa, the Asian sub-continent and the Caribbean, as well as those born in Britain, the black in 'black feminism' inscribed a multiplicity of experience even as it articulated a particular feminist subject position. Moreover, by foregrounding a wide range of diasporic experiences in both their local and global specificity, black feminism represented black life in all its fullness, creativity and complexity.

Black feminism prised open discursive closures which asserted the primacy of, say, class or gender over all other axes of differentiation; and it interrogated the constructions of such privileged signifiers as unified autonomous cores. The point is that black feminism not only posed a very serious challenge to colour-centred racisms, but its significance goes far beyond this challenge. The political subject of black feminism decentres the unitary, masculinist subject of Eurocentric discourse, as well as masculinist rendering of 'black' as a political colour, while seriously disrupting any notion of 'woman' as a unitary category. That is to say that, while constituted around the problematic of 'race', black feminism performatively defies confines of the boundaries of its constitution.

Black feminism did not preclude coalitions across other boundaries, and black women have worked with white women and men, and other categories of people across a spectrum of political opinion on issues of common concern. I fully recognise that the category 'black' as a political colour no longer has the purchase it used to have. As a part of the Left project, it has suffered similar predicaments to the British Left as a whole. The New Right politics which reached their apotheosis during the Thatcher years, the demise of state socialism in Eastern Europe, formation of the European Union, economic restructuring, the rise of political religious movements, the resurgence of new forms of youth cultures, etc., have all made significant impact on all aspects of life. These changes call for new configurations of solidarity. The point, however, is that any alternatives to the political category 'black', such as 'women of colour' or some term as yet not in currency, cannot be willed in the abstract or decided in advance. They can only emerge through new modes of contestation set against a changed economic and political climate.

My proposition that 'black' and 'white' feminisms be addressed as non-essentialist, historically contingent discursive practices implies that black and white women can work together towards the creation of non-racist feminist theory and practice. The key issue, then, is not about 'difference' *per se*, but concerns the question of who defines difference, how different categories of women are represented within the discourses of 'difference', and whether 'difference' differentiates laterally or hierarchically. We need greater conceptual clarity in analysing difference.

DIFFERENCE; WHAT DIFFERENCE?

It is axiomatic that the concept of 'difference' is associated with a variety of meanings in different discourses. But how are we to understand 'difference'? In the analytical framework that I am attempting to formulate here the issue is not about privileging the macro- or the micro-level of analysis, but rather, how articulating discourses and practices inscribe social relations, subject positions and subjectivities. The interesting issue then is how micro- and macro-levels inhere in the above inscriptions. How does difference designate the 'other'? Who defines difference? What are the presumed norms from which a group is marked as being different? What is the nature of attributions that are claimed as characterising a group as different? How are boundaries of difference constituted, maintained or dissipated? How is difference interiorised in the landscapes of the psyche? How are various groups represented in different discourses of difference? Does difference differentiate laterally or hierarchically? Questions such as these raise a more general problematic about difference as an analytic category. I would suggest four ways in which difference may be conceptualised: difference as experience, difference as social relation, difference as subjectivity, and difference as identity.

Difference as experience

Experience has been a key concept within feminism. Women's movements have aimed to give a collective voice to women's personal experiences of social and psychic forces that constitute the 'female' into the 'woman'. The everyday of the social relations of gender – ranging from housework and child care, low-paid employment and economic dependency to sexual violence and women's exclusion from key centres of political and cultural power – have all been given a new significance through feminism as they have been brought out of the realm of the 'taken for granted' to be interrogated and challenged. The personal, with its profoundly concrete yet elusive qualities, and its manifold contradiction, acquired new meanings in the slogan 'the personal is political', as consciousness-raising groups provided the forums for exploring individual experiences, personal feelings and women's own understandings of their daily lives. As Teresa de Lauretis noted, this original feminist insight proclaimed 'a relation, however complex it may be, between sociality and subjectivity, between language and consciousness, or between institutions and individuals...' (de Lauretis 1986: 5).

That there are some considerable limitations to the consciousness-raising method as a strategy for collective action is not at issue. The point is that consciousness-raising foregrounded one of feminism's most powerful insights, which is that experience does not transparently reflect a pre-given reality, but rather is itself a cultural construction. Indeed, 'experience' is a process of signification which is the very condition for the constitution of that which we call 'reality'. Hence, the need to re-emphasise a notion of experience not as an unmediated guide to 'truth' but as a practice of making sense, both symbolically and narratively; as a struggle over material conditions and meaning.

Contrary to the idea of an already fully constituted 'experiencing subject' to whom 'experiences happen', experience is the site of subject formation. This notion is often missing from those discussions about differences between people where difference and experience are used primarily as a 'commonsensical term' (Barrett 1987). Not surprisingly, such discussions flounder or result in 'talking at cross purposes' when dealing with the contradictions of subjectivity and identity. For instance, how are we to deal with the racism of a feminist, the homophobia of someone subjected to racism, or indeed the racism of one racialised group towards another racialised group, each presumably speaking from the vantage point of their experience, if all experience transparently reflected a given 'truth'? Indeed, how can a project such as feminism or anti-racism, or a class movement, mobilise itself as a political force for change if it did not start by interrogating the taken-for-granted values and norms which may legitimise dominance and inequality by naturalising particular 'differences'? Attention to this point reveals experience as a site of contestation: a discursive space where different *and* differential subject positions and subjectivities are inscribed, reiterated, or repudiated. It is essential, then, to address the questions of which ideological matrices or fields of signification and representation are at play in the formation of differing subjects, and what are the economic, political and cultural processes that inscribe historically variable experiences. As Joan Scott argues, 'Experience is at once always already an interpretation *and* is in need of interpretation' (1992: 37).

To think of experience and subject formation as processes is to reformulate the question of 'agency'. The 'I' and the 'we' who act do not disappear, but what does disappear is the notion that these categories are unified, fixed, already existing entities rather than modalities of multi-locationality continuously marked by everyday cultural and political practices.

As I sugggested in the last chapter, it is useful to distinguish difference as a marker of the distinctiveness of our collective 'histories' from difference as personal experience inscribing individual biography. These sets of 'differences' constantly articulate, but they cannot be 'read off' from each other. The meaning attached to a given event varies enormously from one individual to another. When we speak of the constitution of individual into subject through multiple fields of signification we are invoking *inscription* and *ascription* as simultaneous processes whereby the subject *acquires* meaning in socio-economic and cultural relations at the same moment as she ascribes meaning by making sense of these relations in everyday life. In other words, how a person perceives *or* conceives an event would vary according to how 'she' is culturally constructed; the myriad of unpredictable ways in which such constructions may configure in the flux of her psyche; and, invariably, upon the political repertoire of cultural discourses available to her. Collective 'histories' are also, of course, culturally constructed in the process of assigning meaning to the everyday of social relations. But, while personal biographies and group histories are mutually immanent, they are relationally irreducible. The same context may produce several different collective 'histories', differentiating as well as linking biographies through *contingent specificities*. In turn, articulating cultural practices of the subjects so constituted mark contingent collective 'histories' with variable new meanings.

Difference as social relation

The concept of 'difference as social relation' refers to the ways in which difference is constituted and organised into *systematic* relations through economic, cultural and political discourses and institutional practices. That is to say that it highlights *systematicity across contingencies*. A group usually mobilises the concept of difference in this sense when addressing the historical genealogies of its collective experience. Indeed, difference and commonalty are relational signs, interweaving narratives of difference with those of a shared past and collective destinies. In other words the concept of 'difference as social relation' underscores the historically variable articulation of macro and micro regimes of power, within which modes of differentiation such as gender, class or racism are instituted in terms of *structured* formations. The category 'working class', for instance, highlights positioning in structures of class relations. But to say this is not to point simply to the designation of a subordinate location within socio-economic and political structures of power, but also to under-line systems of signification and representation which construct class as a cultural category.

Difference in the sense of social relation may be understood as the historical and contemporary trajectories of material circumstances and cultural practices which *produce the conditions* for the construc-tion of group identities. The concept refers to the interweaving of shared collective narratives within feelings of community, whether or not this 'community' is constituted in face-to-face encounters or imagined, in the sense that Benedict Anderson (1983) suggests. It is the echo of 'difference as social relation' which reverberates when legacies of slavery, colonialism or imperialism are invoked; or when attention is drawn to the 'new' international division of labour and the differential positioning of different groups within its continually evolving systems of production, exchange, and consumption which result in massive inequalities within and between various parts of the globe. But this does not mean that the concept of social relation operates at some 'higher level of abstraction' referencing the 'macro' as opposed to the 'micro' context. The effects of social relations are not confined to the seemingly distant operations of national or global economies, politics, or cultural institutions, but are also present in highly localised arenas of the workplace, the household (which, in some cases, as with homeworkers or highly paid executives 'working from home', becomes both a unit of labour – albeit differentially remunerated – and a place of work), as well as in the interstices of the mind where intersubjectivity is produced and contested. All these spheres have always been interlinked, but they articulate in quite unique ways in the present historical moment. As Donna Haraway argues:

> The home, workplace, market, public arena, the body itself – all can be dispersed and interfaced in nearly infinite, polymorphous ways, with large consequences for women and others – conse-quences that themselves are very different for different people and

which make potent international movements difficult to imagine and essential for survival.... Communication technologies and biotechnologies are the crucial tools recrafting our bodies. These tools embody and enforce new social relations for women world-wide.... The boundary is permeable between tool and myth, instrument and concept, historical systems of social relations and historical anatomies of possible bodies, including objects of knowledge

(Haraway 1991: 164–5)

Social relations, then, are constituted and perform in all sites of a social formation. This means that, in practice, experience as social relation and the everyday of lived experience do not inhabit mutually exclusive spaces. For example, if we speak of 'North African women in France', we are, on the one hand, referring to the social relations of gendered post-coloniality in France. On the other hand, we are also making a statement about the everyday experience of this post-coloniality on the part of such women, although we cannot specify, in advance, the particularity of individual women's lives or how they interpret and define this experience. In both instances, the question of how difference is defined remains paramount. Are perceptions of difference acting as a means of affirming diversity or a mechanism for exclusionary and discriminatory practices? Do discourses of differ-ence legitimise progressive or oppressive state policies and practices? In what ways are different categories of women represented in such discourses? How do women themselves respond to these representa-tions?

When understood in this way, the idea of difference as social relation hopefully sheds any claims of privileging 'structural' as the command centre of a social formation in favour of a perspective which foregrounds articulation of the different elements.

Difference as subjectivity

Issues of difference have been central to the theoretical debate around subjectivity. Much of the contemporary debate is conducted in various critiques of the humanist conceptions of the subject: as a unified, unitary, rational, and rationalist 'point of origin'; as centred in consciousness; and, in terms of the idea of a universal 'Man' as the embodiment of an ahistorical essence. These critiques emerged from several different directions. In the post-World War II period the projects of post-structuralism, feminism, anti-colonialism, anti-imperialism, and anti-racism have all, in one form or another, taken serious issue with universalising truth claims of grand narratives of history which place the European 'Man' at its centre. But although these projects have overlapped in some respects, the problematic they have addressed has not been identical. Nor have they always engaged one another. Indeed, a major source of contention amongst them has been the relative lack of attention or, in some cases, an almost complete amnesia by one project about issues central to the other. For example, as I discuss more fully in Chapter Nine, few early canonical texts of post-structuralism address questions of colonialism or decolonisation, or issues of racism in any systematic way, despite their regular invocation of the 'crisis' of the 'West'. Hence, the importance of powerful critiques of the discourse of European Man which emerged from anti-colonial struggles for independence as women, men, and children expressed defiance in Africa, Asia, the Caribbean and other parts of the world. Fanon instantiated one moment of this critique when he exhorted his readers to:

> Leave this Europe where they are never done talking of Man, yet murder men everywhere they find them, at the corner of every one of their own streets, in all the corners of the globe.... That same Europe where they are never done talking of Man, and where they never stopped proclaiming that they were only anxious for the welfare of Man: today we know with what suffering humanity has paid for every one of their triumphs of the mind.
>
> (Fanon 1967: 251)

Similar critiques surfaced in more recent anti-racist resistance movements and within what is sometimes called 'colonial discourse' theory. These currents in politics and theory intersect with those within feminism, peace movements, environmental campaigns and other similar projects. Together they underscore the notion that the subject does not exist as an always already given, but is produced in discourse. Yet, enabling though this insight into the production of the subject has been, it could not by itself adequately account for non-logocentric operations of subjectivity. As Henriques *et al.* posed the problem, how does one avoid, on the one hand:

> a kind of discourse determinism which implies that people are mechanistically positioned in discourses, a view which leaves no room for explicating either the possibilities for change or indivi-

dual's resistance to change, and which disregards the question of motivation altogether (and, on the other hand, the notion of) a *pre-given* subject which opts for particular subject positions?

(Henriques *et al*. 1984: 204)

Such a predicament led feminists and others to re-visit psychoanalysis (especially its post-structuralist and object-relations variants), and to re-think its relationship to theories of 'deconstruction' and 'micro-politics of power'. There was growing acknowledgement that a person's innermost emotions, feelings, desires and fantasies, with their multiple contradictions, could not be understood purely in terms of the imperatives of the social institutions. The new readings were essential to a more complex account of psychic life. Psychoanalysis disrupts notions of a unitary, centred and rational self by its emphasis on an inner world permeated by desire and fantasy. This inner world is addressed as the site of the unconscious with its unpredictable effects on thought and other aspects of subjectivity. At the same time, psychoanalysis facilitates understanding of the ways in which the subject-in-process is marked by a sense of coherence and continuity, a sense of a core that she or he calls the 'I'.

Jane Flax (1990) argues that, despite the many shortcomings which have been the subject of considerable debate, there are many ambiguities in Freud's thought which have made it accessible to different readings. The ambiguities in the theories of the libido and the unconscious, for instance, have made it possible for the boundaries between ego, superego and id, or those between the psychic, the somatic and the cultural, to be understood as unfixed and permeable. The mind/body dualism is problematised when instinct or drive is conceptualised simultaneously as psychic, somatic and cultural, in that a need, a want or a desire is never purely a bodily sensation but is constituted and regulated within a cultural space. Freud's conceptual-isations of the mind as non-unitary, conflictual, dynamic, embodied and constituted in ways that cannot be 'synthesised or organised into a permanent, hierarchical, organisation of functions or control' (Flax 1990: 60) undermines both rationalist and empiricist concepts of mind and knowledge.

In this type of post-structuralist/feminist appropriation of Freud, the mind's constitutive elements – ego, superego and id – emerge as *relational* concepts constituted in and through 'inner' and 'outer' experience. Hence, the subject is understood as decentred and heterogeneous in its qualities and dynamics. Subjectivity, then, is neither unified nor fixed but fragmented and constantly in process. For feminists, such accounts have proved especially attractive, for they problematise 'sexual difference': sexual difference is something to be explained rather than assumed. Some have turned to Lacan's re-reading of Freud for a non-reductive understanding of subjectivity. Others find a re-working of the object-relations strands of Freud's schema more useful for developing feminist projects. Compelling arguments have been made in favour of the importance of psycho-analysis for feminism against those critics who assume that the notion of a fragmented identity constantly in process is at odds with the feminist project of constructing oppositional consciousness through collective action. Nonetheless, some feminists remain sceptical about psychoanalysis altogether. The debate continues unabated (cf. de Lauretis 1984; Henriques *et al*. 1984; Rose 1986; Weedon 1987; Penley 1989; Flax 1990; Minsky 1990).

Such argumentation is essential and productive given the many difficulties and problems that continue to beset the meta-narrative of psychoanalysis which the protagonists in the debate seek to confront in their own ways. The psychic effects of racism, for instance, only rarely feature in these discussions when the 'race' discourse has been a central element in the constitution of the category 'West'. Fanon's work notwithstanding, engagement with the problematic of racialisa-tion of subjectivity is as yet limited. How would psychoanalytic narratives be disrupted by addressing racism? Hortense Spillers (1987, 1989) interrogates psychoanalysis even as she uses it in her analysis. Her ambivalence is instructive when she says:

> I attempt this writing, in fact, as *the trial* of an interlocking interrogation that I am persuaded in by only 50 percent. Is the Freudian landscape an applicable text (to say nothing of appro-priate) to social and historic situations that do not replicate moments of its own historic origins and movements? The presti-gious Oedipal dis-ease/complex, which apparently subsumes the Electra myth, embeds in the 'heterosexual' nuclear family that disperses its fruits in vertical array. Not only 'one man, one woman' but these two – this law – in a specific locus of economic and cultural means. But how does this model, or does this model, suffice for occupied or captive persons and communities (of African slaves in the Americas) in which the rights and rites of

gender functions have been exploded historically in to sexual neutralities.

(Spillers 1989: 128–9, emphasis added)

Her discourse underlines the point raised by Dalal (1988) in relation to what he claims as the Jungian paradigm's complicity with racialised discourses. It highlights the importance and necessity of paying greater attention to how subjectivity is conceptualised in cultures other than Western and the transcultural traffic between ideas.

Over the years there have been attempts to combine different approaches to the study of subjectivity. Teresa de Lauretis (1984), for example, suggests that semiotics and psychoanalysis might be jointly mobilised in furthering our understanding of subjectivity. She argues the case for 'locating subjectivity in the space contoured by the discourses of semiotics and psychoanalysis, neither in the former nor in the latter, but rather in their discursive intersection' (de Lauretis 1984: 168). The aim is to explore the relationship between personal change and social change without recourse to reductive explanations of simple determination.

In other words, we need conceptual frames which can address fully the point that processes of subjectivity formation are at once *social* and *subjective*; which can help us understand the psychic investments we make in assuming specific subject positions that are socially produced.

Difference as identity

Our struggles over meaning are also our struggles over different modes of being: different identities (Minh-ha 1989). Questions of identity are intimately connected with those of experience, subjectivity and social relations. Identities are inscribed through experiences culturally constructed in social relations. Subjectivity – the site of processes of making sense of our relation to the world – is the modality in which the precarious and contradictory nature of the subject-in-process is signified or *experienced* as identity. Identities are marked by the multiplicity of subject positions that constitute the subject. Hence, identity is neither fixed nor singular; rather it is a constantly changing relational multiplicity. But during the course of this flux identities do assume specific patterns, as in a kaleidoscope, against particular sets of personal, social and historical circumstances. Indeed, identity may be understood *as that very process by which the multiplicity, contra-*

diction, and instability of subjectivity is signified as having coherence, continuity, stability; as having a core – a continually changing core but the sense of a core nonetheless – that at any given moment is enunciated as the 'I'.

As we have already seen, the relationship between personal biography and collective history is complex and contradictory. While personal identities always articulate with the collective experience of a group, the specificity of a person's life experience etched in the daily minutiae of lived social relations produces trajectories that do not simply mirror group experience. Similarly, collective identities are irreducible to the sum of the experiences of individuals. Collective identity is the process of signification whereby commonalties of experience around a specific axis of differentiation, say class, caste, or religion, are invested with particular meanings. In this sense a given collective identity partially erases, but also carries traces of other identities. That is to say that a heightened awareness of one *construction* of identity in a given moment always entails a partial erasure of the *memory or subjective sense* of internal heterogeneity of a group. But this is not at all the same as saying that the power relations embedded in heterogeneity disappear. How and if patterns of social relations change would be contingent upon the power of the political challenges which specific discourses and practices are able to effect.

The partial suppression of a sense of one identity by the assertion of another does not mean, however, that different 'identities' cannot 'co-exist'. But if identity is a process, then it is problematic to speak of an existing identity as if this is always already constituted. It is more appropriate to speak of discourses, matrices of meanings, and historical memories which, once in circulation, can form the basis of *identification* in a given economic, cultural and political context. But the identity that is proclaimed is a *remaking*, a context-specific construction. The *proclamation* of a specific collective identity is a *political* process as distinct from identity as a process *in* and *of* subjectivity. The political process of *proclaiming* a specific collective identity entails the *creation* of a collective identity out of the myriad collage-like fragments of the mind. The process may well generate considerable psychic and emotional disjunction in the realm of subjectivity, even if it is empowering in terms of group politics.

In other words, political mobilisation is centrally about attempts to re-inscribe subjectivity through appeals to collective experience. Paradoxically, the commonalty that is evoked can be rendered meaningful only in articulation with a discourse of difference. The precise ways in which the discourse of commonalty/difference is invoked, and with what effects for different segments of the constituency it seeks to mobilise, or indeed for those it constructs as outside this constituency, varies enormously. But essentially such discourses are renditions of some view – re-memory, re-collection, re-working, re-construction – of collective history and, as such, these discourses of identity (whether they invoke notions of 'culture', or are centred around ideas about 'shared economic or political circumstances') are articulations of subjectivity in what I have called 'difference as social relation'.

All discursive formations are a site of power, but there is no single and overarching locus of power where dominance, subordination, solidarity and affiliation based on egalitarian principles, or the conditions for affinity, conviviality and sociality are produced and secured once and for all. Rather, power is performatively constituted in and through economic, political, and cultural practices. Subjectivities of both the dominant and the dominated are produced in the interstices of these multiple, intersecting loci of power. The precise interplay of this power in specific institutions and interpersonal relations is difficult to predict in advance. But if *practice* is productive of power then *practice* is also the means of challenging the oppressive *practices* of power. This indeed is the implication of the Foucauldian insight that discourse is practice. Similarly, a visual image is also a practice. The visual image is also productive of power, hence the importance of understanding the movement of power in technologies of the eye – visual arts such as painting and sculpture, cinematic practice or dance, and the visual effects of communication technologies. The same holds for the aural register – music and other sounds are productive of power. Indeed, the whole body in all its *physicality, mentality and spirituality* is productive of power, and it is within this relational space that the mind/body dualism disappears. A particular 'identity' assumes shape in political practice out of the *fragmentic relationality* of subjectivity and dissolves to emerge as a trace in another identity-formation. As I have stressed all along, the subject may be the effect of discourses, institutions and practices, but at any given moment the subject-in-process experiences itself as the 'I', and both consciously and unconsciously replays and resignifies positions in which it is located and invested.

The concept of difference, then, refers to the variety of ways in which specific discourses of difference are constituted, contested, reproduced, or resignified. Some constructions of difference, such as racism, posit fixed and immutable boundaries between groups signified as inherently different. Other constructions may present difference as relational, contingent and variable. In other words, difference is not always a marker of hierarchy and oppression. Therefore, it is a contextually contingent question whether difference pans out as inequity, exploitation and oppression *or as* egalitarianism, diversity and democratic forms of political agency.

Stuart Hall regards ethnicity as one potential modality of difference – marking the specificity of collective historical, political and cultural experience – which could possibly interrogate and challenge essentialist constructions of group boundaries. He suggests that it should be possible to retrieve ethnicity from racialised nationalist discourses:

> The fact that this grounding of ethnicity in difference was deployed, in the discourse of racism, as a means of disavowing the realities of racism and repression does not mean that we can permit the term to be permanently colonised. That appropriation will have to be contested, the term disarticulated from its position in the discourse of 'multi-culturalism' and transcoded, just as we previously had to recuperate the term 'black' from its place in a system of negative equivalences.
>
> (Hall 1992: 257)

In practice, however, it is not always easy to disentangle these different moves of power. Nationalist discourses may serve both ends. For instance, ethnicities are liable to be appropriated as signifiers of permanently fixed boundaries. Hence, the 'Englishness' of a particular class can come to represent itself via racism as 'Britishness' against those ethnicities that it subordinates – such as those of the Irish, Scottish, Welsh, black British, or the ethnicities of the formerly colonised world (although, as we noted earlier, white/European ethnicities are subordinated differently from 'non-white', 'non-European' ethnicities). Moreover, ethnicities are always gendered and there is no guarantee that their non-essentialist recuperation will simultaneously challenge patriarchal practices unless this task is made a conscious objective. Indeed, it cannot be taken for granted that the process of recuperation will itself not inscribe essentialist differences. This can be especially problematic for women if the cultural values that the groups in question excavate, recast and reconstruct are those that underscore women's subordination.

Although I have argued against essentialism, it is apparent that it is not easy to deal with this problem. In their need to create new political identities, dominated groups will often appeal to bonds of common cultural experience in order to mobilise their constituency. In so doing they may assert a seemingly essentialist difference. Spivak (1987) and Fuss (1989) have argued in favour of such a 'strategic essentialism'. They suggest that the 'risk' of essentialism may be worth taking if it is framed from the vantage point of a dominated subject position. This will remain problematic if a challenge to one form of oppression leads to the reinforcement of another. It seems imperative that we do not compartmentalise oppressions but instead formulate strategies for challenging all on the basis of an understanding of how they interconnect and articulate. I believe that the framework I have outlined here can help us to do this. It is a perspective that calls for continually interrogating essentialism in all its varieties.

Chapter 6

'Race' and 'culture' in the gendering of labour markets
Young South Asian Muslim women and the labour market

Feminist critiques of gender-neutral approaches to the study of labour markets have demonstrated that gender relations do not simply articulate with, but are part of, the very fabric of labour markets as they have developed. That is, gender is a constitutive element in the formation of labour markets. Studies show that gender inscribes definition of skill, construction of the division between full-time and part-time work, the differential between men's and women's wages, segregation of the labour market into 'men's jobs' and 'women's jobs', the nature and type of hierarchies sustained by cultures of the workplace, and the experience of paid work in the formation of identities (cf. Beechey 1988 for an overview). Much less attention has been paid to 'race', ethnicity, or racialised/ethnicised constructions of 'cultural difference' in the gendering of labour markets (but see Chapter 2; Westwood 1984; Brah 1987; Westwood and Bachu 1989; Phizacklea 1990; Walby 1990; Bhavnani 1991). The point is that modes of differentiation such as 'race', class, gender, sexuality, ethnicity, age or disability are at the heart of the constitution, operations, and differential effects of labour markets.

But how are such links to be theorised? The task is made even more complex by a general tendency in the literature to theorise the 'macro' and 'micro' aspects of analysis as separate, almost 'independent' levels. My own interest resides in trying to understand how 'macro' and 'micro' inhere. The approach suggested here – based upon the framework proposed in the previous chapter – problematises this binary. This approach is offered as part of an effort to theorise more adequately the relationship of Asian young Muslim women to the British labour market, but the framework will have a wider applicability. The chapter explores what the women themselves have to say about the place of paid work in their lives, but, following the discussion of the concept of 'experience' in the last chapter, it bears repetition that narratives are constructions and not transparent guides to 'reality'. That is, they are irreducibly marked by wider economic, political and cultural processes, but they neither directly 'reflect' nor are transparently 'reflected by' them. The self that narrates is already a modality of narration of such economic, political and cultural discourses and practices. In the approach I am advocating, structure, culture and agency are conceptualised as inextricably linked, mutually inscribing formations.

The analysis is based upon both in-depth interviews with individual young Muslim women of Pakistani origin, and group interviews with them. Arguing against a general theory of gender that could then be *applied* to analysing specific instances of paid work, the framework proposed highlights the importance of studying the articulations – between and across relations of gender, class, ethnicity, racism, religion and so on – empirically and historically as contingent relationships. The young Muslim women narrate the contradictory codes of such articulations in their daily lives.

Discussions on the subject of young South Asian Muslim women's employment tend to be dominated by a concern with statistics which point to lower economic activity rates for this category of women compared with other groups of Asian and non-Asian women in Britain. Studies which analyse the realities behind the statistics are as yet limited. Why are young Muslim women under-represented in the labour market? What is the nature and range of factors that limit young Muslim women's fuller participation in the labour market? What are the continuities and discontinuities in the life histories of those young women not engaged in paid work as compared with those who are in employment? What are the similarities and differences in the labour market experiences of different categories of Muslim women, comparing, for example, married women with single women, or women recently arrived from Pakistan with those who have been brought up in Britain? How are educational institutions or government training schemes perceived and experienced by Muslim women? Such questions have rarely been addressed by previous research, but they form the core of a study (Brah and Shaw 1992) from which the interviews discussed here derive.[1]

FRAMING LABOUR MARKETS

Discourses about Muslim women's participation in the labour market are suffused with 'culturalist' explanations. It is generally argued that Muslim women are prevented from taking up paid employment by Muslim men. The racialised themes in such discourses are now well documented (see Chapter Three). Such explanations fail to take account of a variety of aspects – discussed below – that are central to understanding the racialisation of gendered labour markets in contemporary Europe. I do not believe that analyses of women's employment necessarily demand a general theory of gender that can subsequently be deployed in analysing the specific instance of paid work. Rather, I favour a form of analysis which can address historically and culturally specific gendered processes *without* demarcating 'public' and 'private' as separate domains. Social labour is thus understood as gendered in historically variable forms. Such variation is embedded within histories of slavery, colonialism, imperialism and the currently evolving global order that is underpinned by 'G-Sevenism'.

In the light of the previous chapter, I would re-emphasise the importance of studying the articulation between different forms of social differentiation, empirically and historically, as contingent relationships that are the effects of multiple determinations. Accordingly, a study of young Muslim women and the labour market would need to address how the labour of this category of women is:

- socially constructed and represented;
- experienced and figured in the landscapes of subjectivity;
- constituted by and is constitutive of labour markets; and it is
- framed within personal narratives and collective histories.

There is no suggestion here of a binary divide between culture and structure. A concept of culture that is evoked does not 'reference' an already fully constituted and fixed array of customs, values and traditions. Rather, culture is understood as a process; a nexus of intersecting significations; a terrain on which social meanings are produced, appropriated, disrupted and contested. Cultural specificities remain important but they are construed as fluid modalities, as motile boundaries constructed within a multiplicity of sites, structures and relations of power. Structure and culture are construed as relational processes. The one is not privileged over the other so that the focus shifts to how structures – economic, political, ideological –

emerge and change over time in and through systems of signification, and how they in turn shape cultural meanings.

In order to understand the relationship of young Muslim women in Britain to the labour market using this approach, it would be necessary to deconstruct the concept of 'Muslim woman' as it has been constituted in British discourse. We would need to consider to what extent and in what ways these social representations construct 'Muslim woman' as a racialised category; that is, how stereotypes might serve to transmute diverse groups of Muslim women into a subject position as a racialised unit of labour. Such deconstruction would highlight discursive processes whereby labour markets are constituted as racially gendered. At the same time, analysis of women's interviews would foreground their positionality as self-narrated selves. How these self-narrations relate to 'Muslim woman' as a category of 'representation' in British discourse would, of course, be subject to empirical variation. What light do women's personal narratives throw on the way in which such 'representations' are implicated in their social identities? Do women occupy oppositional or non-oppositional subject positions within such discourses? Do their own perceptions of themselves reinforce or contest social meanings coded in such discourses?

The point I wish to stress is that it is crucial to make a distinction between 'Muslim woman' as a discursive category of 'representation' *and* Muslim women as embodied, situated, historical subjects with varying and diverse personal or collective biographies and social orientations.

There are *at least* seven dimensions which would seem critical to understanding the form, extent and patterns of Muslim women's participation in British labour markets. These are:

1 the histories of colonialism and imperialism which shaped the patterns of post-World War II migrations into Western Europe;
2 the timing of migration;
3 the post-war restructuring of the national and global economies;
4 changing structure of the regional and local labour markets;
5 state policies, especially on immigration control;
6 racism in the labour market;
7 segmentation of the labour market by gender, class, age and ethnic background.

I elaborate this framework below by drawing out its implications and by thinking it through the study referred to above (Brah and Shaw

1992). In the first section I consider how the seven dimensions listed above inscribe the terrain on which young Muslim women's relationship to the labour market is shaped and negotiated. The second section addresses the social imagery through which Muslim women are socially constructed in Britain, and the impact this field of representation has on how young Muslim women are positioned in social relations. This is followed by an analysis of women's narratives.

How would the proposed framework inform a study of young Muslim women and the labour market, such as the one we made?

First, the emphasis on historical perspective draws attention to the colonial background that frames the formation of South Asian communities in Britain. The colonial encounter, as is now well known, was a complex and contested arena of economic, political and cultural relations marked by gendered forms of racism. As Mies (1986) points out, colonial regimes of accumulation were centrally implicated in class-mediated changes in the organisation and structure of families and households in metropolitan societies as much as they were in the colonies. The emergence of the notion of a 'family wage' in Western societies, Mies argues, owes not a little to the extraction of surplus from the colonies. Certain weaknesses in parts of her argument notwithstanding (cf. Walby 1990), Mies demonstrates the centrality of gender and racialisation processes as constitutive elements in the development of a global economy. She shows how patriarchal systems of colonisers and colonised have been interconnected since long before the post-World War II migrations from the sub-continent.

A historical perspective also draws attention to the conditions under which immigrant labour was deployed in post-war Britain. The economic boom from 1945 until the late 1960s that helped to draw a growing number of white British women into the labour force also led to the recruitment of workers from Britain's former colonies. Both sets of workers were employed predominantly in low-wage sectors of the economy. Segregation of the labour market by gender meant, however, that male and female workers were concentrated in different sectors of the economy. Asian women experienced the labour market not simply through their gender but also as racialised subjects. Even within a gender-segregated labour market they occupy a distinctive profile compared with white women. As we have already seen, overall, a higher proportion of women than men in Britain are engaged in part-time work. This pattern of employment is often taken as a major contributory factor towards women's low pay. However, a higher proportion of Asian women than white women are in full-time employment. Yet their earnings are lower compared with those of white women. Whereas the overall pattern for women in Britain is that they are concentrated in the service industries, Asian women are more commonly found in low-paid, semi-skilled and unskilled work in the manufacturing sector, particularly in the clothing and textile industries which have recently been in decline. Even in those industries where women predominate, Asian women are concentrated in the lowest level jobs, and unemployment rates among Asian women are much higher compared with white women (see Chapter Three).

In the early phase of post-war migration, Pakistani men had arrived predominantly without their female kin. The class position of these men as low-wage workers resident in declining inner areas of British cities was to have a crucial effect on the type of employment available to Pakistani women as they began to arrive. The argument that fewer Pakistani women entered the labour market primarily due to 'cultural reasons' warrants interrogation rather than dismissal without consideration. I set this issue aside for the moment, and discuss the effects of timing of migration, economic change, immigration control and racism in shaping the structure of job opportunities for Pakistani women.

Timing of immigration and post-war socio-economic change

Pakistani women migrated to Britain later than women from India (who were mostly Sikhs and Hindus). The former arrived mainly in the late 1960s and early 1970s, whereas Asian women who entered the labour market in the early phase of the post-war migrations were mainly Sikh and Hindu women. These Asian women took up paid employment at a time of economic growth and relative stability. Mass production concentrated in factories, and centralised forms of work organisation and managed national markets were a key feature of this phase. Most Asian women, including the small number of Muslim women in employment at this time, found paid work doing semi-skilled and unskilled jobs generated by this form of production.

From the 1970s, economies of the advanced industrial societies began to undergo fundamental restructuring. The global economy became increasingly transnationalised, creating new forms of the international division of labour alongside the older ones. In Britain, the decline in the old manufacturing sector, where Asian workers had been concentrated, led to large-scale job loss. These economic changes entailed a rise of 'flexible specialisation', leading to more decentralised forms of labour process and a greater emphasis on the contracting out of functions and services. New types of small businesses proliferated within national economies. There was a growth of jobs in the service sector, but the increase was concentrated primarily in low-status, part-time work and a variety of forms of 'homeworking' (Mitter 1986; Allen and Massey 1988; Jensen *et al.*1988; Hall and Jacques 1989; Phizacklea 1990; Nazir 1991).

It will be evident from the above that Muslim women arriving in Britain in the late 1960s and early 1970s would have encountered the labour market in a period of major economic restructuring and recession. While this resulted in the contraction of certain types of jobs, there was an expansion of small businesses, especially those which rely upon the 'putting out' system. The ready availability of paid work that could be carried out from home would have held a strong appeal for Muslim women with young families to care for. Over a period of time, as 'homeworking' became an established pattern, more and more women were likely to be drawn into it through kinship and friendship networks. In other words, the growing involvement of Muslim women in 'homeworking' during this period could not be explained simply in terms of 'cultural constraints'.

The relationship of Pakistani women to the labour market cannot be fully understood without an appreciation of the significance of region and locality. The South Asian groups are concentrated in specific regions. The highest concentrations of Pakistanis are found in London and the South East, with substantially large settlements also in Yorkshire, Humberside and in the North West. Our study (Brah and Shaw 1992) was made in the city of Birmingham in the West Midlands. During the 1980s, major job losses occurred in the West Midlands, especially in manufacturing where there has been a concentration of Asian workers. In the city of Birmingham, this pattern was even more pronounced. Between 1981 and 1984, Birmingham City declined twice as fast as the region as a whole (Birmingham City Council 1988). The devastating impact of this change on Asian households may be gauged given that, according to the 1971 census, just over 60 per cent of male workers of Pakistani and Indian origin in the West Midlands worked in the manufacturing industries. Asian women, too, have been concentrated in manufacturing, principally in textiles and clothing. While there has been a relative increase in employment in the service sector, this is primarily in those enclaves where the Asian workforce is as yet under-represented.

Moreover, according to Birmingham City Council's 1986 Review of Economic Strategy, such expansion mainly consists of growth in low-paid employment, and self-employment at lower levels of the income scale. Such regional and local trends have been crucial to the type, range and extent of employment available to young women.

Immigration control

The impact of immigration legislation on Asian families is now well documented. As we saw in Chapter Three, social constructions of Asian marriage and family relations as a 'problem for British society' have been pivotal in the legitimation of British immigration policy. Images of 'tidal waves' of Asian men scheming to circumvent immigration restrictions through the arranged marriage system were commonly invoked in the justification of immigration control. While the Asian male was defined as a prospective worker posing a threat to the employment prospects of white men, Asian women were defined in immigration law as 'dependants'. This social imagery of Asian women as hapless dependants who would most likely be married off at the earliest possible opportunity has played an important role in constructing the 'commonsense understandings' which teachers, employment advisers, training officers, and other professionals might hold of young Muslim women's education and employment prospects. Such professionals have an important role to play in encouraging or discouraging young Muslim women from pursuing certain types of education or employment (Cross *et al.* 1990; Brah and Shaw 1992).

There is now an extensive literature that documents direct and indirect discrimination in the labour market in terms of access to employment, promotion and training (cf. Daniel 1968; Brooks and Singh 1978; Brown 1984; Drew *et al.* 1991). Such discriminatory practices are constituted in and through a variety of racialised discourses and practices that construct the racialised group as inherently 'different'. Just as patriarchal discourses may represent women's labour as 'different' and/or inferior, racialised discourses call into question the abilities, aptitudes, cultural attributes, and the general suitability of a group for certain types of jobs and positions within the employment hierarchy. Research shows that teachers, careers officers and employers can all be implicated in practices that have life-long adverse consequences for individuals (Lee and Wrench 1983; Cross *et al.* 1990; Drew *et al.* 1991; see also Chapter Three).

Images, representations, and lived culture

Where Asian women are concerned, racialised constructions articulate with those of gender, ethnicity, religion and class in the social representations of this category of women in Britain. There is a long history of orientalised discourses embedded in literature, paintings, drawings, photography, 'scientific' discourse, political debate, state policies and practices and in 'commonsense'. The 'oriental female', especially the Muslim woman, came to occupy a position of the quintessential 'Other' in this discursive space of desire (cf. Said 1978; Alloula 1986). Whether she is exoticised, represented as ruthlessly oppressed and in need of liberation, or read as a victim/enigmatic emblem of religious fundamentalism, she is likely to be cast as the bearer of 'races' whose 'alien' cultures continually threaten to disrupt 'civilised values'. She excites Western fantasies of transgression: mystique, lust, danger. The 'veil' is the ultimate icon of this fantasmatic field, frustrating the Western gaze by its opaqueness and its apparent dismissal and disregard for its hegemonic moves. 'Veil' is the metaphor for the orientalisation of the contradictions of gender and imperialism. But orientalisation is a process, and there is no one-to-one direct correspondence either between colonial representations of groups who were 'orientalised' (Arabs, Turks, Indians, for example, have been orientalised in different ways), or between colonial representations and contemporary discourses. There are continuities as well as discontinuities across this discursive field. Hence, social images of Pakistani women in present day Britain may in part derive from colonial representations of Muslims in colonial India, but, essentially, they are an integral component of the field of representation associated with the Pakistani presence in post-war Britain. Such social imagery connects also with discourses of 'the Muslim' in Western Europe as a whole. There would seem to be substantial overlap in the available imagery of young Muslim women in different parts of Western Europe (see Chapter Three; Parmar 1982; Brah and Minhas 1985; Lutz 1991).

But how do such images of Muslim or other categories of Asian women affect their employment trajectories? They do so when, as noted above, these stereotypes are translated into institutional practices with adverse consequences for women's position in the labour market. For example, the discourse of 'cultural constraints on Muslim women' is played out within a myriad of practices on the part of teachers, education and training guidance providers, recruitment and personnel officers, youth workers, social workers, and so on. The general currency of such ideas on a wide scale through the media means that they have become sedimented into a collective common-sense. Their influence can be all-pervasive, although the precise meaning and significance attached to them would depend upon how they articulate under given circumstances.

To highlight the discourse of 'cultural constraints' as ideology is not to deny the importance of culture. But what do we mean when we speak of cultural constraints? In discussions of Muslim women the 'cultural' constraint that is most frequently invoked is the institution of 'purdah' – a series of norms and practices which limit women's participation in public life. It is important to point out that this social concept signifies practices which vary enormously from one historical period to another, from one country to another, and from one social group to another. Even within the same social group its patterns of observance can differ considerably along class, caste and other dimensions (El Sadawi 1980; Sharma 1980). Nor is this institution confined to Muslims in the Asian sub-continent. Versions of 'purdah' are also observable among Hindus and Sikhs. Indeed, Sharma (1980) argues that, in terms of its broader meaning as a sign for the complex of discourses and practices which circumscribe women's participation in public life, the concept may have some applicability in all societies. In this sense, the segregation of the labour market by gender in Britain, for instance, could be understood as a set of patriarchal ideologies and practices that are not entirely different from 'purdah'. Nevertheless, it is important to acknowledge the specificity of Islamic forms of 'purdah', but without viewing the institution as uniform, fixed, or unchanging. The important issue, then, is how 'purdah' is played out differently among different Muslim groups and other South Asian communities in Britain, and how it articulates with other British patriarchal ideologies and practices. The point I wish to stress is that 'Asian' patriarchal discourses and practices in Britain are not exogenous to British society; they are very much an internal dynamic of the British social formation.

The lived cultures that young Muslim women inhabit are highly differentiated, varying according to such factors as country of origin, rural/urban background of households prior to migration, regional and linguistic background in the sub-continent, class position in the sub-continent as well as in Britain, and regional location in Britain. Asian–British cultures are not simply a carry-over from the sub-continent but are now 'native' to different regions and localities of

Britain. Asian cultures of London, for example, may be distinguished from those of Birmingham. Similarly, East London Asian cultural life has its own distinctive features compared with the local cultures of West London. There are some commonalties, of course, depending upon which particular modality – religion, region, language, class, etc. – is singled out. For example, Panjabi cultures have their own specificities compared with Gujerati or Bengali cultures. On the other hand, all Muslim groups, be they Panjabi, Gujerati or Bengali, share certain cultural specificities. But each case is simultaneously a dimension of region and locality – of 'Englishness', 'Scottishness', 'Welshness', 'Irishness', or of 'Geordiness', 'Cockneyness', 'Yorkshireness', and so on. In the everyday lives of women, these are not separate but enmeshing realities. They can not be disaggregated into 'Asian' and 'British' components. They are fusions such that 'Asian–British' is a new ensemble created and played out in the everyday life world.

Therefore, as I said earlier, it is crucial to distinguish between 'young Pakistani women' as a generalised object of social discourse and young Pakistani women as embodied historical subjects. The latter are a diverse and heterogeneous category of people who occupy a multiplicity of subject positions. As is the case with other subjects, their everyday lives are constituted in and through matrices of power embedded in intersecting discourses and material practices. The next section examines how the respondents to the study are constituted by and in turn elaborate the discourse of women's paid and unpaid labour. We examine the ways in which women's narratives represent a range of responses and strategies – of accommodation, complicity, resistance, struggle, transgression – as they negotiate the many and varying facets of power in their everyday lives. The aim is to explore how wider social structures are implicated in the lived cultures that the women inhabit.

NARRATING SELF AND THE REST

It is axiomatic that paid employment is only one form of work. Although wage labour has existed for many centuries, the almost total dependence of households on a wage is a relatively recent phenomenon. In Europe, where it is now the dominant pattern, it only dates from the nineteenth century (Pahl 1988). It is a commonplace to say that women have always worked. In most societies, however, some of the most demanding work that women perform, i.e. housework, child care and caring work for other members of the family, is rarely regarded as 'work', such that the notion of 'work' is now a synonym for paid work. While many women are engaged in paid forms of work, whether inside the household in some form of homeworking or on an employer's premises, the ideology of the male breadwinner is still pervasive in advanced industrialised societies (cf. Leonard and Speakman 1986; McRae 1989; Hall 1992).

In less industrialised countries, the subsistence sector is comparatively large and the demarcation between 'productive' work and work for creation of 'use values' is less clear. Women may be involved in a variety of tasks which simultaneously form part of the market economy and in the production of goods and services directly for consumption within the household (Beneria and Sen 1981; Young and Wolkowitz 1981; Redclift 1985). In South Asia, women perform a wide range of economic activities both inside and outside the household. In urban Pakistan, women may work in a variety of professions such as teaching, medicine and social work. Women may also be found in some of the lowest status forms of paid work, including road and building construction, municipal street sweeping and domestic service. In rural areas, women are likely to be responsible for the care of domestic animals and the processing of food for preservation and storage; they may undertake specialised forms of agricultural work such as the transplanting of rice, and take part in general sowing and harvesting of crops; and they may weave, sew and produce handicrafts alongside other domestic and child care responsibilities (Papaneck 1971; Nazir 1991). In other words, Pakistani women who migrated to Britain are likely to have been involved in a variety of economic activities prior to migration. What would be new when they migrated would not be the prospect of 'working' but rather the experience of paid work in an advanced industrialised society.

There is a dearth of research case lore from which to develop a systematic picture of the labour market realities of young Muslim women. Much of the research carried out relates to the immigrant generation (Dhaya 1974; Saifullah-Khan 1974; Jeffery 1976; Anwar 1979). One exception is a pilot study involving a dozen households where the author interviewed daughters, mothers and grandmothers in the city of Bradford (Afshar 1989). In this account, we encounter women employed largely as homeworkers, although some women had worked in mills before the birth of their children, or as unpaid workers in a family business – and, in some cases, as 'career women'. Clearly, these women were economically active, although few would be included in formal statistics.

In our study we interviewed five categories of women: those who were not looking for paid employment; those engaged in paid work (both those working on employers' premises and homeworkers); unemployed women; trainees on Government Training Schemes; and students in courses of further or higher education. This range of women were interviewed because, in order to fully understand why some Muslim women do not enter the labour market, we needed to know why others already have done so. Also, it is important to know what perceptions and aspirations are represented among women enrolled on courses of education and training.

To work or not to work?

This question held different significance depending upon whether the respondent was a student or a trainee, an unemployed young woman, a woman with young children weighing the advantage of an income against the cost of paying a childminder or nursery fee, or someone already engaged in paid work outside the home or as a 'homeworker'. The most striking common aspect of the responses we received was that the women overwhelmingly supported women's right to paid work. Irrespective of whether or not they themselves wished, or were in a position, to find employment, this support was consistently echoed in the interviews. It represents a serious critique of patriarchal discourses which privilege male income and construct women's labour as singularly appropriate to caring responsibilities in the household. It interrogates the hegemonic claims of such ideologies. Women's earnings were considered by our respondents as an indispensable contribution to the income of households. Paid work was also valued for offering women a measure of independence and a sense of confidence.

When performed outside the household, paid work was thought to provide a much needed network of contacts beyond those of family and kinship. Employment outside the home was considered an antidote to the boredom and isolation of staying at home. Workplace friendships were experienced as a source of fun. Women talked about the joy of sharing a joke, teasing, engaging in casual banter, sharing out items of lunch brought from home, gossiping, offering a sympathetic ear to workmates experiencing domestic or other problems, sharing 'a moan' against employers, and so on.

Contradictions of gender, ethnicity, racism, class and generation seemed to be played out in all their complexity in these workplace cultures. The importance attached by women to workplace cultures is also attested by ethnographic studies of women in the workplace (cf. Pollert 1981; Westwood 1984).

Barriers to employment

If the great majority of women emphasised the importance of paid work for women, why were some of them not looking for employment? All the women who fell into this category – both married and single – cited housework and other caring responsibilities as taking up most of their time. The single women often had to share responsibility for looking after their younger brothers and sisters, or, in some cases, their nephews and nieces. In instances where a mother suffered ill health, the single woman had to assume the overall responsibility for the household. There was no doubt that, for these women, housework and other forms of caring work including child care, care of elderly parents-in-law, or that of other members of the extended family, constituted 'work' *par excellence*:

> How can I look for other work, I can't even finish my housework. I have plenty of work to do: wash, iron, make dinner and all that. My mum can't do it because of poor health, so I have to do the housework.
>
> (18-year-old single woman)

> Housework takes up all my time. There are eight of us at home. Cooking, cleaning the house, washing clothes, ironing – it never finishes.
>
> (20-year-old single woman)

> I have four children, three boys and a girl. I have my hands full. . . . Besides, if I did work I would have to place the children in a nursery. That costs more than the wage I would earn.
>
> (Young married woman)

Of course, there is a sense in which these narratives might be understood as being typical of any woman under such circumstances. But while these women are not alone in finding domestic responsibilities onerous, there are two factors that have a particular bearing on this group. First, these women often had responsibility for larger-than-average households, which sometimes included members of the extended family. Second, domestic appliances such as washing machines or dishwashers that might relieve the pressures of housework were not a common feature of many households, especially those facing difficult material circumstances in a period of high unemployment. A similar finding is reported by Shaw (1988). It is worth bearing in mind that both during *and* since the last decade, Pakistani households in Birmingham have been one of the hardest hit by job losses in the area. In our study, we came across families where several members of the household were unemployed. Moreover, even when a household might not be directly affected by unemployment, low income might still be a problem due to the concentration of Pakistanis in low-paid jobs. Moreover, the financial demands of mutual obligations amongst extended kin may further deplete disposable household income.

It is sometimes suggested that South Asians from rural Pakistan, as compared to those from urban centres, might be more inclined to restrict women's entry in the labour market. However, we did not find any major differences in family background prior to migration between women who were not searching for a job and those who were 'economically active' – that is, who were either unemployed or employed. The families of the majority of women in all three categories migrated from rural parts of Pakistan. Rural origin in itself, therefore, could not account for whether or not young Pakistani women would take up employment. Nor did marital status emerge as a particularly important determinant of women's propensity to seek paid work. Although single women were more likely to be economically active, they were also strongly represented among those not looking for paid work.

One factor that did seem to have a clear influence on the likelihood of a woman participating in the labour market was her length of stay in Britain. We found that the great majority of women who were active in the labour market were born here or arrived here as children. In contrast, most of the women who were not pursuing employment came to Britain as teenagers or later and, as a consequence, their experience of schooling in Britain was limited. In Pakistan they had attended mainly village schools. In Britain the majority had left school without achieving any formal qualifications, and some experienced difficulty in using English. Such women often perceived their lack of formal qualifications and their limited facility in the English language as a barrier to 'good jobs'.

Sitting at home you get bored. But finding jobs is not easy. I have to learn English first.

At the moment I don't know. When I have learnt English and other things I'll see whether I want to work or not. English is a big problem for me.

These women were not unaware of jobs in the secondary sector of the labour market, especially in the clothing industry in Birmingham where employers asked no questions about knowledge of English or other types of formal qualification. But the young women categorised these as 'bad jobs' with low rates of pay and poor working conditions. Such jobs held no attraction for the women, since they would merely impose an extra burden on existing demands on their time from domestic responsibilities, without any of the advantages of a well-paid job with good working conditions.

I said earlier that women's position in the labour market is defined, not simply by the structure of the labour market or the needs of the economy, but also by patriarchal ideologies which define women's position in society. Social norms about 'women's work' and 'men's work' are constitutive of the unequal division of labour in the household, occupational segregation of the labour market by gender, and the possibility that a substantial number of women may never enter the labour market. Patriarchal ideologies have a bearing on all women in Britain, but they may take specific forms in relation to young Muslim women. Notions of 'purdah', as has already been pointed out, vary enormously among Muslim groups. But where families do wish to observe such norms the prospect of women going out to perform paid work causes deep concern because it is thought to signal the inability of men to provide for the economic maintenance of the household. The generalised ideology of the male as breadwinner, common in Britain and other Western countries, emerges in this system of signification as 'family honour'. The prospect of young women working away from home unchaperoned is understood as providing fertile ground for malicious gossip. Such gossip is considered a serious threat to a woman's reputation. As we saw in Chapter Three, Sue Lee's work demonstrates the power of gossip and innuendo in casting doubts on a young woman's reputation in British schools. A white girl who has been constructed as a 'slag' may redeem her reputation by finding a steady boyfriend. Such possibility of patriarchal 'redemption' through the heterosexual economy of desire is not available to young Asian women. They must have a reputation of no sexual involvement prior to marriage if they are to help maintain their 'family honour', something that was not generally uncommon in Britain that long ago. The point is that both instances are exemplars of patriarchal practices.

What is interesting in terms of our study is that only about a quarter of our respondents gave their families' opposition to women holding jobs away from the home on the grounds of 'izzat' and 'purdah' as the major reason why they were not doing paid work. But when opposition did occur constraints could be quite stringent:

> My parents want me to stay at home. . . . The relatives are the same as well. They say she shouldn't go out. . . . I don't even sign on. I think they wouldn't mind me doing homeworking. . . . If I was at home they could keep an eye on me. If I went to a factory they might think I will go somewhere else with a friend, or I might find a boyfriend.

> My parents didn't let me out of the house. Straight home from school, do the housework and stay in. Didn't see my friends. My Mum is stricter than my Dad. Dad used to say 'let them go out', but she wouldn't. She said people would talk.

Patriarchal norms and practices cannot, however, be regarded simply as 'external constraints'. As we saw in the last chapter and in the first part of this one, at any given moment our subjectivity is marked by the discursive field of complex articulation between the psychic and the social. We have different investments in different political positions. That is, women may be positioned or even consciously position themselves differently within patriarchal discourses, not because they are either 'oppressed' or 'forced' to do so or because they are propelled by an enlightened self-referencing agency, but because they are emotionally, psychically, subjectively invested in specific positionalities where the effects of the social dynamics of power are non-reductively interiorised into the contradictory modalities of the mind. So, how did the young women who were not looking for employment construct themselves in terms of the cultural practices that serve to exclude women from the labour market? In some cases the young women echoed the gender-specific injunctions that mark the concept of 'izzat'. As one woman observed:

> When women work outside the home it brings 'Be Izzti' (dishonour) on the family. I do not think women should work outside the home. I would not want a daughter of mine to work! [translated]

But other women opposed the idea that women should not hold jobs outside the home. Their responses to the personal circumstances that had led to their own exclusion from the labour market differed considerably. One single woman, currently unable to take up paid work due to the opposition of her parents, lived in the hope that her future partner would be more liberal on the subject. A second young woman, whose parents had not considered it appropriate for unmarried women to work outside the home, and who was married soon after leaving school, found that her husband too was not in favour of her finding a job. Feeling isolated and bored at home, she feels quite disenchanted with this aspect of her life. But she is determined to ensure that when she has children her daughter will get similar opportunities to a son. Her own life might have been constrained by the normative construction of the male as breadwinner, but she is keen to negotiate a different future for her daughter. A third woman, who was a twenty-four-year-old young mother with three children, could not take up employment because of child care responsibilities, but she was planning to train as a nursery nurse when her children were older. Her husband and in-laws were supportive of her job aspirations. It is clear that young Pakistani women who are outside the labour market constitute a diverse and differentiated category of individuals.

Dilemmas of paid work

Muslim women may be under-represented in those forms of paid work which are accessible to statistical collation. But they are far from absent in the labour market. As we saw earlier, evidence suggests that a substantial proportion of these women may be engaged in 'homeworking'. On the other hand, Muslim women are also employed in a range of manual, office and clerical, as well as professional, jobs in Britain. This range was reflected among our employed respondents, with three of them working in a clothing factory, one self-employed as a graphic designer, one a primary school teacher. Another respondent worked for the local authority in a middle-range advisory/managerial post, three worked in the voluntary sector as community workers or advice workers, and two worked from home as 'homeworkers'. Another twelve women were unemployed. A common characteristic of both employed and unemployed women was their determination to find a job. They placed great emphasis on the need for women to be economically active:

> I think men and women should have equal rights. If men work why can't women? Women are not just there to do the housework.

> I strongly disagree with those who think that women should not work outside the home. Well, why should they stay at home? Why can't men stay at home?

> I think that both men and women should work. You can't live on one person's income.... It is important to me not to be dependent on anyone – my Mum or husband. I am ambitious for myself.

A substantial proportion of our respondents belonged to families who were quite flexible about women holding jobs. In such instances, parents had been at the very least non-obstructive and, in several cases, positively encouraging about the education and career ambitions of their daughters:

> When I decided to look for jobs my parents were not overjoyed. But they didn't stop me either.

> My parents left the choice to me: you can stay at home or go to work just as long as you don't give me a bad name and people can't point the finger.

> My parents were very encouraging. They said, 'do what you want to do'.

Where families were initially reluctant, the women used a variety of strategies of persuasion to obtain consent, often recruiting the support of sympathetic relatives or family friends to help negotiate a desired outcome. Academic and professional jobs are especially highly regarded among Asian groups. Even those parents who might at first be ambivalent about a daughter pursuing higher education/ professional qualifications for fear that the young woman may become 'wayward', as one respondent put it, will feel quite proud once she has achieved such qualifications.

Not surprisingly, economic necessity emerged as one of the most effective persuaders:

> At first I didn't work because my parents didn't want me to. Dad is unemployed now. It is hard. I am looking for work now.

> Well it is hard because my Mum doesn't really want me to have a job. But we have been forced to because we've got no money. . . . My

parents want me to sew at home [homeworking]. Loads of girls my age [17] do it around here. But I don't want to.

When my father retired of ill health we actually had to support ourselves. . . . There's no way my sisters could have got married – right – the dowry, the jewelry and hiring the hall, feeding the guests – all that – without previous employment.

The effects of immigration legislation were also cited as influencing women's decision to participate in the labour market. Our respondents argued that the law discriminates against Asians, and the young women are particularly caught up in this through the 'primary purpose' clause which places the onus on an applicant from the Asian sub-continent married to a British-born Asian woman to provide the burden of proof that the marriage was not contracted primarily for the purpose of immigration to Britain. The immigration rules also stipulate that persons wishing to bring their spouses over to live in Britain must be able to support them without recourse to public funds. Families are often divided across continents due to these laws, and the women who wish to sponsor a spouse must find employment in order to provide proof of being able to support a spouse without recourse to public funds (cf. Sondhi 1987).

Whatever the reasons given for holding a job, and irrespective of the level of social importance attached to women's right to employment by individual women, paid work was not always experienced as an unequivocal advantage. Managing the 'double-shift' of domestic responsibilities alongside paid work was likely to be exhausting (see Chapter Two). For most women combining these two types of work the day could start as early as five or six o'clock in the morning, and may not end until ten or eleven o'clock at night after all the household chores, or the tasks related to paid work (e.g. marking student essays or preparing for the next day's lessons, in the case of a teacher; or completing the piece-work quota for the day in the case of a 'homeworker') had been completed (see case studies in Brah and Shaw 1992).

Our interviews with 'homeworkers' support the evidence from other studies which points to low wages, insecurity of employment, boredom and isolation, unbearable pressures resulting from sudden deadlines imposed at short notice by suppliers, and overall lack of employment protection, as characteristic features of 'homeworking' (cf. Bisset and Huws 1984; Allen and Wolkowitz 1987; Phizacklea 1990). This should not be taken to imply, however, that women working at employers' premises considered themselves as being better off. Indeed, several women working outside the home in low-waged, non-unionised sectors of the economy complained bitterly about conditions of work. Any attempts at unionisation of the workforce, they said, could result in dismissal. Fear of 'the sack' was a powerful deterrent against collective action. As one woman put it:

> They treat you like animals but everyone fears the sack because you can't get a job that fast.

Poor working conditions – whether associated with 'homeworking' or with work carried out from employers' premises – were deplored across the board. Women condemned such conditions even though they may have no option themselves but to accept such employment through necessity and lack of available options.

Overall, 'homeworking' was regarded by the women as the least favoured form of paid work. They described it as sheer drudgery and exploitation. They saw it as reinforcing social isolation and leading to loneliness, and in some cases to acute forms of depression. Correspondingly, low-skilled forms of 'factory work' or non-manual work were also met with little enthusiasm, although they were generally preferred over homeworking. Women wanted 'good jobs with decent pay' and a creative and positive working environment. Yet they possessed a fairly realistic assessment of the limited range of jobs available to the majority of Asian women. Living in working-class areas of decaying urban centres, women were fully aware of the limitations of the local labour market. They spoke of how 'homeworking', certain types of factory work or, at best, low-skilled low-paid non-manual work in the service sector had become the norm for Asian girls in the minds of local employers, teachers, education and guidance advisers, as well as among sections of the Asian communities. There is not the space here to discuss our respondents' experiences of education, the Government Training Schemes, and the education and training guidance services. Suffice it to say that the young women reported low expectations and stereotypic perceptions of Asian girls, their aspirations, abilities and parental cultures, on the part of educational professionals. The professional gaze in which a young Muslim woman is always an object rather than a subject of her own destiny was seen by our interviewees as a major obstacle to Asian girls' success in the labour market.

Racism and discrimination were cited as another huge barrier to entry and success in the labour market:

Racism is a problem. It is easier for white people to get jobs. If a white person advertised a job he would probably want a white person to do it.

It is difficult for us. They give the white people jobs first and then us last.

There are some white people who do not like Asian people. When they see them on the streets they shout abuse and swear words. It makes me really angry. Some employers don't like to give jobs to Asians.

CONTINGENT POSITIONALITY

It is clear from women's narratives that they are 'situated' differently and differentially across a variety of discourses. While some women endorse a woman's right to employment and thereby pose a challenge to patriarchal notions of the male as breadwinner, other women's narratives reiterate patriarchal values. There was no direct correspondence between, on the one hand, their views on women's participation in the labour market as a desirable and desired general goal and, on the other hand, individual women's own involvement in paid forms of work. The latter was circum-scribed by such aspects as the form and extent of their caring responsibilities, the financial circumstances of the household, the structure of opportunities available through the local market, encouraging/discouraging attitudes on the part of relations/tea-chers/employment advisers, and racism and racial discrimination in employment. But the point is that women's experience is not unmitigated uni-directional 'oppression', nor are their narratives a straightforward codification of 'social orientation' waiting to 'burst out' as voluntaristic agency.

Rather, the narratives 'perform' variable modalities of *subjectivity* as the site of 'social' and 'psychic' simultaneity of *positionality*. Women's views about paid employment narrate articulating but distinctive and differentiated gender identities. As previously dis-cussed, identity may be understood as that process whereby the instability and contradiction of the subject-in-process is *signified* as having stability and coherence as a 'core' which is enunciated as the 'I'. The 'I' is non-identically but relationally installed as the 'we' across the discursive space of subjectivity and institutional power and practice. In this sense, the collective agency of the women we interviewed was deeply marked by different political subject positions, but not necessarily those which neatly fit certain received notions of the 'political', where political agency signals a certain kind of 'consciousness' and a certain kind of 'action'. By placing a strong emphasis on the importance of women having access to well-paid jobs with good working conditions, our respondents articulated a gendered discourse of social equity and justice. As we have seen, some of these young women were not 'economically active' themselves, but they persisted in the pursuit of everyday strategies that would facilitate and strengthen the opening up of socially just options for women, even if, as in their own cases, such a goal had to be deferred for a generation and achieved through daughters, or partially gained by supporting friends or female relatives. Women who already held jobs created cultural spaces where the pleasures of sociality could be experienced in the everyday minutiae of life in the workplace. Paid work embodied all the contradictions of class, gender, ethnicity and racism as women sought to balance the 'double-shift' of combining domestic responsibilities with a job. In their varying capacity either as 'homeworkers', workers in low-waged occupations on employers' premises, or doing various clerical, managerial and professional jobs, women came face-to-face with gendered forms of racialised class exploitation. Their everyday life world whispered myriad configurations of power relations.

Overall, the young women's relationship to the labour market was constructed by a multiplicity of discourses and institutional practices, such as the impact of the global and the national economy on the local labour markets; discourses about women's suitability for caring responsibilities and women's own positionality in such discourses – how they might 'feel' and 'think' about them; the role of education in the social construction of gendered job aspirations, and racism. In other words, 'structure', 'culture' and 'agency'; the social and the psychic are all implicated. They are all integral to the framework I have outlined.

NOTE

1   The study upon which this chapter is based was funded by the Department of Employment. It focuses upon young women of predominantly Pakistani background living in Birmingham. It is a qualitative study, carried out during 1988/89, which involved 55 in-depth interviews with individuals

and group discussions with 50 women in the age group 16–24. The women had family origins in the Mirpur district of Azad Kashmir or in the Panjab. Most of the families came to Britain from rural parts of the sub-continent, but about a sixth of them had urban backgrounds prior to migration. The young women's parents worked mainly in manual occupations in Britain (Brah and Shaw 1992).

Chapter 7

Re-framing Europe
Gendered racisms, ethnicities and
nationalisms in contemporary Western Europe

We are living in a period marked by profound changes. The political upheavals of recent times in Eastern Europe, the Soviet Union, South Africa, Central and South America – to note a few examples – and the aftermath of the Gulf War, signal major realignments in the structuring of the world political order. There has been a fundamental transformation in the political economy of late twentieth-century capitalism with a growing dominance of transnational capital, an increasing consolidation of global markets, the development of new techniques in production and distribution systems, the formation of a 'new' international division of labour, and a revolution in the technologies of communication. In the cultural sphere, the homogenising tendencies of mass cultural consumption across transnational boundaries are paralleled by a reassertion of the local aesthetic, political and ethnic tradition, and a call for a recognition of heterogeneity and cultural difference.

In Western Europe, '1992' has come to signify a new phase in the relations between the twelve members of the European Community. On 1 January 1993, the internal borders of the twelve states officially came down, with the intent of allowing the free movement of capital, goods, services and certain categories of people. The emerging configuration that is increasingly described as the 'new Europe' is as yet difficult to define. What will this new configuration be? Is the new Europe primarily a constellation of economic interests emerging in the face of growing competition, especially from Japan and the USA? To what extent will Eastern European countries become Western Europe's new colonies? What will be the impact of such realignments of European countries on the 'Third World'? What will be the place of Europe in the wake of the Gulf War now that the USA emerges as the undisputedly dominant global military power? Will the 'new Europe' be an inherently unstable formation with its interstate conflicts over economic and political power, and tribal rivalries between different European ethnic groups which currently result in untold bloodshed and genocide? Such questions have a critical bearing on the construction of new European identities.

Significantly, 1992 was also the fifth centennial of Columbus's arrival in the Americas on 12 October 1492. And 1492 was also the year of the fall of Granada in Spain, which marked the end of seven hundred years of power and influence of the 'Moors' in Europe – an anniversary that places into relief the historical contestation between Judaism, Christianity and Islam, and how such contestations are reconfiguring in contemporary Europe. Such historical events constituted inaugural moments in the evolution of a world economic system in which Western dominance became inextricably linked with the history of transatlantic slavery, colonialism and imperialism. Throughout the five hundred years of European expansion and colonisation, the idea of 'Europe' as in some sense a unified category has been persistently challenged by intense European conflicts and rivalries, as testified this century by the two World Wars and the subsequent Cold War between capitalist and 'socialist' power blocs. In such political landscapes, ideals of a pan-European identity were continually interrogated by the processes of national identity formation, themselves subject to internal contradictions of gender, class, regional and ethnic specificities.

Yet Europe did exist as a conglomerate power on the world stage: as a concrete reality for all those whom it subordinated. Indeed, as Balibar (1991) noted, until the middle of the twentieth century, the principal meaning of the term 'European' referred to groups of colonisers in the colonised regions of the world. The processes of conquest, colonisation, empire formation, permanent settlement by Europeans of other parts of the globe, nationalist struggles by the colonised, and selective decolonisation constitute the terrain on which Europe constructed itself and its 'others'. It is against this background that current changes in the global economic and political order are taking shape and a 'new Europe' is emerging.

In this 'new Europe', we are presently faced with a growing resurgence and intensification of racism, nationalism, and a genocide that unabashedly asserts itself as 'ethnic cleansing' while it wreaks rape, death and torture. This makes it politically imperative that, as we rethink the concept of ethnicity, we consider its affirmative inscriptive possibilities as well as its susceptibilities to potential recuperation in racism and nationalism. Under what circumstances does ethnicity become racialised? How does racism articulate with nationalism? How do gender and class inscribe these intersections? This chapter is an attempt to explore some theoretical and political aspects of the problematics constituted by such questions. In the first part I discuss conceptual categories and debates addressing such questions. In the second part I examine the political ramifications of economic and cultural processes inscribing the Europe of a 'Single European Market'.

I develop my analysis with a focus on racism, but explore its relationship to other axes of differentiation. The point is that racism, ethnicity, nationalism and class represent gendered phenomena; and that their changing configurations are immanent within the broader shifts associated with the transition from 'modernity' to what is variously described as 'post-industrialism', 'post-modernity', or 'late capitalism'. I examine the concept of 'neo-racism' and suggest that its analytical usefulness is dependent upon the extent to which it is possible to establish criteria which could be utilised as a basis for distinguishing its 'newness' from older forms of racisms in Europe. I emphasise the need to address the plurality of racisms in Europe and argue a case for treating these as articulating, rather than parallel, dynamics of power. I use the term 'differential racisms' (as distinct from Balibar's notion of 'differentialist racisms') to analyse the discursive space of:

- intersectionality within, between, amongst and across different racisms;
- articulations of racism with socio- economic, cultural and political relations of gender, class and other markers of 'difference' and differentiation;
- relationality of subjectivity and identity in and through these fields.

Finally, I foreground the need to be attentive to new configurations of ethnicities.

RACISM, GENDER AND CLASS: A PROBLEM OF DEFINITION?

There has been some considerable controversy and protracted debate in Britain about the use of the concept of race and the definition of racism. Should the concept of race be assigned analytical value given the weight of evidence against its validity as a 'biological' category?

How is its importance as a 'social' category to be addressed? Is racism an 'ideology' or can it also be understood as 'structure'? Such questions remain far from settled (Gilroy 1987; Miles 1989; Donald and Rattansi 1992). But it is generally agreed that the concept of race signifies a historically variable nexus of social meanings. That is to say that 'race' is a social construction. Any number of markers – colour, physiognomy, culture, gene pools – may be summoned, singly or in combination, as signifiers of 'race'. Certain forms of racism will highlight biological characteristics as indicators of supposed 'racial' difference. Other forms may single out cultural difference as the basis of presumed impervious racial boundaries between groups. Cultural racism may be silent or even deny any notion of biological superiority or inferiority, but what characterises it specifically as racism is the subtext of innate difference that implicitly or explicitly serves to denote a group as a 'race'. In other words racism constructs 'racial' difference.

It is not necessary for biological characteristics to be fore-grounded in each and every racism, but, if a phenomenon is to be identified as racism, the collectivity signified within it must be represented as being 'inherently different'. Contrary to positions which construct racism as a transparent technology of suppression and oppression, processes of racialisation do not always occur in a matrix of simple bipolarities of negativity and positivity, superiority and inferiority, or inclusion and exclusion. While racialised encounters have certainly been predicated against a history of exploitation, inferiorisation and exclusion, they have equally inhabited spaces of deep ambivalence, admiration, envy and desire. Desire for the racialised 'Other' is constructed and codified in and through patriarchal regimes of power, even as heterosexual cultural norms, values and conventions are continually disrupted by lesbian, gay, and other sexualities. At the same time all sexualities in a racialised context are inscribed by racialised matrices of power. In other words the 'Other' of racism is not an unequivocal obverse of 'self'; 'otherness' may be constructed primarily, but not exclusively, in antithetical terms. Moreover, racial and sexual otherness are inti-mately connected, the one is immanent in the other (Bhabha 1986b). I shall return to this point below.

There is a tendency in some analyses of racism to confine the use of the concept of racism exclusively to an 'ideological phenomenon', as distinct from 'social practices'. Such categorical distinctions are deeply problematic. If discourses, in the Foucauldian sense, are 'orders of knowledge' and 'regimes of power' which 'are not in a position of exteriority with respect to other types of relations (economic processes, knowledge relationships, sexual relations) but are immanent in the latter' (Foucault 1984: 94), it follows that they are constitutive elements in the formation of different forms of subjectivity and social practices. Consequently, processes of signification such as racism cease to be a mere 'surface' phenomenon in contradiction to some 'deep structural phenomenon'. Rather, the focus of attention is shifted to the ways in which racialised 'regimes of power' articulate with those of gender, class, or other modalities' differentiation as they are played out in economic, political, cultural and psychic spheres.

Given the amazing profusion – perhaps, even *con*-fusion – in studies of racism which remain oblivious to the centrality of gender and sexuality in the constitution of racism, it is necessary to reiterate explicitly that racism is always a gendered and sexualised phenomenon. First, the *idea* of 'race' is essentially an *essentialist narrative of sexualised difference*. It is an allegory of centring Western dynastic genealogies of the 'ascent' and 'descent' of 'Man'. That is, it is a trope for the 'Western' heterosexual economy of desire. Discourses of 'racial difference' are saturated with metaphors of origin, common ancestry, blood, kith and kin. The figure of woman is a constitutive moment in the racialised desire for economic and political control.

Racism constructs the female gender differently from the male gender (cf. Greenberger 1969; Davin 1978; bell hooks 1981; Davis 1981; Carby 1982; Mackenzie 1984; Mani 1987; Haraway 1989; Hall 1992; Ware 1992). Not only are men and women from one racialised group differentiated from those of another racialised group, but the male from a subordinated group may be racialised through the attribution of 'feminine qualities', or the female may be represented as embodying 'male' qualities. Thus, for instance, Bengali men in colonial India were characterised as 'effete' or 'feminine' in contrast to the macho self-image of the self-assured and heroic British male. Similarly, black women slaves in the Americas were racialised *vis-à-vis* white women by the attribution of 'masculine qualities' which were thought to set them apart from 'the gentility of white womanhood'. Given the gendered 'nature' of 'culture', racism is also experienced differently by men and women. *That is, racism encodes gendered differentiations while seeming to subsume them.* The process of subsumption is significant in that it imposes an 'imagined' and imaginary unity upon the racialised group, while simultaneously inscribing patriarchal regimes of power. Racism and patriarchal discourses/practices are similar, in that both forms of signification serve to naturalise certain ascriptive differences: racism constructs human variation as codifying inherent and immutable difference, represents it as 'racial' and maps this imputed difference on to social collectivities; patriarchal moves invoke sex as a pre-given 'fact' that represents men and women as 'naturally' different, such that women's subordinate position is legitimised as deriving from innate differences between men and women. Both sets of significations figure the body as a bearer of immutable difference whether or not this putative difference is represented as biological or cultural.

The sex/gender distinction that emerged as a result of feminist attempts to critique the biology-is-destiny formulation was invoked in some feminist accounts to differentiate between 'racism' and 'sexism'. It was argued that, whereas racism inscribed inequality through a mobilisation of biological notions of 'races' when none existed except as social categories, sexism utilised the already existing biological sexual difference as the basis for institutionalising unequal treatment of the sexes. Butler (1990), among others, takes issue with the sex/gender distinction. She asks whether ostensibly natural facts of sex might not also be historically produced discursive formations, so that, if the immutable character of sex is contested, perhaps the construct labelled sex is as much a cultural construction as gender. As she observes:

> On some accounts, the notion that gender is constructed, suggests a certain determinism of gender meanings inscribed on anatomic-ally differentiated bodies, whereas those bodies are understood as passive recipients of an inexorable law. When the relevant 'culture' that 'constructs' gender is understood in terms of such a law or set of laws, then it seems that gender is as determined and fixed as it was under the biology-is-destiny formulation. In such a case, not biology but culture becomes destiny.
>
> (Butler 1990: 8)

For Butler, gender is not merely a cultural inscription of meaning on a pre-given sex, it is also the very means by which the sexes themselves are established as 'prediscursive', prior to culture, as a politically neutral surface on which culture adds. On this view, 'sex' is no less a cultural construction than 'race' or 'gender' is. As such, any distinc-tion between them is essentially a matter of the particular signifier of 'difference' that each of the consructs mobilises, the historically specific cultural meanings that are brought into play by each narration, and their differing effects for different categories of people. Butler's account is silent on issues of racism or class. But her question: 'To what extent does the body come into being in and through the mark(s) of gender?' may be reformulated as: 'To what extent does the body come into being in and through the mark(s) of gender, "race", or class?'; so that there would then be an implosion of boundaries between the physical and the social body.

The question of how best to theorise the link between racism and class has been the subject of considerable debate in Britain, but much of this literature has been virtually silent on the relationship of racism and class to gender. This combined theme has been the subject of major controversy in feminist discourses where, until recently, the general tendency had been to analyse gender without taking systematic account of racism (see Chapter Five for an overview of these debates). The main concern of this debate was whether racism and patriarchal relations should be understood as autonomous of social class, as reducible to social class, or as having separate histories but articulating with class relations in a given historical context. My own position is that racism is neither reducible to social class or gender, nor is it wholly autonomous, and while it can have independent effectivity it does not constitute an independent form of domination. As conceptual categories, racism, gender or class address the articulations between discourses and practices as contingent and situated relationships across a variety of sites. The late twentieth-century constructions and representations of the categories of 'race', class or gender are embedded in the contemporary changing 'world order', refashioned by what Donna Haraway (1991) calls the 'Informatics of Domination'.

Thus far, I have explored the conceptualisation of 'race' and racism and their articulation with gender and class. Next, I examine how the interlinks between racism, nation, ethnicity and gender may be theorised, before going on to consider some of their configurations in the 'New Europe'.

NATIONALISM, RACISM, ETHNICITY AND GENDER

The concept of 'nation' has been the focus of some considerable debate in both the liberal and Marxist historiography (Nairn 1977 [1990]; Seton-Watson 1977; Anderson 1983; Chatterjee 1986 [1993]; Nazir 1986b; Hobsbawm 1990; Smith 1991). The term is in general associated with different meanings in different discourses. At times, it is used in order to designate a broad category of persons who are presumed to have a common culture. In other discourses, it invokes a political entity embodied in a state. Alternatively, it may hail the will and institutions of 'the people'. Benedict Anderson describes the 'nation' as an 'imagined political community'. He attributes the rise of nationalism to the historical conditions of the late eighteenth century, arguing that the development of certain 'cultural artefacts' – most notably print-language as a commodity in the form of texts – was crucial to the construction and circulation of the European discourse of 'nation-ness' and nationalism: ' the convergence of capitalism and print technology on the fatal diversity of human language created the possibility of a new form of imagined community, which in its basic morphology set the stage for the modern nation' (Anderson 1983: 49). But, while scholars such as Anderson view nationalism as a 'modern' phenomenon closely allied to the development of the nation-state, for others (see Van den Berghe 1979) nations are primordial rather than historical constructions.

Partha Chatterjee (1986) points to an influential tendency in the analysis of nationalism which mobilises 'typology' as a heuristic mode for addressing nationalism. He identifies it especially in the work of scholars such as John Plamenatz and Hans Kohn. Plamenatz speaks of 'two types' of nationalism: one type is described as 'Western', presumed to have emerged primarily in Western Europe, and the other 'Eastern', thought to be flourishing in Eastern Europe, in Asia, Africa, and also in Latin America. Kohn makes a somewhat similar distinction between 'Western' and 'non-Western' nationalisms. More recently, the work of A. D. Smith resonates a similar theme. Smith (1991) proposes a 'civic' and an ethnic 'model' of the nation. He characterises the 'civic model' as a 'Western' model and identifies its main features as: the possession of a historic territory; a sense of a legal–political community that is subject to common laws and institutions; a presumption of legal and political equality among members of such a community; and identification with a common culture. By contrast, the 'ethnic' conception of the nation – associated by Smith primarily with Eastern Europe and Asia – emphasises a common descent and ties based on kinship, vernacular languages, customs and traditions.

Is this 'civic' and 'ethnic' distinction helpful? Posed in this way the question fails to interrogate an important *subtext* of the Smith discourse. Leaving aside for the moment the problem of 'binaries' discussed in other chapters of the present volume, there is certainly a sense in which such a distinction between the two *constructions* of 'nation' is useful in elucidating certain specific features of a determinate discourse. But we may dissent from Smith's use of the various terms, indeed the terms themselves. For example, is 'model' an appropriate or even useful device for analysing processes which patently defy 'emmodelification'? What is signified by the categories of 'East', 'West' and 'Asia' in Smith's work? Do they inscribe geographical territories or political communities? How are Africa, South America or Australia – about which Smith's text remains silent – constituted in the gaps of this silence? Smith ostensibly represents the 'non-Western model' as a form of resistance in that, as he says: 'Historically it challenged the dominance of the Western model and added significant new elements, more attuned to the very different circumstances and trajectories of non-Western communities.' Yet, in the same breath, he continues:

> We can term this non-Western model an 'ethnic' conception of the nation. Its distinguishing feature is its emphasis on a community of birth and native culture. Whereas the Western concept laid down that an individual had to belong to some nation *but could choose to which he or she belonged*, the non-Western or ethnic concept allowed *no such latitude*. Whether you stayed in your community or emigrated to another, you remained ineluctably, organically, a member of the community of your birth and were *forever* stamped by it. A nation in other words was first and foremost a community of common descent.... This emphasis on presumed family ties helps to explain the strong popular or demotic element in the ethnic conception of the nation. Of course the 'people' figure in the Western model too. But there they are seen as a *political community subject to common laws and institutions.*
>
> (Smith 1991: 11–12, emphasis added)

There is not the space here to undertake a more detailed deconstruction of Smith's work. But one may reasonably ask how much choice the Jewish people in Europe had when faced with the Holocaust? Why should 'civic' be treated as synonymous with 'Western' and 'ethnic' with 'non-Western'? Are 'non-Western' conceptions of the nation *really* devoid of a notion of political community subject to common laws and institutions? Especially if it is also his contention that these conceptions are part of a derivative discourse: 'Western experience has exerted a powerful, indeed the leading, influence on our conception of the unit we call the "nation"' (ibid.: 11).

Smith's distinction between 'civic' and 'ethnic' conceptions of the 'nation' can be helpful, however, if it is de-coupled from the Western/ non-Western binary. He rightly suggests that nationalisms almost always combine 'civic' and 'ethnic' conceptions, and that ethnic processes are constitutive elements in the formation of a nation. He argues that the emergence of many polyethnic nation-states, such as Britain, has been predicated against the coming to dominance of a particular ethnic community: in the British case, the English ascendancy over the Irish, the Scottish and the Welsh, although this hegemony has been continually contested.

How is nationalism best understood? Do we need a general theory of nationalism? Reviewing Marxist and non-Marxist analyses of nationalism, Nazir argues that 'there cannot be a general or universal definition or a general theory of nation, nationality, or nationalism. An attempt to arrive at a conclusive definition or general theory would be inappropriate... [for] no universal definitions are possible, and that, instead of identifying essences, we need to explore concrete sets of historical relations and processes in which these ideologies become meaningful' (Nazir 1986b: 494–501). It is an empirical question, then, what form is assumed by a particular nationalism, what circumstances and social conditions contour its shape and trajectory, or how ethnicity is mobilised within a given nationalism.

The nationalist struggle for independence in India, for example, involved the construction of a sense of a nation among a people who were ethnically extremely heterogeneous. The forging of this national identity required an emphasis upon the common condition of being a colonised people struggling for the right of self-determination. Initially, the nationalists underplayed the particularities of religion, regional languages, local customs and traditions in order to invent a new set of allegiances to a nation-state. But this nationalism became internally fractured when religion emerged as a focus for mobilisation in the political movement for the creation of Pakistan. Different modalities of ethnicity were invoked in the two instances: in the first case the notion of a common Indian culture was highlighted as a syncretic entity, a collective endeavour of all constituent ethnic groups; in the second case a cultural identity centred around religion was brought to the fore as the primary basis of ethnic identification. It bears reminding that nationalism can be mobilised for very different purposes, and that nationalist discourses construct and embody a variety of contradictory political and cultural tendencies. Whether the outcomes are empowering and progressive or reactionary and oppressive – in practice they are always a mix rather than simply one or the other, not least since, by definition, 'progressive' and 'reactionary' are cultural/political constructions – is dependent upon the historical and contemporary contingencies.

In the light of the preceding discussion it is clear that the idea of ethnicity is central to discourses of nation. Ethnicity is a relatively new construct compared to that of race and nation. Glazer and Moynihan (1975) note its absence in the 1933 edition of the *Oxford English Dictionary*, but that it makes an appearance in the *OED*'s 1972 *Supplement*, where the first usage recorded is that of American sociologist David Reisman in 1953. They point out how the 1973 edition of the *American Heritage Dictionary* defines it as: '1. The condition of belonging to a particular ethnic group; 2. Ethnic pride'. The above dictionary attempt at 'capturing meaning' implicitly acknowledges the continual articulation of the subjective and the social in the sign of ethnicity, even if 'pride' might not be the only 'structure of feeling' (to use Raymond Williams's incisive and evocative conceptual category) at play. Glazer and Moynihan encountered ethnicity as a term 'still on the move'. There is a sense in which, two decades later, it is *still* on the move, a point I shall consider more fully in the last chapter, with specific reference to the recent discourse of 'new ethnicity'. Suffice it to say here that ethnicity – in terms of an analytical category – addresses changing signifying/political practices.

The concept of ethnicity embodies another signifier, namely 'ethnic'. In contrast to ethnicity the term 'ethnic' has a very old trajectory. It derives from the Greek *ethnos* (in turn derived from *ethnikos*), which originally meant 'heathen' or 'pagan', replete with the echoes of 'otherness'. It was used in this sense in English from the mid-fourteenth century until the mid-nineteenth century, when it gradually came to acquire racialised connotations. At around the time of World War II in the USA, the term 'ethnic' became a polite way of referring to Jews, Italians, Irish and other groups in contrast to the dominant group who were largely of British descent (Eriksen 1993). The European groups defined as 'ethnics' were inferiorised in relation to the 'Anglo-Saxon' which served as the norm. At the same time, these European descent 'ethnics' were differentiated from Americans of African descent who were constructed as a 'racial' group.

In post-war Britain, the term 'ethnic group' became embedded in the concept of 'minorities'. Sometimes it subsumed all those construed as minorities, but in its most common usage the term became a code for British citizens from Africa, the Asian sub-continent and the Caribbean, and their British-born children. There was thus an implicit collusion between the idea of 'ethnic group' and that of 'coloured people', itself a re-worked colonial construct. This racialisation of 'ethnic group' meant that 'coloured people' were now discursively re-invented as 'ethnics', whereas ethnic groups of European descent were rarely invoked in these terms. This is partly borne out by the fact that during the time of Ken Livingstone's administration of the Greater London Council, 'minorities' of European descent found themselves having to stake out a claim to be recognised as 'ethnic groups' for purposes of receiving funds; their status in this discourse was clearly far from unambiguous.

Fredrik Barth's conceptualisation of ethnicity has exercised a major influence on British studies of ethnicity. According to Barth (1969), ethnic groups are categories of self-identification and ascription by others. He emphasises social processes by which ethnic groups identify themselves as distinctive entities and maintain boundaries with others. An ethnic group is best defined not by its cultural characteristics but by reference to the process of boundary formation. Ethnic boundaries may be constructed and maintained around a range of signifiers articulating in varying combinations under specific situations. These may include a belief in common ancestry, claims to a shared history that gives shape to feelings of shared struggles and shared destinies, attachment to a 'homeland' which may or may not coincide with the place of residence, and a sense of belonging to a group with a shared language, religion, or social customs and traditions.

In other words, ethnicity is primarily a mechanism of boundary maintenance between groups. Barth takes issue with earlier formulations of ethnicity for assuming that ethnicity was about communicating a pre-given, already existing cultural difference. Instead, he foregrounds context and process which mark the emergence of specific signifiers of difference as constituting ethnic distinctiveness. Ethnicity is understood as *relational* and it is construed in terms of a *process*. What is central to ethnicity is not some objective criterion of cultural difference. Rather, it is the process whereby one group constructs its distinctiveness from another. Of course, processes of boundary construction, maintenance and dissolution vary over time. They are subject to the forces of socio-economic and political change.

Since they are historical products, bonds of ethnicity may shift in meaning, may be strengthened, weakened or dissolved, and they will have varied salience at different points in an individual's or a group's biography.

It is clear that ethnic groups *do not* constitute a category of primordial ties. But this does not mean that, under particular political circumstances, they cannot come to be represented in such terms. Ethnic groups are both formed and exist within and through discursive and material practices inscribing economic, political and cultural modalities of power. They are heterogeneous categories differentiated along a variety of axes such as gender, religion, language, caste or class. But political mobilisation of ethnicity in nationalist or racist discourses may serve to conceal precisely such social divisions. Discourses of ethnic distinctiveness, 'race' and nation, are all able to call upon metaphors of blood, kith and kin, heritage and sexuality. To the extent that they may share a common content or generalised object, they are subject to articulation in particular forms in a specifiable context (Miles 1989).

For example, a particular nationalism may construct the 'nation' as having mythic origins, and it may invoke dreams of historical destinies through visions of 'racial purity'. The ethnicities of the dominant and subordinate groups may now come to be represented as constituting immutable hierarchical boundaries. Indeed, it is precisely the power of such imagery that can give these types of discourses a special purchase on the popular imagination. And concerns about 'racial contamination' may stir patriarchal fears about women's sexuality. It is no coincidence, therefore, that women occupy a central place in the processes of signification embedded in racism and nationalism (see Davin 1978; Enloe 1989; Yuval-Davis and Anthias 1989; Anthias and Yuval-Davis 1992; Parker *et al.* 1992). These and other studies demonstrate how women are crucial to the construction and repro-duction of nationalist ideologies. Women may serve as the symbolic figuration of a nation. They are also seen as embodiments of male honour, and as such become a site of contestation for this honour. Hence, the defence of women and children becomes a rallying slogan of men going to war, while the women themselves from opposing factions fall victim to rape and other sexual atrocities. When represented as guardians of the 'race' and nation, women not only signify and demarcate juridical, political, cultural and psychic boundaries of a national collectivity, they inscribe these boundaries in and through a myriad of cultural practices, their assumption of particular feminised subject positions, their relationship to the upbringing of children, and their involvement in religious and other ritualistic practices that construct and reproduce particular notions of tradition. In racialised contexts these processes are inscribed through racism positioning different groups of racialised women differently in the field of representation of a national collectivity.

RETHINKING THE 'NEW EUROPE'

Having established certain broad parameters for analysing the linkages between racism, ethnicity, nationalism and class as gendered formations, I now explore some of these articulations as they are figured in contemporary Western Europe while the Single European Market goes into effect. How is the 'new Europe' being constituted economically, juridically, politically and culturally in and through 'race'? Who is a 'European'? How is the juridical conception of the 'European' effected in and through immigration and citizenship law? What is the likely impact of the Single European Market upon women and other groups discursively represented as minorities? How is 'European-ness' figured in racist and nationalist discourse, and in what ways are these constructions challenged and contested by the emergent new ethnicities? Is 'neo-racism' a useful analytical category in understanding new configurations of racism in Europe today? How does this concept compare with that of 'new racism'? These are some of the questions that frame this section.

I begin with the concept of 'new racism' as it was elaborated in Britain in the early 1980s, before addressing its relationship to the concept of 'neo-racism' where Western Europe of the 1990s has formed the focus of analysis.

New racism

In Britain, the 'new racism' thesis emerged in the wake of the hegemonic success of Powellism and its institutionalisation in the politics of the New Right. Martin Barker (1982) proposed that this new racism was essentially a theory of human nature linking 'race' and nation. It was a racism that combined a disavowal of biological superiority or inferiority with a focus on 'a way of life', of cultural difference as the 'natural' basis for feelings of antagonism towards outsiders. Within this discourse, national consciousness came to be understood as an instinct for self-preservation and national survival.

This analysis provided some important insights into racialised discourses that emerged from a realignment of different forces on the right of the political spectrum, both inside and outside the Conservative Party. But what signals the 'newness' of this racism from a previous racism, I would suggest, was not so much its espousal of a 'pseudo-cultural' racism, for this was not an infrequent phenomenon in the past. For example, cultural difference as a signifier of innate difference was a particularly strong strand in colonial discourses on India (Hobsbawn and Ranger 1983; Mackenzie 1984; Mani 1987; Mohanty 1989). Rather, the distinctiveness of this specific brand of cultural racism resides in its emergence in the metropolitan in a post-World War II era where it articulates with a New Right discourse. This discourse develops against a background of economic restructuring, high levels of unemployment, youth rebellions, and strikes in such sectors as the National Health Service, the mining industry and newspaper publishing.

The New Right discourse, especially as articulated in the ideological matrix of Thatcherism, deployed notions of 'nation' and 'people' against class, trade unions, and 'scroungers on the welfare state'. It combined a free-market philosophy with social authoritarianism centred around a concern to uphold traditional morality and preserve the British nation from the presumed dangers of cultural decline and disintegration of law and order (Hall and Jacques 1983; Jessop et al. 1988). It celebrated 'traditional family values', exalted motherhood as a vocation, espoused 'pro-life' programmes, fiercely attacked lesbian and gay relationships as 'unnatural' and generally sought to villify feminism (David 1983; Harding 1990: Phoenix 1990). The New Right constructed the essence of being British to be white, without explicitly proclaiming to do so, by deploying the language of 'immigrants' and 'swamping' which, in an earlier phase during the post-war period, had become a code for people of African and Asian descent. These groups had already been described by Enoch Powell as social collectivities who could be 'in Britain' but not 'of Britain'. The use of the metaphors of 'nation', 'family' and the 'British way of life' in the New Right ideology resonated with a long history of racialised exclusions as a centrepiece of British identity. These metaphors invoked pathologised notions of Afro-Caribbean and Asian households (Carby 1982; Phoenix 1987), constructing these groups as the 'Other' of the 'British Character' which, according to Margaret Thatcher, is presumed to have 'done so much to civilise the world'. It was easy within this ideological frame to represent the lived cultures of

African-Caribbean and Asian people as not only different from, but a serious threat to, the 'British way of life', despite the fact that these cultures are inextricably interwoven into the British economic and political fabric.

To the extent that Irish, Scottish and Welsh identities occupy a somewhat contradictory and ambiguous relationship to 'Britishness', their positioning within this discourse remained obscure, as did the positioning of the ethnicities of other European groups settled in Britain such as the Italians, the Poles and the Greeks; and as, indeed, has been the case with the European Jewish collectivity which also remains outside the 'nation' in so far as the 'nation' is represented as Christian. But the New Right ideology did not mobilise these European 'differences' to any significant extent, although, in a different political discourse, the representations of the Irish continued to be linked with 'terrorism'. However, such discursive ambiguity is not inconsequential, for it simultaneously incorporates and differentiates between these European ethnicities. Their precarious and ambivalent location within the discourse of Britishness means that they may be inferiorised in relation to 'Englishness' or with respect to one another. Conversely, these ethnicities may be mobilised in unison *vis-à-vis* 'non-Europeans'.

Neo-racism

Facing a growing resurgence of popular as well as institutionalised forms of racism, nationalism and fascist activity in Europe, with officially sanctioned policies of 'ethnic cleansing' stalking parts of the landscape, commentators have increasingly come to utilise the concept of 'neo-racism' to refer to contemporary configurations of racialised formations (see Balibar 1991). But how are these new formations to be understood? What are the particularities of this neo-racism? How is this racism to be distinguished from older forms?

I would emphasise that we are dealing not with one but several racisms in Europe. There are a variety of colour-centred racisms directed at groups defined as 'non-white'. Other forms of racism include anti-Jewish, anti-Muslim, anti-Arab, anti-Turk, anti-African (itself internally differentiated in terms of how it constructs peoples from North Africa and those from sub-Saharan Africa), and anti-Gypsy racism. Each of these has its own specific history, its own characteristic features, and each has undergone various transformations during the course of its development. This suggests that we consider:

- how each racism has changed over different historical periods;
- what shape and form each of them presently assumes in Europe;
- how each differs from the other, as well as from its previous forms in content, structure, and its mode of signification;
- and, how they currently intersect both within individual European countries and at a pan-European level.

Anti-Jewish racism, for example, has an ancient history but, not only has its trajectory varied in different countries of Europe, its post-World War II manifestations are framed against the background of Nazism and the creation of Israel, as well as the present-day turmoil following the political change in Eastern Europe, Germany and the former Soviet Union. One aspect, then, that distinguishes contemporary anti-Jewish racism from its previous forms is its emergence in this changed historical context. It would also be important to examine (and this is subject to empirical verification) whether there has been a discursive shift in the nature of representation of Jewish people. Hence, a second specific feature of present-day anti-Jewish racism may be signalled by the questions: how are anti-Jewish discourses presently structured and what forms of signification do they articulate? What are the continuities and differences in the way Jewish women and men are differentially represented? Furthermore, we would need to understand the specificity of present-day anti-Jewish racism in different European countries, while taking into account also the constitutive elements of a more generalised pan-European anti-Jewish racism.

As another example, we may consider the case of South Asians in Britain. The racism directed against these groups was initially elaborated within a colonial encounter. It has been reworked in post-World War II Britain within a context, at first, of an economic boom in which South Asian labour was recruited and deployed in low-skilled and low-waged sectors of the economy; and subsequently that of an economic recession, the arrival of Asian refugees from East Africa, and a relative growth in small businesses owned by Asians. More recently, it has been elaborated with reference to the events surrounding the 'fatwah' against Salman Rushdie. A characteristic feature of this racism has been its focus on cultural difference as the primary signifier of a supposed immutable boundary: a view of the Asian as the 'alien' *par excellence*; the ultimate 'Other'.

The racialisation of religion with respect to South Asians is in itself not a new phenomenon. Creation of racialised categories through religion was a significant part of colonial discourses and political practices. Muslims and Hindus, for instance, were attributed distinctive qualities that were imbued with connotations of innate/natural difference. The gender of Muslim and Hindu women was differentially constructed with the vocabulary of 'purdah' and 'sati' becoming emblematic means of signifying the presumed religious differences inscribing their womanhood. However, present-day racialisation of Islam since the 'fatwah' represents a new discursive formation. It inheres within fundamental realignments in the global economic and political order following the dismantling of socialism as an economic and state structure in the former Soviet Union and Eastern Europe, the Gulf War and other major political upheavals. It marks a period when most of the old certainties are in deep crisis. Even as liberal democracy declares itself triumphant, Western rationality and secularism stands challenged by religious movements of all manners and types. In these religious movements the world over – whether they are Christian, Hindu, Jewish, Muslim, or Sikh – reinvigoration of patriarchy and the control of women is central (see Yuval-Davis and Saghal 1992). Racism directed against South Asians in post-Rushdie Britain can thus be seen to differ from its previous forms partly because of the particular circumstances of the late twentieth century. It differs also because it represents a reconstitution of the discourse of 'the Asian' (itself a peculiar construction of post-war Britain referring only to South Asians) through a foregrounding of 'the Muslim', the latter having certain very particular pan-European and global connotations.

It is not sufficient, however, to delineate the transformations that each racism has recently undergone. They are not merely parallel racisms but constitute intersecting configurations. It is critical, therefore, that we examine how these different racisms articulate in present-day Europe, and how they position various categories of people differentially in relation to one another. For example, the Irish represent a subordinate racialised category within anti-Irish racism in Britain, but as 'Europeans' they occupy a discursive space of dominance via a racism that constructs all non-Europeans as the 'Other'. White European Jews, too, would be positioned in a relatively 'privileged' position *vis-à-vis* non-Europeans by such a discourse, but their positioning will be interrogated by anti-Jewish racism. A black Jewish woman, for example, would be simultaneously positioned

within anti-black racism and anti-Jewish racism. The specific consequences for an individual or a group who is the bearer of multiple
racialised significations would depend upon which particular
racism(s) achieve prominence in a given context.

What is new about the 1990s, then, is not that there is a single neo-
racism in Europe, but that a variety of racisms (some of which had
become less salient) are being reconstituted into new configurations.
They are not old forms in new guises but new forms which – in the
process of their own reconstruction – subsume selective elements of
the old. These neo-racisms across Europe may or may not overlap
with the discursive shifts analysed in Britain via the concept of 'new
racism'. Some of these racisms, as for instance anti-Semitism,
emerged in Europe and were directed at populations inside Europe,
whereas others, such as the racism against people of African descent,
were elaborated in the context of slavery and colonialism. I am
reluctant to use Balibar's schema of distinguishing between them by
designation of the former as 'racism of the interior' and the latter as
'racism of the exterior' because I believe that this could perpetuate the
erroneous view that European racisms directed against peoples
outside Europe were not an internal dynamic of the historical
constitution of 'Europe'. Be that as it may, what is particular about
the present moment is that many of the groups who were previously
racialised outside Europe are now in Europe. The nature and form of
struggles against these racisms will be set against a major restructuring of European and world economies and labour markets, marked
changes in the composition of the labour force, the emergence of new
supranational state structures across the EEC countries, and fundamental shifts in cultural formations.

A Single European Market in labour?

The creation of the Single European Market is likely to have a
profound economic, political and social impact. The post-war
economic boom that resulted in the use throughout Europe of
'migrants' or 'immigrants' as replacement labour in the low-wage
sectors of the economy, where they were largely consigned to perform
unskilled or semi-skilled work, also helped to draw a growing number
of women into the labour force at lower levels of the occupational
hierarchy. That class, gender, age, ethnicity and racism intersect as
constitutive elements in the formation of labour markets is amply
demonstrated by feminist research. It has been shown, for instance,

how such intersections underpin the definition of skill, the construction of the division between full-time and part-time work, division of occupations into 'men's' and 'women's' jobs, differences in men's and women's earnings, cultures of the workplace, and the meaning of paid work in the construction of identities (see Chapter Six).

More recently, the economies of the advanced capitalist societies have undergone major restructuring. Flexible specialisation has been identified as a key characteristic of contemporary developments in methods of production. Technological changes making small-batch production economical have led to a growing decentralisation of production. Parts can now be produced in many different locations and ordered for assembly in small batches, thus by-passing the need for large, inflexible holdings of inventories. General purpose machinery and adaptable labour can be used to produce semi-customised goods to suit differing markets, and segments within different markets. This method contrasts with the large-scale production aimed at the mass market. It enables firms to deal relatively easily with changing and uncertain demand, and it is attractive as much to multinationals as it is to small firms (see Allen and Massey 1988; Hirst 1989). As a consequence, labour has become decentralised while a new gendered division of labour has emerged both internationally and within the national economies. Workers in Third World countries, especially women, as well as specific categories of the population in the advanced capitalist world, such as black and other 'minority' groups, and women as a general category, have been drawn into this new division of labour at the lower rungs as cheap, semi-casualised, relatively disposable labour (see Mitter 1986). Creation of the Single European Market is both predicated against and constitutive of these trends.

Current forecasts suggest that completion of the Single European Market will result, especially in the early stages, in large increases in job losses within Britain in specific industries such as textiles, food industries and telecommunications, and in particular regions, most notably Yorkshire, Greater Manchester, Merseyside and Strathclyde. This is likely to have an adverse impact on the employment prospects for black and other 'minority' men and women, as well as other categories of women with a history of employment in such industries. It is also predicted that the impact of restructuring will be uneven in relation to the size of the firms. While large-scale multinational capital will emerge stronger, small and medium-sized firms will be the hardest hit. This will have a disproportionate impact upon 'minority' businesses, since they are mostly concentrated in small firms. The small firm is also where a substantial proportion of women from these communities are employed. Although there are some important variations in the position of different 'minority' groups, both within and between different Western European states, there are major similarities in their structural location in Western economies. In other words, peripheralisation processes underlying the formation of the Single European Market are realised in and through processes of gender, 'racial' and other modalities of subordination. That is to say that *such economic processes are simultaneously political and cultural*. Slogans such as 'they are taking our jobs' are easily mobilised in racialised/patriarchal discourses which, in turn, may articulate with nationalist discourses.

Immigration law and citizenship

One of the main aims of the Single European Market is to facilitate the freedom of movement of people across national boundaries of the member states. However, this freedom will not be available to all groups of people. Citizenship rights in Europe are currently under-pinned by a racial division between *citizens, denizens* (people with established residential and civic rights in one of the member states but with 'Third Country' nationality) and *migrants*, who essentially have extremely limited rights. In Britain, its former colonial subjects were initially accorded full citizenship rights. However, these rights have been persistently eroded since 1948 through the introduction of increasingly restrictive immigration legislation. The history of immigration control in Britain serves as a constant reminder of how commonsense racism became appropriated and institutionalised into the parliamentary politics of the post-war era. Racialised notions of 'culture', 'marriage', and 'family systems' have been organising themes in the debates surrounding the introduction of immigration control. The ideological construction of women as the 'privileged bearers of their race and culture' means that white women and black or other 'ethnic minority' women have been differentially positioned in the discourses surrounding immigration issues. Black and other 'ethnic minority' women have been singled out as a serious problem for the state as a potential source of primary male immigration through marriage. It is worth noting that the Immigration Rules governing the entry of foreign husbands or fiancés were changed five times between 1969 and 1983 to curtail the rights of 'non-patrial' (read non-white) women to have their partners join them in Britain, while allowing white women to enjoy this right. The current legislation on immigration divides the world into those with a 'British ancestry' through a parent or a grandparent born in Britain (and these individuals have normal rights of citizenship), and others who are 'non-patrials' and as such are subject to immigration control, deportation and restriction on taking up employment.

This means that, while a majority of the three million people from Britain's former colonies and their descendants are currently citizens, there are almost a million who are classed as 'Third Country' nationals. The rights of residence in Britain of the latter ensure them entitlements to work, housing, education, health care, pensions, etc. But the rest of Europe has no such arrangements, and it appears that the rights of these people will not be transferable throughout the EC. If such people move to other parts of Europe, they are liable to be classified as 'migrants' or 'aliens', with the corresponding loss in political and social rights. For example, like many Algerians in France, they will not have any rights to take part in local and national elections. In Brussels, they may encounter laws excluding them from living in certain parts of the city. Europe contains some 7.5 million such people, mainly from the Third World countries, and these women, men and children bear the brunt of hostility, discrimination and economic exploitation throughout Europe (see *Race and Class* 1991; *New Community* 1991).

The impact of '1992' will also be adversely felt by people seeking asylum or refugee status. Asylum-seekers from Third World countries are often seen as economic migrants rather than individuals escaping political persecution. New measures to curtail this flow of people include fines of £2,000 sterling to be paid by airlines bringing in passengers without valid documentation, and restricting the asylum-seekers' right to movement in EC countries by stipulating that they can claim asylum only in the country in which they first arrived.

In the process of its formation, the 'new Europe' is instituting a wide variety of measures to keep out immigrants and refugees from the Third World, while simultaneously strengthening its internal controls. Such measures are being introduced via *ad hoc* and secretive bodies and intergovernmental arrangements, e.g. the Trevi Group of Ministers, the Scheniegen Accord, and the Ad Hoc Group on Immigration. The proceedings of these agencies of the state are as yet not subject to democratic control. Their attempts at harmonising policies on immigration, terrorism, drugs, public order issues and policing pose serious challenges to the civil liberties and social rights of 'minorities'. For example, these activities could lead to greater police powers to stop and question people about their immigration status, to an increasingly closer linking of entitlements of welfare benefits and services with immigration status, and they could result in more stringent enforcement of workplace surveillance which would require employers to check the immigration status of people applying for work. Such internal controls already operate in Britain and other parts of Europe, but 1992 has seen their imposition on a much more coordinated, systematic and trans-European basis (*Race and Class 1991; New Community 1991*).

Such super-national political and administrative operations are part of the formation of new state structures to regulate economic, juridical and social domains in order to manage the interest of the member states under new regimes of accumulation. The relationship of national states to the institutions of this super-national entity is at an evolutionary stage and is likely to be subjected to all manner of stress and strain. The realm of politics and culture will remain crucial sites where much of the power of state institutions in differentially structuring economic, political and social rights of different groups will be contested.

WHICH WAY ETHNICITY?

Europe is struggling to re-cast its self-image in the face of tumultuous changes across the globe. In the process, different European ethnicities confront one another as much as those that 'Europe' has defined as the 'Other'. It is a precarious encounter, with its outcomes not as readily predictable or inevitable as they might at first seem. We noted earlier that under specific circumstances ethnicity may become racialised. We also considered how nationalist discourses may potentially draw upon discourses of 'race' or ethnicity. One significant outcome is the growing entrenchment of different racisms or ethnicisms constructing essentialist discourses figuring Africans, Arabs, Asians, Jews, Muslims, Gypsies, Turks, and so on. In practice these categories are not all mutually exclusive, but they are likely to be represented as such. To varying degrees and in different ways nationalist discourses may include or exclude such groups as part of or outside the 'nation'. Hence there is the potential for considerable polarisation and division.

However, those defined in discourse as being outside the 'nation' could be experienced as part of the 'nation', especially when faced with people from another part of Europe. I am reminded of an incident during an exchange visit in the early 1980s by a group of mainly African-Caribbean and Asian youth and community workers to Germany. One evening, as we sat chatting outside a downtown café, the black Liverpudlian youth-worker was warmly greeted by a group of white Liverpudlians on holiday in Germany. His accent provided his fellow Liverpudlians with a clue to his 'origins', and they spent a pleasant half-hour engaged in Scouse rites of male bonding. In that moment their Scouse ethnicity, forged in the lived experience of working-class masculinity, was the most salient. The coming into play of this ethnicity did not erase the history of anti-black racism in Liverpool, but it interrogated and challenged its hegemonic tendencies as it simultaneously operated within and across invisible boundaries of Scouse/not Scouse, German/British, and black/white. Such examples could easily be dismissed by some as anecdotal trivia, but I believe that they are important in signifying precisely the complex and contradictory relationship between discursive representations and the lived experience of, for instance, class, gender, religion and locality – the very crucible in which personal identity, however fragmented or fragmentary, connects with social identities, and where politically identities are assumed and proclaimed.

As we have already discussed, ethnicities are not fixed but constantly in process. They reference contingent, conditional and provisional specificities. The boundaries of ethnicity may be drawn around a variety of criteria – language, religion, memories of a shared history and visions of a shared destiny, a belief in common origins – so that one may be positioned within more than one field of ethnicity depending upon the criteria in play within a particular context. The processes of boundary construction and the specific criteria invoked in a given situation are subject to political, cultural and economic contingencies. The question of when and where these borders are imagined and instituted, or how they may shift, change, weaken or dissolve is critical. Equally important is how formations of ethnicity are played out: in terms of a non-hierarchical difference or as a means of representing its distinctiveness as natural and superior, as is the case, for example, of a nationalist discourse of Englishness. But Englishness does not have to be constructed invariably in racialised terms. Whether or not it does is a matter of struggle over policies, practices, and cultural meanings. Hence, as Hall (1988) notes, the politics of representation are central to the contestation over ethnicities.

To reiterate a point made earlier, ethnicities are always gendered in terms of both how they construct sexual difference and how they are lived. Furthermore, they inscribe and are inscribed by relations of class and other modalities of differentiation. This means that they are also a site for contestation over patriarchal, class and other inscriptions of power. This applies to both dominant and dominated ethnicities. That is, as women from dominant and dominated ethnicities, we need to be attentive to how we are positioned in and through these relations of power among ourselves and *vis-à-vis* men from these groups. In Europe this demands the complex task of addressing the relational positioning of a diverse set of ethnicities. Among other things, we will need to distinguish between 'difference' as a process of acknowledging specificities of the social and cultural experience of a group, 'difference' as a contestation against oppression and exploitation, and a situation where 'difference' itself becomes the modality in which domination articulates (see Chapter Four).

Resistance to the processes of exclusion may come from many sources, not least from those excluded, and such resistance may take many forms – from workplace struggles, through campaigning against specific state policies and, importantly, through culture: music, art, literary production, cinematic practices, fashion. For example, young African-Caribbean and Asian women in Britain seem to be constructing diasporic identities that simultaneously assert a sense of belonging to the locality in which they have grown up, as well as proclaiming a 'difference' that marks the specificity of the historical experience of being 'black', or 'Asian', or 'Muslim'. And all of these are changing subject positions. The precise ways and with what outcomes such identities are mobilised is variable. *But they speak as 'British' identities with all the complexity, contradiction, and difficulty this term implies.*

The ongoing debate over the 'new Europe' in the media, educational institutions, organisations of employers and employees and in a variety of other sites, may serve to create a new awareness of commonalties that potentially hold the promise of interrogating parochial and xenophobic tendencies. On the other hand, given the particular histories of the different nation-states of Europe, their internal differentiations and divisions, and their differing positioning within the global social order, the emerging New Europe is likely to be an unstable complex of competing interest groups. The economic and political uncertainties of the present conjuncture provide fertile ground for the growth of racisms and xenophobia, and their articulation with nationalist imaginations. The future outcomes would seem largely to depend on the nature and forms of political struggle in the 1990s and beyond, at all levels of the social formation.

Chapter 8

Diaspora, border and transnational identities

As we approach the beginning of the twenty-first century we witness a new phase of mass population movements. There has been a rapid increase in migrations across the globe since the 1980s. These mass movements are taking place in all directions. The volume of migration has increased to Australia, North America and Western Europe. Similarly, large-scale population movements have taken place within and between countries of the 'South'. More recently, events in Eastern Europe and the former Soviet Union have provided impetus for mass movements of people. Some regions previously thought of as areas of emigration are now considered as areas of immigration. Economic inequalities within and between regions, expanding mobility of capital, people's desire to pursue opportunities that might improve their life chances, political strife, wars, and famine are some of the factors that remain at the heart of the impetus behind these migrations. People on the move may be labour migrants (both 'documented' and 'undocumented'), highly-qualified specialists, entrepreneurs, students, refugees and asylum seekers, or the household members of previous migrants. In 1990, the International Organisation for Migration estimated that there were over 80 million such 'migrants'. Of these, approximately 30 million were said to be in 'irregular situations' and another 15 million were refugees or asylum seekers. By 1992, some estimates put the total number of migrants at 100 million, of whom 20 million were refugees and asylum seekers (Castles and Miller 1993). The notion of 'economic migrant' as referring primarily to labour migrants was always problematic, not least because it served to conceal the economic proclivities of those who were likely to be placed outside such a definition, for example industrialists or commercial entrepreneurs. However, these new migrations call this construct even more seriously into question, as global events increasingly render untenable such distinctions as those held between the so called 'political' and 'economic' refugees.

These population movements are set against major re-alignments in the world political order. As I have already noted in previous chapters, new transnational configurations of power articulate with fundamental transformations in the political economy of late twentieth-century capitalism. Globalising tendencies set in motion centuries ago acquire new meanings in a world characterised by the increasing dominance of multinational capital; the flexible specialisation of labour and products; and the revolutionising impact of new technologies in production, distribution, and communication. The emergent new international division of labour depends quite crucially upon women workers. Indeed, whether working in electronics factories, textile sweatshops, performing outwork from their homes, or (rather more untypically) holding jobs in the commanding heights of the economy – women have become emblematic figures of contemporary regimes of accumulation. It is not surprising, therefore, that women comprise a growing segment of migrations in all regions and all types of migrations. This feminisation of migration is especially noticeable in particular instances. For example, women form the majority of Cape Verdian workers migrating to Italy, Filipinos to the Middle East, or Thais to Japan. Similarly, women predominate in a number of refugee movements (Castles and Miller 1993).

These recent migrations are creating new displacements, new diasporas. In the context of a proliferation of new border crossings the language of 'borders' and of 'diaspora' acquires a new currency. A variety of new scholarly journals have one or the other of these terms in their titles. Yet, surprisingly, there have been relatively few attempts made to theorise these terms. This is partly because, as James Clifford (1994) rightly observes, it is not easy to avoid the slippage between diaspora as a theoretical concept, diasporic 'discourses', and distinct historical 'experiences' of diaspora. They seem to invite a kind of 'theorising', Clifford continues, that is always embedded in particular maps and histories. Yet, perhaps this embeddedness is precisely why it becomes necessary to mark out the conceptual terrain that these words construct and traverse if they are to serve as theoretical tools.

This chapter is just such an attempt to explore the analytical purchase of these terms. It delineates specific features which may serve to distinguish diaspora as a theoretical concept from the historical 'experiences' of diaspora. *Inter alia* I suggest that the concept of diaspora should be understood in terms of historically contingent 'genealogies' in the Foucauldian sense; that is, as an ensemble of investigative technologies that historicise trajectories of different diasporas, and analyse their relationality across fields of social relations, subjectivity and identity. I argue that the concept of diaspora offers a critique of discourses of fixed origins, while taking account of a homing desire which is not the same thing as desire for a 'homeland'. This distinction is important, not least because not all diasporas sustain an ideology of 'return'. In examining the subtext of 'home' which the concept of diaspora embodies, I analyse the problematic of the 'indigene' subject position and its precarious relationship to 'nativist' discourses.

Inscribed within the idea of diaspora is the notion of 'border'. The second part of this chapter is organised around the theme of borders. I address border as a political construct as well as an analytical category, and explore some of the strengths and limitations of the idea of 'border theory', especially as it has been mobilised via Gilles Deleuze and Felix Guattari's concept of 'deterritorialisation' and applied to the analysis of literary texts.

The concepts of border and diaspora together reference the theme of location. This point warrants emphasis because the very strong association of notions of diaspora with displacement and dislocation means that the experience of *location* can easily dissolve out of focus. The third section of the chapter is centred on this topic and explores the contradictions of and between location and dislocation. As a point of departure, I use the long-standing feminist debate around issues of home, location, displacement and dislocation which came up with the concept of a *'politics of location'* as locationality in contradiction . Self-reflexive autobiographical accounts often provide critical insights into the politics of location. I use two such accounts – an essay by Minnie Bruce Pratt and the autobiography of Angela Davis – as narratives enunciating a white and a black woman's feminist subject position. They do so through an intricate unravelling of those manifold operations of power which have the effect of naturalising identities, and the different costs involved in maintaining or relinquishing lived certainties attendant upon such identities. What is also crucially important for the discussion at hand is the way in which these autobiographical accounts demonstrate how the same geographical and psychic space comes to articulate different 'histories' and how 'home' can simultaneously be a place of safety and of terror.

The concepts of *diaspora, border,* and *politics of location* together offer a conceptual grid for historicised analyses of contemporary trans/national movements of people, information, cultures, commodities and capital. The three concepts are immanent. Part four of the chapter discusses a new concept that I wish to propose, namely that of *diaspora space,* as the site of this immanence. Diaspora space is the intersectionality of diaspora, border, and dis/location as a point of confluence of economic, political, cultural and psychic processes. It addresses the global condition of culture, economics and politics as a site of 'migrancy' and 'travel' which seriously problematises the subject position of the 'native'. My central argument is that diaspora space as a conceptual category is 'inhabited' not only by those who have migrated and their descendants but equally by those who are constructed and represented as indigenous. In other words, the concept of *diaspora space* (as opposed to that of diaspora) includes the entanglement of genealogies of dispersion with those of 'staying put'.

Throughout the chapter I have emphasised power relations embedded within discourses, institutions, and practices. In so doing I have mobilised a multi-axial performative conception of power. The chapter concludes with the idea of 'creolised theory' which is central to the kind of analysis I have been developing in this book.

THINKING THROUGH THE CONCEPT OF DIASPORA

First, a note about the term 'diaspora'. The word derives from the Greek – *dia*, 'through', and *speirein*, 'to scatter'. According to Webster's Dictionary in the United States, diaspora refers to a 'dispersion from'. Hence the word embodies a notion of a centre, a locus, a 'home' from where the dispersion occurs. It invokes images of multiple journeys. The dictionary also highlights the word's association with the dispersion of the Jews after the Babylonian exile. Here, then, is an evocation of a diaspora with a particular resonance within European cartographies of displacement; one that occupies a particular space in the European psyche, and is emblematically situated within Western iconography as the diaspora *par excellence*. Yet, to speak of late twentieth-century diasporas is to take such ancient diasporas as a point of departure rather than necessarily as 'models', or as what Safran (1991) describes as the 'ideal type'. The dictionary juxtaposition of what the concept signifies in general as against one of its particular referents, highlights the need to subject the concept to scrutiny, to consider the ramifications of what it connotes or denotes, and to consider its analytical value.

At the heart of the notion of diaspora is the image of a journey. Yet not every journey can be understood as diaspora. Diasporas are clearly not the same as casual travel. Nor do they normatively refer to temporary sojourns. Paradoxically, diasporic journeys are essentially about settling down, about putting roots 'elsewhere'. These journeys must be historicised if the concept of diaspora is to serve as a useful heuristic device. The question is not simply about *who travels* but *when, how, and under what circumstances*? What socio-economic, political, and cultural conditions mark the trajectories of these journeys? What regimes of power inscribe the formation of a specific diaspora? In other words, it is necessary to analyse what makes one diasporic formation similar to or different from another: whether, for instance, the diaspora in question was constituted through conquest and colonisation as has been the case with several European diasporas. Or it might have resulted from the capture or removal of a group through slavery or systems of indentured labour, as, for example, in the formation respectively of African and Asian diasporas in the Caribbean. Alternatively, people may have had to desert their home as a result of expulsion and persecution, as has been the fate of a number of Jewish groups at various points in history. Or they may have been forced to flee in the wake of political strife, as has been the experience of many contemporary groups of refugees such as the Sri Lankans, Somalis and Bosnian Muslims. Perhaps the dispersion occurred as a result of conflict and war, resulting in the creation of a new nation state on the territory previously occupied by another, as has been the experience of Palestinians since the formation of Israel. On the other hand, a population movement could have been induced as part of global flows of labour, the trajectory of many, for example African-Caribbeans, Asians, Cypriots, or Irish people in Britain.

If the circumstances of leaving are important, so, too, are those of arrival and settling down. How and in what ways do these journeys conclude, and intersect in specific places, specific spaces, and specific historical conjunctures? How and in what ways is a group inserted within the social relations of class, gender, racism, sexuality, or other axes of differentiation in the country to which it migrates? The manner in which a group comes to be 'situated' in and through a wide variety of discourses, economic processes, state policies and institutional practices is critical to its future. This 'situatedness' is central to how different groups come to be relationally positioned in a given context. I emphasise the question of relational positioning for it enables us to begin to deconstruct the regimes of power which operate to differentiate one group from another; to represent them as similar or different; to include or exclude them from constructions of the 'nation' and the body politic; and which inscribe them as juridical, political, and psychic subjects. It is axiomatic that each empirical diaspora must be analysed in its historical specificity. But the issue is not one that is simply about the need for historicising or addressing the specificity of a particular diasporic experience, important though this is.

Rather, the *concept* of diaspora concerns the historically variable forms of *relationality* within and between diasporic formations. It is about relations of power that similarise and differentiate between and across changing diasporic constellations. In other words, the concept of diaspora centres on the *configurations of power which differentiate diasporas internally as well as situate them in relation to one another*.

Diasporas, in the sense of distinctive historical experiences, are often composite formations made up of many journeys to different parts of the globe, each with its own history, its own particularities. Each such diaspora is an interweaving of multiple travelling; a text of many distinctive and, perhaps, even disparate narratives. This is true, among others, of the African, Chinese, Irish, Jewish, Palestinian and South Asian diasporas. For example, South Asians in Britain have a different, albeit related, history to South Asians in Africa, the Caribbean, Fiji, South East Asia, or the USA. Given these differences, can we speak of a 'South Asian diaspora' other than as a mode of description of a particular cluster of migrations? The answer depends crucially upon how the relationship between these various components of the cluster is conceptualised.

I would suggest that it is the *economic, political and cultural specificities linking these components that the concept of diaspora signifies*. This means that these multiple journeys may configure into one journey via a *confluence of narratives* as it is lived and re-lived, produced, reproduced and transformed through individual as well as collective memory and re-memory. It is within this confluence of narrativity that 'diasporic community' is differently imagined under different historical circumstances. By this I mean that the identity of the diasporic imagined community is far from fixed or pre-given. It is constituted within the crucible of the materiality of everyday life; in the everyday stories we tell ourselves individually and collectively.

All diasporic journeys are composite in another sense too. They are embarked upon, lived and re-lived through multiple modalities: modalities, for example, of gender, 'race', class, religion, language and generation. As such, all diasporas are differentiated, heterogeneous, contested spaces, even as they are implicated in the construction of a common 'we'. It is important, therefore, to be attentive to the nature and type of processes in and through which the collective 'we' is constituted. Who is empowered and who is disempowered in a specific construction of the 'we'? How are social divisions negotiated in the construction of the 'we'? What is the relationship of this 'we' to its 'others'? Who are these others? This is a critical question. It is generally assumed that there is a single dominant Other whose overarching omnipresence circumscribes constructions of the 'we'. Hence, there tends to be an emphasis on bipolar oppositions: black/ white; Jew/Gentile; Arab/Jew; English/Irish; Hindu/Muslim. The centrality of a particular binary opposition as the basis of political cleavage and social division in a given situation may make it necessary, even imperative, to foreground it. The problem remains, however, as to how such binaries should be analysed. Binaries can all too readily be assumed to represent ahistorical, universal constructs. This may help to conceal the workings of historically specific socio-economic, political and cultural circumstances that mark the terrain on which a given binary comes to assume its particular significance. That is, what are actually the effects of institutions, discourses and practices may come to be represented as immutable, trans-historical divisions. As a consequence, a binary that should properly be an object of deconstruction may gain acceptance as an unproblematic given.

It is especially necessary to guard against such tendencies at the present moment when the surfacing of old and new racisms, violent religious conflicts and the horrors of 'ethnic cleansing' make it all too easy to slide into an acceptance of contexually variable phenomena as trans-historical universalisms that are then presumed to be an inevitable part of human nature. On the contrary, the binary is a socially constructed category whose trajectory warrants investigation in terms of how it was constituted, regulated, embodied and contested, rather than taken as always already present. A bipolar construction might be addressed fruitfully and productively as an object of analysis and a tool of deconstruction; that is, as a means of investigating the conditions of its formation, its implication in the inscription of hierarchies, and its power to mobilise collectivities.

The point is that there are multiple others embedded within and across binaries, albeit one or more may be accorded priority within a given discursive formation. For instance, a discourse may be primarily about gender and, as such, it may centre upon gender-based binaries (although, of course, a binarised construction is not always inevitable). But this discourse will not exist in isolation from others, such as those signifying class, 'race', religion or generation. The specificity of each is framed in and through fields of representation of the other. What is at stake, then, is not simply a question of some generalised notion of, say, masculinity and femininity, but whether or not these representations of masculinity and femininity are racialised; how and in what ways they inflect class; whether they reference lesbian, gay, heterosexual or some other sexualities; how they feature age and generation; how and if they invoke religious authority. Binaries, thus, are intrinsically differentiated and unstable. What matters most is how and why, in a given context, a specific binary – e.g. black/white – takes shape, acquires a seeming coherence and stability, and configures with other constructions, such as Jew/Gentile or male/female. In other words, *how these signifiers slide into one another in the articulation of power.*

We may elaborate the above point with reference to racialised discourses and practices. The question then reformulates itself in terms of the relationship at a specific moment between different forms of racism. Attention is shifted to the forms in which class, gender, sexuality or religion, for instance, might figure within these racisms, and to the specific signifier(s) – colour, physiognomy, religion, culture, etc. – around which these differing racisms are constituted. An important aspect of the problematic will be the relational positioning of groups by virtue of these racisms. How, for instance, are African, Caribbean, South Asian and white Muslims differentially constructed within anti-Muslim racism in present-day Britain? Similarly, how are blacks, Chicanos, Chinese, Japanese, or South Koreans in the USA differentiated within its racialised formations? What are the economic, political, cultural and psychic effects of these differential racialisations on the lives of these groups? What are the implications of these effects in terms of how members of one racialised group might relate to those of another? Do these effects produce conditions that foster sympathetic identification and solidarity across groups, or do they create divisions? Of central concern in addressing such questions are the power dynamics which usher racialised social relations and inscribe racialised modes of subjectivity and identity. My argument, as stated in preceding chapters, is that these racisms are not simply parallel racisms but are intersecting modalities of *differential racialisations marking position-ality across articulating fields of power*. It is important to note that my use of the term 'differential racialisation' differs from Balibar's use of *'differentialist* racism'. Following P. A. Taguieff, Balibar describes 'differentialist racism' as 'a racism whose dominant theme is not biological heredity but the insurmountability of cultural differences, a racism which, at first sight, does not postulate the superiority of certain groups or peoples in relation to others but only the harmfulness of abolishing frontiers, the incompatibility of life-styles and traditions'(Balibar 1991: 21). Balibar's definition is close to what Barker (1982) describes as the 'new racism'. I, on the other hand, wish to use *differential racialisation* as a concept for analysing processes of *relational multi-locationality within and across forma-tions of power marked by the articulation of one form of racism with another, and with other modes of differentiation*. In my schema, 'new racism' would feature as but one instance of a historically specific racism (see previous chapter).

If, as Khachig Tölölian (1991) suggests, contemporary diasporas are the 'exemplary communities of the transnational moment', and the term now overlaps and resonates with meanings of words such as migrant, immigrant, expatriate, refugee, guest worker or exile, then the *concept* of diaspora that I am seeking to elaborate is *an interpretive frame referencing the economic, political and cultural dimensions of these contemporary forms of migrancy*. As such, it interrogates other discourses surrounding the social relations of migrancies in this phase of late twentieth-century capitalism. I now briefly consider how the debate over the construct 'minority' pans out in relation to the concept of diaspora.

DIASPORA AND MINORITY

In Britain there has been a tendency to discuss diaspora primarily along a 'majority/minority' axis. This dichotomy surfaced in post-war Britain as an element underpinning the processes of racialisation. The term 'minority' was applied primarily to British citizens of African, Caribbean and Asian descent – a postcolonial code that operated as a polite substitute for 'coloured people'. The elaboration of the discourse of 'minorities' marks the fraught histories, now widely documented, of immigration control, policing, racial violence, infer-iorisation and discrimination that has become the hallmark of daily life of these groups. This discourse also resonates with older connotations of the term in classical liberal political theory, where women, subjugated colonial peoples and working classes tend to be associated with the status of being a 'minor in tutelage' (Spelman 1988; Lloyd 1990; Phillips 1991). Even when the majority/minority dichotomy is mobilised in order to signal unequal power relations, as is the case in studies that document discrimination against 'minorities', its usage remains problematic. This is partly because the numerical referent of this dichotomy encourages a literal reading, reducing the problem of power relations to one of numbers, with the result that the repeated circulation of the discourse has the effect of naturalising rather than challenging the power differential. Moreover, conceptualising social relations primarily in terms of dichotomous oppositions, as I have pointed out above, fails to take full account of the multidimensionality of power.

In the USA, there has been a degree of serious and sustained attempt by some scholars to re-valorise the term from a different perspective. Since I am broadly in agreement with their arguments but also hold some reservations, it is, perhaps, necessary to ask where my argument situates itself with respect to the concept of 'minority discourse' which they offer. This concept was first proposed by JanMohammed and Lloyd in 1986, at a conference entitled 'The Nature and Context of Minority Discourse', held at the University of California, Berkeley. The papers presented at this conference were published in an edited collection of the same title (JanMohammed and Lloyd 1990). This is a theoretically and politically engaged volume whose influence in the USA in sanctioning the concept of 'minority discourse' has been far reaching. The editors define 'minority discourse' as follows:

> By 'minority discourse' we mean a theoretical articulation of the political and cultural structures that connect different minority cultures in their subjugation and opposition to the dominant culture.
>
> (JanMohammed and Lloyd 1990: ix)

One of the stated aims of the conference was 'to define a field of discourse among various minority cultures'. The project was conceived as a means of 'marginalising the center' and displacing the 'core-periphery model'. As Barbara Christian, invoking the works of other black women such as June Jordan and Audre Lorde, argues in the same volume, it is crucial to 'distinguish the desire for power from the need to become empowered' (ibid.: 47), and hence to critique any moves to want to be at the centre. JanMohammed is careful to point out that a minority location is 'not a question of essence (as the stereotypes of minorities in dominant ideologies would want us to believe) but a question of position, subject position that in the final analysis can be defined only in "political" terms – that is, in terms of the effects of economic exploitation, political disenfranchisement, social manipulation, and ideological domination on the cultural formation of minority subjects and discourses' (ibid.: 9). Similarly, David Lloyd's contribution to the collection addresses *inter alia* the interplay of 'race', gender and class in the construction of minorities as political and cultural categories within the liberal theory of political representation. Pointing to an inextricable linkage of aesthetic and political concepts of representation in '. . . a western discourse of "the human" conceived as universally valid but effectively ethnocentric' (ibid.: 379), Lloyd examines the challenge posed to such hegemonic exercises of power when, as in the works of Jean Genet, there is a refusal of these modes of 'subjection'.

My overall sympathy for this project will be evident from what I have argued so far, not least because JanMohammed and Lloyd are far from endorsing a conception of 'minorities' that does not foreground socio-economic and cultural relations of power. Yet I am less than convinced about the use of the concept of '*minority* discourse'. I have already expressed my concern with respect to the more literal readings that the word minority tends to engender, as well as the related issue to which David Lloyd also draws attention, namely the association in classical liberal political theory of certain categories of 'minorities' with the status of being a 'minor in tutelage'. These connotations have yet to disappear. Moreover, there is a tendency to use the term 'minority' primarily to refer to racialised or ethnicised groups, and I believe that this tendency is not confined to Britain. The discourse then becomes an alibi for pathologised representations of these groups. In other words, given the genealogy of signifying practices centred around the idea of 'minority', the continuing use of the term is less likely to undermine than to reiterate this nexus of meanings.

I am aware that it is possible to turn a term on its head and imbue it with new meanings, and that the construction of this new discourse of 'minority discourse' is intended as just such a project. Nevertheless, in the absence of a political movement such as the Black Power Movement which successfully dislodged the negative associations of black in racist representations, I presently remain sceptical that, irrespective of intent, any moves that perpetuate the circulation of the minority/majority dichotomy will not serve to reinforce the hegemonic relations that inscribe this dichotomy. What category of person is 'minoritised' in a specific discourse? Are dominant classes a 'minority' since, numerically, they are almost always in the minority? If the aim is to use the term as a synonym for subordination and thereby to become all-inclusive by bringing all subordinate classes, genders, ethnicities or sexualities within its orbit, then there would seem to be even less to gain by jettisoning the language of subordination which, at the very least, signals inequities of power. As an alternative, I do not wish to offer some all-embracing panacea, but rather to insist that, in so far as it is possible, the conceptual categories we employ should be able to resist hegemonic cooptation.

The concept of diaspora that I wish to propose here is embedded within a multi-axial understanding of power; one that problematises the notion of 'minority/majority'. A multi-axial performative conception of power highlights the ways in which a group constituted as a 'minority' along one dimension of differentiation may be constructed as a 'majority' along another. And since all these markers of 'difference' represent articulating and performative facets of power, the 'fixing' of collectivities along any singular axis is called seriously into question. In other words, 'minorities' are positioned in relation not only to 'majorities' but also with respect to one another, and vice versa. Moreover, individual subjects may occupy 'minority' and 'majority' positions simultaneously, and this has important implications for the formation of subjectivity.

What this means is that where several diasporas intersect – African, Jewish, Irish, South Asian, and so on – it becomes necessary to examine how these groups are similarly or differently constructed vis-à-vis one another. Such relational positioning will, in part, be structured with reference to the main dominant group. But, there are aspects of the relationship between these diasporic trajectories that are irreducible to mediation via metropolitan discourse. India and Africa, for instance, have connections that pre-date by many centuries those initiated via British colonialism. In contemporary Britain, too, the act of conversion to Islam by people of African-Caribbean descent, for instance, cannot be understood exclusively as a reaction to British racism, any more than the positionality of an African, Arab or South Asian Jew in Britain can be encapsulated solely within the European discourse of anti-semitism. There are other transnational histories, diasporic connections – where Europe is not at 'the centre' – which retain a critical bearing on understanding contemporary diasporic formations and their inter-relationships.

By this I do not mean to refer only to those social formations which came under direct European colonial rule. The reconfiguration in modern times of the ancient link between China and Japan, for instance, has not been refracted entirely through the 'Western prism', although the global expansion of both capitalist relations and Western imperialism have, of course, played their part. Chinese and Japanese diasporas in America, therefore, are the bearers of these already entangled histories reconstituted in the modalities of labour migrations to the USA, the politics of World War II (when, for instance, American citizens of Japanese descent were rounded up and interned), the Cold War that followed, in which China was demonised as a communist country, and the present conjuncture when both Japan and China assume, albeit in different ways, a central position in the global social order. The heterogeneity, multiplicity and hybridity of this Asian–American experience, insightfully theorised by Lowe (1991b), articulates these many and varied similarities and differences. What I wish to stress is that the study of diasporic formations in the late twentieth century – as in the case of Chinese and Japanese diasporas in the California of the 1990s – calls for a concept of diaspora in which different historical and contemporary elements are understood, not in tandem, but *in their dia-synchronic relationality*. Such analyses entail engagement with complex arrays of contiguities and contradictions; of changing multilocationality across time and space.

THE HOMING OF DIASPORA, THE DIASPORISING OF HOME

As we noted earlier, the concept of diaspora embodies a subtext of 'home'. What are the implications of this subtext? First, it references another – that of the people who are presumed to be indigenous to a territory. The ways in which indigenous peoples are discursively constituted is, of course, highly variable and context-specific. During imperial conquests the term 'native' came to be associated with pejorative connotations. In the British Empire the transformation of the colonised from native peoples into 'the Native' implicated a variety of structural, political and cultural processes of domination, with the effect that the word Native became a code for subordination. The British diasporas in the colonies were internally differentiated by class, gender, ethnicity (English, Irish, Scottish, Welsh) and so on, but discourses of Britishness subsumed these differences as the term 'British' assumed a positionality of superiority with respect to the Native. The Native became the Other. In the colonies, the Natives were excluded from 'Britishness' by being subjected as natives. But how does this particular nativist discourse reconfigure in present-day Britain? Of course, there is no overt evocation of the term 'native' but it remains an underlying thematic of racialised conceptions of Britishness. According to racialised imagination, the former colonial Natives and their descendants settled in Britain are not British precisely because they are not seen as being native to Britain: they can be 'in' Britain but not 'of' Britain. The term 'native' is now turned on its head. Whereas in the colonies the 'colonial Native' was inferiorised, in Britain the 'metropolitan Native' is constructed as superior. That is, nativist discourse is mobilised in both cases, but with opposite evaluation of the group constructed as the 'native'.

The invocation of native or indigenous status, however, is not confined to discourses of nationalism. Oppressed peoples such as Native Americans or Native Australians may also mobilise a concept of the positionality of the indigenous, but with quite a different aim. Here, the native positionality becomes the means of struggle against centuries of exploitation, dispossession and marginality. This native subject position articulates a subaltern location. It is important, therefore, to distinguish these claims from those that go into the constitution of structures of dominance. However, it does not always follow that this subaltern location will provide automatic guarantees against essentialist claims of belonging. It cannot be assumed in advance that the hegemonic processes of subordination will invariably be resisted without recourse to the indigene subject position as *the* privileged space of legitimate claims of belonging. What is at stake here is the way in which the indigene subject position is constructed, represented and mobilised. Oppositional politics from a subaltern location must contend with all manner of contradictions. Can 'first nationhood' be asserted as a 'native' identity while renouncing nativism? How precisely is the 'first nationhood' of subaltern groups to be distinguished from the claims to this status by groups in positions of dominance? How do subaltern indigenous peoples place themselves *vis-à-vis* other subordinate groups in a locale? For instance, how do the claims for social justice by Native Americans articulate with and become 'situated' in relation to those made by black Americans? Are such claims marked by a politics of solidarity or competitive antagonism and tension? In one sense, the problematic can only be fully addressed by studying particular cases. But the answer will depend, at least in part, upon the way that the question of 'origins' is treated – in naturalised and essentialist terms, or as historically constituted (dis)placements?

Where is home? On the one hand, 'home' is a mythic place of desire in the diasporic imagination. In this sense it is a place of no return, even if it is possible to visit the geographical territory that is seen as the place of 'origin'. On the other hand, home is also the lived experience of a locality. Its sounds and smells, its heat and dust, balmy summer evenings, or the excitement of the first snowfall, shivering winter evenings, sombre grey skies in the middle of the day... all this, as mediated by the historically specific everyday of social relations. In other words, the varying experience of the pains and pleasures, the terrors and contentments, or the highs and humdrum of everyday lived culture that marks how, for example, a cold winter night might be differently experienced sitting by a crackling fireside in a mansion as compared with standing huddled around a makeshift fire on the streets of nineteenth-century England.

If, as is quite possible, the reader pictured the subjects of this cold winter scenario as white English men and women, it bears reminding that this would not invariably be the case. The group huddled on the street might easily have included men and women brought over to England as servants from Africa and India; the descendants of Africans taken as slaves to the Americas; as well as Irish, Jewish and other immigrants. What effects might this type of intra-class differentiation have in the marking of affinities and antagonisms *amongst* those on the street and *between* the street and the mansion? What range of subjectivities and subject positions would have been produced in this crucible? What are the implications for late twentieth-century Britain of certain ways of imaging 'Englishness' that erases such nineteenth-century, and indeed earlier, 'multicultur-alisms'? The question of home, therefore, is intrinsically linked with the the way in which processes of inclusion or exclusion operate and are subjectively experienced under given circumstances. It is centrally about our political and personal struggles over the social regulation of 'belonging'. As Gilroy (1993) suggests, it is simultaneously about roots and routes.

The *concept* of diaspora places the discourse of 'home' and 'dispersion' in creative tension, *inscribing a homing desire while simultaneously critiquing discourses of fixed origins.*

The problematic of 'home' and belonging may be integral to the diasporic condition, but how, when, and in what form questions surface, or how they are addressed, is specific to the history of a particular diaspora. Not all diasporas inscribe homing desire through a wish to return to a place of 'origin'. For some, such as the South Asian groups in Trinidad, cultural identification with the Asian sub-continent might be by far the most important element.

We noted earlier that diasporas are not synonymous with casual temporary travel. Nor is diaspora a metaphor for individual exile but, rather, diasporas emerge out of migrations of collectivities, whether or not members of the collectivity travel as individuals, as households or in various other combinations. Diasporas are places of long-term, if not permanent, community formations, even if some households or members move on elsewhere. The word diaspora often invokes the imagery of traumas of separation and dislocation, and this is certainly a very important aspect of the migratory experience. But diasporas are also potentially the sites of hope and new beginnings. They are contested cultural and political terrains where individual and collective memories collide, reassemble and reconfigure.

When does a location *become* home? What is the difference between 'feeling at home' and staking claim to a place as one's own? It is quite possible to feel at home in a place and, yet, the experience of social exclusions may inhibit public proclamations of the place as home (Brah 1979; Cohen 1992; Bhavnani 1991; Tizzard and Phoenix 1993). A black British young woman of Jamaican parentage may well be far more at home in London than in Kingston, Jamaica, but she may insist upon defining herself as Jamaican and/or Caribbean as a way of affirming an identity which she perceives is being denigrated when racism represents black people as being outside 'Britishness'. Alternatively, another young woman with a similar background might seek to repudiate the same process of exclusion by asserting a black British identity. The subjectivity of the two women is inscribed within differing political practices and they occupy different subject positions. They articulate different political positions on the question of 'home', although both are likely to be steeped in the highly mixed diasporic cultures of Britain. On the other hand, each woman may embody both of these positions at different moments, and the circumstances of the moment at which such 'choices' are made by the same person are equally critical.

Clearly, the relationship of the first generation to the place of migration is different from that of subsequent generations, mediated as it is by memories of what was recently left behind, and by the experiences of disruption and displacement as one tries to re-orientate, to form new social networks, and learns to negotiate new economic, political and cultural realities. Within each generation the experiences of men and women will also be differently shaped by gender relations. The reconfigurations of these social relations will not be a matter of direct superimposition of patriarchal forms deriving from the country of emigration over those that obtain in the country to which migration has occurred. Rather, both elements will undergo transformations as they articulate in and through specific policies, institutions and modes of signification.

The *concept* of diaspora signals these processes of *multi-location-ality across geographical, cultural and psychic boundaries.*

It bears repeating that the double, triple, or multi-placedness of 'home' in the imaginary of people in the diaspora does not mean that such groups do not feel anchored in the place of settlement. When a British politician such as Norman Tebbit, the former Conservative Cabinet Minister, argues that young British Asians cannot feel allegiance to Britain if they support a visiting cricket team from India or Pakistan, his 'cricket test' is more a reflection of the politics of 'race' in Britain than an indicator of British Asians' subjective sense of their own 'Britishness'. It is unlikely that Tebbit would question the allegiance of populations of European origin in the Americas, Australia, Canada or New Zealand to their countries of adoption. Or that he would consider them less rooted in those places for having ancestors that came there from Europe. It would be interesting to see if Tebbit would describe Irish Americans or Italian Americans as less committed to the USA because they had enthusiastically supported Irish or Italian football teams in the 1994 World Cup. Paradoxically, racialised forms of nationalism which discourses such as that initiated by Tebbit inhabit are precisely the ones which might engender responses whereby to call oneself Bangladeshi, Indian, Pakistani, or Sri Lankan becomes a mode of resistance against racist definitions of 'Asian-ness'. But the assertion of such 'identity' cannot be taken as a measure of the processes of 'identification' operating among these collectivities. Norman Tebbit's restricted vision of Britishness is seriously inter-rogated and called into question by all kinds of old and new diasporic identities in Britain. These identity formations challenge the idea of a continuous, uninterrupted, unchanging, homogeneous and stable British identity; instead, they highlight the point that identity is always plural and in process, even when it might be construed or represented as fixed.

THE LOCAL AND THE GLOBAL OF DIASPORA

A combination of the local and the global is always an important aspect of diasporic identities. But the relationship between these elements varies. The diasporas proliferating at the end of the twentieth century will be experienced quite differently, in some respects, in this age of new technologies and rapid communications compared with the time when it took months to travel or communicate across the seas. The impact of electronic media, together with growing opportunities for fast travel, invests Marshall McLuhan's idea of 'the global village' with new meanings. Simultaneous transmission to countries linked by satellite means that an event happening in one part of the world can be 'watched together' by people in different parts of the globe. Electronic information 'super-highways' usher new forms of communication unimaginable only two decades ago. These developments have important implications for the construction of new and varied 'imagined communities'. Having said this, it does not necessarily follow that there will be a single overarching one-way process of cultural homogenisation, not least because global consumption of visual or other forms of culture is mediated in complex ways (Hall et al. 1992)

The effects are not totally predictable, for there can be many and varied readings of the same image. The same image can elicit a diversity of meanings, signalling the effects of personal biography and cultural context on processes of meaning production. In other words, the compression of time and space and the consequent 'shrinking' of the world can have contradictory outcomes. There are, on the one hand, possibilities for greater awareness of global inequalities leading to transnational modes of cooperation in the development of strategies to combat such inequalities. New forms of political solidarity and activism could emerge to meet the challenges of this era. There could be the release of much creative energy, resulting in transformation in politics, art, music, literature and other forms of cultural production. On the other hand, globalism today is the very means of encoding the changing post-Cold War world order. It is the vehicle for securing cultural hegemony in the age of 'G-Eightism' now that, as of July 1994, Russia has been admitted to the political, if not yet the economic, inner sanctum of the Group of Seven. This globalism of late capitalism inscribes the economic and political terrain against which the new migrations are taking place, a terrain with which both the old and new diasporas must contend, a point I develop further in the next section.

Diasporic identities are at once local and global. They are networks of transnational identifications encompassing 'imagined' and 'encountered' communities.

WHITHER DIASPORA?

The term diaspora can be very general and all-embracing. This is both its strength and its weakness. Its purchase as a theoretical construct rests largely on its analytical reach; its explanatory power in dealing with the specific problematics associated with transnational movements of people, capital, commodities and cultural iconographies. I have argued that diasporas ought not to be theorised as transhistorical codifications of eternal migrations, or conceptualised as the embodiment of some transcendental diasporic consciousness. Rather, the concept of diaspora should be seen to refer to historically contingent 'genealogies', in the Foucauldian sense of the word. That is to say that the term should be seen as conceptual mapping which defies the search for originary absolutes, or genuine and authentic manifestations of a stable, pre-given, unchanging identity; for pristine, pure customs and traditions or unsullied glorious pasts.

I have indicated that diasporas are composite formations with members of a single diaspora likely to be spread across several different parts of the world. What enables us to mobilise the word diaspora as a conceptual category in analysing these composite formations, as opposed to using it simply as a description of different migrations, is that the concept of diaspora specifies a matrix of economic, political and cultural inter-relationships which construct the commonalty between the various components of a dispersed group. The concept of diaspora delineates a field of identifications where 'imagined communities' are forged within and out of a confluence of narratives from annals of collective memory and re-memory. It is important to stress that diaspora is a pan-*ic* concept.

As a description of distinct historical experiences diaspora represents a heterogeneous category differentiated along the lines of class, gender, and so on. I have argued that the concept of diaspora addresses this internal differentiation as much as the one which exists across globally scattered parts of a particular diasporic population. Throughout the discussion I have emphasised circuits of power embedded within discourses, institutions and practices that inscribe diasporic experiences. In so doing I have mobilised a multi-axial performative conception of power: power is understood as relational, coming into play within multiple sites across micro and macro fields.

Following Tölöian, I understand contemporary diasporas as 'exemplary communities' of late twentieth-century forms of migrancy. They resonate with the meaning of words such as immigrant, migrant, refugee and asylum-seeker. This does not mean that the term diaspora is a substitute for these varying conditions underlying population movements. Not at all. Rather, the concept of diaspora signals the similarity and difference of precisely these conditions. I have stressed that the study of diasporas calls for a concept of diaspora in which historical and contemporary elements are understood in their *diachronic relationality*.

In examining the subtext of 'home' which the concept of diaspora embodies I have analysed the problematic of the indigene subject position and its precarious relationship to nativist discourses. A key issue here is whether the question of 'origins' is treated in essentialist terms or as a matter of historical displacements. I argue that the concept of diaspora offers a critique of discourses of fixed origins, while taking account of a homing desire. The homing desire, however, is not the same as the desire for a 'homeland'. Contrary to general belief, not all diasporas sustain an ideology of return. Moreover, the multi-placedness of home in the diasporic imaginary does not mean that diasporian subjectivity is 'rootless'. I argue for a distinction between 'feeling at home' and declaring a place as home. Processes of diasporic identity formation are exemplars *par excellence* of the claim that identity is always plural, and in process. The relationship between the two is subject to the politics in play under given sets of circumstances. In other words, the concept of diaspora refers to *multi-locationality* within and across territorial, cultural and psychic boundaries.

The concept of diaspora then emerges as an *ensemble of investigative technologies* that historicise trajectories of different diasporas, map their relationality, and interrogate, for example, what the search for origins signifies in the history of a particular diaspora; *how* and *why* originary absolutes are imagined; how the materiality of economic, political and signifying practices is experienced; what new subject positions are created and assumed; how particular fields of power articulate in the construction of hierarchies of domination and subordination in a given context; why certain *conceptions of identity* come into play in a given situation, and whether or not these conceptions are reinforced or challenged and contested by the *play of identities*.

THINKING THROUGH BORDERS

Embedded within the concept of diaspora is the notion of the border, and, indeed, it is not possible to address the concept of diaspora without considering its relationship to the idea of borders. It is to this construct that I now turn.

Borders: arbitrary dividing lines that are simultaneously social, cultural and psychic; territories to be patrolled against those whom they construct as outsiders, aliens, the Others; forms of demarcation where the very act of prohibition inscribes transgression; zones where fear of the Other is the fear of the self; places where claims to ownership – claims to 'mine', 'yours' and 'theirs' – are staked out, contested, defended, and fought over.

Gloria Anzaldua's theorisation of border and borderlands provides important insights. Two are especially important for my purposes here. First, she uses these terms as a means to reflect upon social conditions of life at the Texas–US Southwest/Mexican border where, as she says, 'the Third World grates against the first and bleeds' (Anzaldua 1987: 3). She invokes the concept of the border also as a metaphor for psychological, sexual, spiritual, cultural, class and racialised boundaries. If understood in terms of my discussion of 'difference' in Chapter Five, the Anzaldua text speaks of borders simultaneously as social relation, the everyday lived experience, and subjectivity/identity. Borders are arbitrary constructions. Hence, in a sense, they are always metaphors. But, far from being mere abstractions of a concrete reality, metaphors are part of the discursive materiality of power relations. Metaphors can serve as powerful inscriptions of the effects of political borders.

Each border embodies a unique narrative, even while it resonates with common themes with other borders. Such metaphoric materiality of each border calls attention to its specific features: to the geographical and/or psychic territories demarcated; to the experiences of particular groups of people who are sundered apart or affected in other ways by the creation of a certain border zone; or to the old and new states which may be abolished or installed by the drawing of particular boundaries. How is a border regulated or policed? Who is kept out and why? What are the realities for those stigmatised as *undesirable* border-crossers? The realities, for instance, of proclaiming a gay or lesbian identity in a social context saturated with homophobia and heterosexism, as Anzaldua shows. Or the realities of present-day labour migrants negotiating the immigration apparatus of the state: difficulties of gaining visas, confronting immigration checks, detentions and deportations, and even facing the possibility in some circumstances of losing one's life.

The USA/Mexico border typifies the conditions of contemporary migrancy. It encapsulates certain common thematics which frequently come into play whenever the 'overdeveloped' countries institute measures to control selectively the entry of peoples from economically 'underdeveloped' segments of the globe. This border speaks the fate of formerly colonised people presently caught up in the workings of a global economy dominated by transnational capital and mediated by politics of 'G-Sevenism' or 'G-Eightism'. These new regimes of accumulation are characterised by 'flexibility' (or what perhaps will increasingly be referred to as 'adaptability', the term favoured by the G7 summit of 10 July 1994) in labour processes, labour markets, commodities, and in patterns of consumption. There is an intensification in the segmentation of the labour market into a comparatively small sector of highly skilled core staff at managerial and professional level, and a much larger group of employees who are often called 'peripheral' workers but whose labour is in fact central to the functioning of the global economy. The core staff hold well-paid full-time permanent jobs with good promotion and re-training prospects. They are expected to be flexible and adaptable and, when required, geographically mobile, but any inconvenience that this may generate is offset by the security of entitlement to pensions, insurance and other benefits. The so-called 'peripheral' employees working in the 'secondary labour market' are generally low paid, and they comprise two distinct sub-groups. The first of these consists of full-time employees performing skilled or semi-skilled jobs. High turnover rates are fairly typical of this type of employment. Providing an even greater level of flexibility is the second group that includes a wide variety of part-timers, temporary staff, fixed-term contract holders, job sharers, and homeworkers. Not surprisingly, as we noted in the last chapter, there is a predominance of women, immigrant and migrant workers (both male and female) and their descendants, as well as other low-paid categories of worker in this secondary labour market.

The late twentieth-century forms of transnational movement of capital and people usher new kinds of diasporic formations. The rapid rate of technological, commercial, and organisational innovation is accompanied by a proliferation of new methods of production, new markets, new products and services, and new systems of financing. The accelerated mobility of capital to wherever profitability can be maximised within domestic boundaries or overseas has a particular bearing on population movements. A combination of offshore and onshore relocation of jobs, alongside a continuing demand for migrant labour for certain kinds of low-paid work in the economically advanced 'cores', is resulting in an eruption of new borders, while the old borders are subjected to processes of entrenchment or erosion (Sassen 1988; Rouse 1991; Miles 1993).

Roger Rouse, for example, provides a telling example of the shifting nature of such borders in the face of 'late' capitalism. Using as a case in point his study of US-bound migration since the early 1940s from a rural *municipio* of Aguilla in Mexico, he shows how these migrants have increasingly become part of a transnational network of settlements. By the early 1980s, almost every family in the *municipio* had a member who had worked abroad, and the local economy was heavily dependent on migrant remittances. In time these migrants have established several outposts in the United States, working largely in the service sector as cleaners, dishwashers, gardeners, hotel workers, housekeepers and child care workers. There is frequent traffic and communication between these outposts in the USA and Aguilla, with 'homes' dispersed in several places. In a sense they are *simultaneously migrants and settlers*, negotiating their personal agendas in a political context in which the demand for their labour has been set against increasing political pressure for tighter immigration controls.

The growing polarisation of the labour market in the United States has increased demand for Mexican workers to fill the lowest layers of jobs, in agriculture, on the assembly line and in the service sector. At the same time, new legal restrictions designed to regulate the flow of migrants have been imposed in the face of intensification of racism and growing political pressure against a background of job losses in certain sectors of the economy. Racism is fuelled also by the fact that certain elements of capital find it increasingly more lucrative to locate some aspects of the labour process in Mexico. Mexican workers now suffer resentment for 'taking our jobs' in the USA *and* in Mexico.

These tropes of resentment construct the worker as an embodiment of capital rather than its contradiction. Thus there emerges the paradox of the *'undocumented worker' – needed to service lower rungs of the economy, but criminalised, forced to go underground, rendered invisible; that is, cast as a phantom, an absent presence that shadows the nooks and crannies wherever low-paid work is performed.*

The contradictions surrounding 'undocumented workers' within racialised patriarchal formations in the heart of advanced economies was brought into sharp focus by the controversy that became known as the 'Nannygate Scandal' (*Newsweek*: 1 Feb. 1993) over the employment of an 'undocumented' Peruvian couple by President Clinton's nominee for Attorney-General, Zoe Baird. When the news about this employment practice broke out, Zoe Baird, the first female nominee for the position of Attorney-General, a corporate lawyer with a reported annual salary of $500,000 and a stately home, used the difficulties of finding good child care as an explanation of why she hired a Peruvian couple who were illegally resident in the USA. She paid the couple $500 a week to take care of her child and to provide other household help. Her appeals for sympathy on the grounds of the dilemma facing 'working mothers' did little to advance her case with her male colleagues. Arrangements for child care – a rather mundane issue for many of them – could hardly compete in the league table of importance with 'matters of state'. This is not surprising, of course, given that child care is globally still perceived primarily as the responsibility of women. Women's groups in the USA, such as the National Organisation for Women, pointed to a double standard working against women in public office. As the editorial of the *New York Times* (9 Feb. 1993) argued, a male senator whose wife had employed workers without legal rights of residence would be unlikely to have been disqualified from office.

On the other hand, opposition to Zoe Baird was not confined to men. Women with incomes much lower than Baird's pointed to her class privilege, arguing that they could not accept her explanation since she had all the financial and other resources at her command to employ a nanny without breaking the law. There was some comment in the print and visual media about the problems of child care faced by households in which both parents are employed. However, public opinion seemed to have been far more strongly galvanised against Baird's evasion of tax laws due to her failure to pay social security taxes for her employees. The general view seemed to hold that someone with her income and legal background who can readily afford to pay taxes should not breach her legal obligations.

The debate centred mainly on the question of the employment of 'illegal immigrants' and the non-payment of social security taxes by a prospective minister of the state who would be responsible for administering the Immigration and Naturalisaton laws. Baird's testimony generated very little comment or discussion on the subject of the exploitation of migrant workers in low-wage sectors of the economy, despite the presentation of a variety of statistics in the media that clearly demonstrated this aspect. The *Newsweek* article cited above pointed out that violation of the 1986 law prohibiting employment of illegal immigrants was common at all levels of society. The employment of such workers was not confined to upper-class American households. The article referred to a survey conducted by the Families and Work Institute in New York that showed how assembly-line workers in Texas hire Mexican women coming across the border as domestic workers at ten dollars a day. In Chicago a child care placement firm, Nannies Midwest, claimed that 60–70 per cent of the nannies in the area were 'undocumented' workers. A majority of them are likely to work very long hours cooking, cleaning and taking care of the children. Some of them hold university degrees or professional qualifications. They come not only from the Caribbean, Central and South America and the Pacific Rim countries but also from Eastern Europe.

According to the US Internal Revenue Service, of the two million households in the USA that employ domestic help, only one quarter pay social security taxes for them. Following the uproar over the case of Zoe Baird, the Clinton administration introduced screening procedures in order to discover if potential candidates for presidential appointments had been culpable of employing 'illegal aliens' (*New York Times*: 9 Feb. 1993). This incident served to bring into the public domain the complicity of public and private institutions and people in all walks of life in the maintenance of an informal economy embedded within the interstices of local and global inequalities. But, far from challenging the discourse of the 'undocumented worker', this public furore re-inscribed it, pathologising the migrant workers as *the* problem. *In other words the exclusionary practices that underlie constructions of the 'undocumented worker' as a juridical subject were naturalised alongside a simultaneous legitimation of the very legal processes that had produced the juridical category in the first place.*

Immigration policies such as the employer sanctions contained in

US immigration law and equivalent measures operated by immigration control agencies in Britain and elsewhere create border zones not only at the port of entry but also internally. In Britain, business premises are known to have been raided by immigration agencies in search of suspected 'illegal immigrants'. There are cases when all those *assumed* by the immigration officers to be 'immigrant' workers – that is, someone not white, or seeming as if they were from an 'underdeveloped' country – were questioned during these 'fishing raids', even if they were legally settled in Britain (Gordon 1985).

In these situations, colour or 'looks' often serve as the racialised signifier in and through which economic inequalities and state policies articulate. There are no such barriers to the mobility of capital. Rather, multinational companies receive special dispensations for offshore production in countries with low-wage economies. The new intersections between global flows of capital and transnational circuits of migrations interrogate the boundaries presupposed by such concepts as core and periphery, centre and margin, rural and urban, or First and Third World, even as the inequities that these concepts were presumed to signal persist on a wide scale. This is part of the terrain on which contemporary diasporic social relations are constituted and lived.

The idea of 'border theory'

Increasingly, the idea of 'border theory' is invoked to refer to scholarship that addresses 'borders' both in their geographical and analytical sense. The concept of 'deterritorialisation' proposed by Gilles Deleuze and Felix Guattari has been used in a number of analyses of literary texts presumed to constitute 'border writing' (Lloyd 1990; Hicks 1991; Calderon and Salvidar 1991). Deleuze and Guattari have identified 'deterritorialisation' as a distinctive feature of what they call 'minor literature' – that is, literature with its primary characteristics defined in opposition to canonical writing. Minor literature, they contend, is marked by 'the deterrititorialisation of language, the connection of the individual to a political immediacy, and the collective assemblage of enunciation' (Deleuze and Guattari 1986 [1975]: 13). The concept of deterritorialisation is understood as describing the displacement and dislocation of identities, persons and meanings, with the moment of alienation and exile located in language and literature. It refers to the effects of a rupture between signifier and signified, so that 'all forms come undone, as do all the significations, signifiers, and signifieds to the benefit of an unformed matter of deterritorialised flux, of nonsignifying signs' (ibid.).

While the attraction of such a term in analysing literary texts is understandable, its generalised applicability is much more problematic. The literary trope of 'border writing' can be important in elucidating certain aspects of border encounters. As Emily Hicks suggests, border writing articulates a textual strategy of translation as opposed to representation. She argues that it enacts non-synchronous memory and offers the reader the possibility of practising multi-dimensional perception. The reader enters a multi-layered semiotic matrix, and experiences multi-lingual, cross-cultural realities. I agree with Hicks that 'border writing' offers a rich, multi-faceted and nuanced depiction of border histories. My cautionary note here is aimed at the tendency to conflate 'border theory' with analysis of 'border writing', especially when the latter is used as a synonym for literary texts. Literary texts constitute but one element of border textualities. The concept of 'territory' as well as its signifieds and significations is a contested site in diaspora and border positionalities, where the issue of territorialisation, deterritorialisation or reterritorialisation is a matter of political struggle. The outcomes of these contestations cannot be predicted in advance. *In other words, the move from a literary text to 'world as text' is much more fraught, contradictory, complex and problematic than is often acknowledged.*

BORDER, DIASPORA AND THE POLITICS OF LOCATION

Together, the concepts of border and diaspora reference a politics of location. This point warrants emphasis, especially because the very strong association of notions of diaspora with displacement and dislocation means that the experience of *location* can easily dissolve out of focus. Indeed, it is the contradictions of and between location and dislocation that are a regular feature of diasporic positioning. Feminist politics have constituted an important site where issues of home, location, displacement and dislocation have long been a subject of contention and debate. Out of these debates emerges the notion of a 'politics of location' as *locationality in contradiction* – that is, a positionality of dispersal; of simultaneous situatedness within gendered spaces of class, racism, ethnicity, sexuality, age; of movement across shifting cultural, religious and linguistic boundaries; of journeys across geographical and psychic borders. Following a strand of the discussion in earlier parts of this chapter I would describe the politics of location *as a position of multi-axial locationality*. But politics is the operative word here, for multi-axial locationality does not predetermine what kind of subject positions will be constructed or assumed, and with what effects.

Self-reflexive autobiographical accounts often provide critical insights into political ramifications of border crossings across multiple positioning. One such account, an essay by Minnie Bruce Pratt entitled 'Identity: Skin, Blood, Heart' (Pratt 1984), has attracted attention in feminist analysis for its commitment to unravelling operations of power that naturalise identities inscribed in positions of privilege, and the different costs involved in maintaining or relinquishing lived certainties attendant upon such positions. This text reveals what is to be gained when a narrative about identity continuously interrogates and problematises the very notion of a stable and essential identity by deconstructing the narrator's own position, in this case that of a white, middle-class, lesbian feminist raised as a Christian in the southern United States. Pratt is able to hold her various 'homes' and 'identities' in perpetual suspension even as she tries to recapture them in re-memory. She enacts her locationality from different subject positions, picking apart her position of racialised class privilege simultaneously as she works through her own experiences of coming out as a lesbian and confronting heterosexism in its many and varied manifestations. A critical strategy that enables this narrative to refuse reductive impulses is that it works at a number of different levels, addressing *the linked materiality of the social, the cultural, and the subjective.* As Biddy Martin and Chandra Talpade Mohanty point out:

> the narrative politicises the geography, demography, and architecture of these communities – Pratt's homes at various times of her history – by discovering local histories of exploitation and struggle. These histories are quite unlike the ones she is familiar with, the ones she grew up with. Pratt problematises her ideas about herself by juxtaposing the assumed histories of her family and childhood, predicated on the invisibility of the histories of people unlike her, to whom these geographical sites were also home.
>
> (Martin and Mohanty 1986: 195)

Pratt examines how her sense of safety in the world was largely related to her unquestioning acceptance of the normative codes of her social milieu, and the structures of legitimation that underpinned these norms. She is particularly attentive to the workings of racism as one of the central dynamics binding this Southern community together. The tenuous nature of her security and sense of belonging is revealed to her when, as a lesbian mother fighting for the custody of her children, she comes face-to-face with the heterosexism embedded not only in state structures but also in the everyday cultural practices taken for granted by her family, friends and the people she had considered as her 'community'. The withdrawal of emotional support by those whom she had previously loved throws into total disarray the concept of home and community which she had hitherto envisioned. Engulfed by a sense of dislocation and loss, Pratt 'moves home', and she chooses this moment of cultural and psychic journeying to learn about the processes which sustain social relations and subjectivities that had been at the centre of the world she had taken for granted.

While Pratt's narrative addresses the social universe of a white woman growing up in Alabama during the civil rights struggles, Angela Davis's autobiography articulates the positionality of a black woman growing up in Alabama at about the same time. A juxtaposition of these two narratives is helpful in offering related accounts of the operations of racism and class in the constitution of gendered forms of white and black subjectivity against the backdrop of a turbulent period in recent American history. Both women invoke the segregated South of their childhood, but their memories construct an experiential landscape charted from opposite sides of the racial divide. Pratt speaks of the terror endemic in the racist cultural formations of the South. Angela Davis recounts how this terror was unleashed on the black people in her hometown. She relates how she felt when, at the age of four, her family moved into an all-white area:

> Almost immediately after we moved there the white people got together and decided on a borderline between them and us. Center street became the line of demarcation. Provided we stayed on 'our' side of the line (the east side) they let it be known we would be left in peace. If we ever crossed over to their side, war would be declared. Guns were hidden in our house and vigilance was constant.
>
> (Davis 1974 [1990]: 78)

Racism was experienced by this four-year-old in the form of hostility from the white elderly couple who now became their neighbours:

> the way they stood a hundred feet away and glared at us, their refusal to speak when we said 'Good Afternoon' . . . sat on the

porch all the time, their eyes heavy with belligerence. . . . When a
black minister and his wife transgressed the racial border and
bought the house next door to the white elderly couple, the
minister's house was bombed. As more black families continued
to move in the bombings were such a constant response that soon
our neighborhood became known as Dynamite Hill.

(ibid.: 79)

Davis draws attention to class and gender differences both amongst
and between black and white people, and to the conditions under
which solidarities across these differentiations are made possible. One
of the most poignant moments in the text is when, as a student in
France, Davis reads a newspaper report about the racist bombing of a
church in Birmingham, Alabama, and realises that the four girls
named as killed are her friends. Her fellow students show sympathy
but fail to grasp the systematic impact of racism as an institutional
and cultural phenomenon underlying such violence, and instead treat
the incident as one would a sudden 'accident' – 'as if my friends had
just been killed in a crash'. Davis's account, quite rightly, does not
ascribe this lack of understanding to their being white, but rather to
the absence of an awareness on their part of the history of racism in the
USA. Yet, awareness alone might still not have produced an understanding of this history. A deeper engagement with this history would
inevitably call for a radical shift in subject position, of the kind that
Pratt's narrative demonstrates. The point is that the issue is not simply
one of acquiring knowledge but of deconstructing 'whiteness' as a
social relation, as well as an experiential modality of subjectivity and
identity (see Chapter Five on 'difference'; also Breines 1992; Ware
1992; Hall 1992; Frankenberg 1993).

What is especially important for the present discussion about these
autobiographical accounts is the way in which they reveal how the
same geographical space comes to articulate different histories and
meanings, such that 'home' can simultaneously be a place of safety
and terror. They also underscore what I have suggested before, namely
that diasporic or border positionality does not *in itself* assure a
vantage point of privileged insight into and understanding of
relations of power, although it does create a space in which
experiential mediations may intersect in ways that render such
understandings more readily accessible. It is essentially a question
of politics. Diasporic identities cannot be read off in a one-to-one
fashion straightforwardly from a border positionality, in the same

way that a feminist subject position cannot be deduced from the
category 'woman'. This point deserves emphasis especially because
the proliferation of discourses about 'border crossings' and 'diasporic
identities' might be taken to imply a common standpoint or a
universalised notion of 'border consciousness'. Rather, there are
multiple semiotic spaces at diasporic borders, and the probability of
certain forms of consciousness emerging are subject to the play of
political power and psychic investments in the maintenance or erosion
of the status quo.

DIASPORA SPACE AND THE CREOLISATION OF THEORY

The concepts of diaspora, borders, and multi-axial locationality
together offer a conceptual grid for historicised analyses of contemporary trans/national movements of people, information, cultures, commodities and capital. The concept of diasporas
presupposes the idea of borders. Correspondingly, the concept of
border encapsulates the idea of diasporising processes. The two are
closely intertwined with the notion of the politics of location or
dislocation. The three concepts are immanent. I wish to propose the
concept of *diaspora space* as the site of this immanence. Diaspora
space is the intersectionality of diaspora, border, and dis/location as a
point of confluence of economic, political, cultural, and psychic
processes. It is where multiple subject positions are juxtaposed,
contested, proclaimed or disavowed; where the permitted and the
prohibited perpetually interrogate; and where the accepted and the
transgressive imperceptibly mingle even while these syncretic forms
may be disclaimed in the name of purity and tradition. Here, tradition
is itself continually invented even as it may be hailed as originating
from the mists of time. What is at stake is the infinite experientiality,
the myriad processes of cultural fissure and fusion that underwrite
contemporary forms of transcultural identities. These emergent
identities may only be surreptitiously avowed. Indeed, they may even
be disclaimed or suppressed in the face of constructed imperatives of
'purity'. But they are inscribed in the late twentieth-century forms of
syncretism at the core of culture and subjectivity (Hall 1990; Coombes
1992).

The concept of diaspora space references the global condition of
'culture as a site of travel' (Clifford 1992) which seriously problematises the subject position of the 'native'. Diaspora space is the point

at which boundaries of inclusion and exclusion, of belonging and otherness, of 'us' and 'them', are contested. My argument is that diaspora space as a conceptual category is 'inhabited', not only by those who have migrated and their descendants, but equally by those who are constructed and represented as indigenous. In other words, the concept of *diaspora space* (as opposed to that of diaspora) includes the entanglement, the intertwining of the genealogies of dispersion with those of 'staying put'. The diaspora space is the site where *the native is as much a diasporian as the diasporian is the native*. However, by this I do not mean to suggest an undifferentiated relativism. Rather, I see the conceptual category of diaspora space in articulation with the four modes of theorising of difference that I have proposed in Chapter Five, where 'difference' of social relation, experience, subjectivity and identity are relational categories situated within multi-axial fields of power relations. The similarities and differences across the different axes of differentiation – class, racism, gender, sexuality, and so on – articulate and disarticulate in the diaspora space, marking as well as being marked by the complex web of power.

In the diaspora space called 'England', for example, African-Caribbean, Irish, Asian, Jewish and other diasporas intersect among themselves as well as with the entity constructed as 'Englishness', thoroughly re-inscribing it in the process. Englishness has been formed in the crucible of the internal colonial encounter with Ireland, Scotland and Wales; imperial rivalries with other European countries; and imperial conquests abroad. In the post-war period this Englishness is continually reconstituted via a multitude of border crossings in and through other diasporic formations. These border crossings are territorial, political, economic, cultural and psychological. This Englishness is a new ensemble that both appropriates and is in turn appropriated by British-based African-Caribbean-ness, Asian-ness, Irishness and so on. Each of these formations has its own specificity, but it is an ever-changing specificity that adds to as well as imbues elements of the other. What I am proposing here is that border crossings do not occur only across the dominant/dominated dichotomy, but that, equally, there is traffic within cultural formations of the subordinated groups, and that these journeys are not *always* mediated through the dominant culture(s). In my schema such cultural ensembles as British Asian-ness, British Caribbean-ness, or British Cypriot-ness are cross-cutting rather than mutually exclusive configurations. The interesting question, then, is how these British identities take shape; how they are internally differentiated; how they interrelate with one another and with other British identities; and how they mutually reconfigure and decentre received notions of Englishness, Scottishness, Welshness, or Britishness. *My argument is that they are not 'minority' identities, nor are they at the periphery of something that sees itself as located at the centre, although they may be represented as such.* Rather, through processes of decentring, these new political and cultural formations continually challenge the minoritising and peripheralising impulses of the cultures of dominance. Indeed, it is in this sense that Catherine Hall (1992) makes the important claim that Englishness is just another ethnicity.

I have argued that feminist theorisation of the politics of location is of critical relevance to understanding border positionalities. This, however, is not to minimise the importance of other theoretical and political strands in illuminating diasporising border processes. Insights drawn from analyses of colonialism, imperialism, class, and gay and lesbian politics, for instance, are equally indispensable. Earlier, we noted the growing currency of the term 'border theory' to reference analytical perspectives that, *inter alia*, address some of these aspects. This term jostles with others, such as 'post-colonial theory' and 'diaspora theory'. Here, I am less concerned about the overlaps or differences between and across these conceptual terrains. The point I wish to stress is that these theoretical constructs are best understood as constituting *a point of confluence and intersectionality* where insights emerging from these fields inhere in the production of analytical frames capable of addressing multiple, intersecting, axes of differentiation. In other words, it is a space of/for theoretical crossovers that foreground processes of power inscribing these interrelationalities; a kind of *theoretical creolisation*. Such creolised envisioning is crucial, in my view, if we are to address fully the contradictions of modalities of enunciation, identities, positionalities and standpoints that are simultaneously 'inside' and 'outside'. It is necessary in order to decode the polymorphous compoundedness of social relations and subjectivity. The concept of diaspora space which I have attempted to elaborate here, and my analysis of 'difference' in a previous chapter, are firmly embedded in a theoretical creolisation of the type described above.

Chapter 9

Refiguring the 'multi'
The politics of difference, commonalty and universalism

This book is about the figuration of power in its multiple modalities. It is an attempt to grapple with the intersectionality across some of these modalities: class, gender, 'race' and racism, ethnicity, nationalism, generation and sexuality. It is part of my ongoing struggle to find ways of thinking about the *relationship* between and across these distinctive fields of power as they are played out in the constitution and transformation of social relations, subjectivity and identity. Each of these constructs – class, gender, racism . . . – signifies a *specific type of power relation* produced and exercised in and through a myriad of economic, political and cultural practices. The previous chapters have been concerned with the kinds of inclusion or exclusion sanctioned by specific articulations of power. They have concerned the question of how power is exercised through specific state policies, structures and modes of governance. They address what types of subject positions, subjectivities and identities are constructed and contested within the interstices of particular configurations of power. And they explore what kinds of politics are inscribed, and what forms of fantasies, desires, ambivalences and contradictions are performed in, through or by particular dynamics of power. In all this, the key question underpinning my attempts at analysis has been: 'How are realms – that we heuristically define as cultural, economic, political, psychic or social – marked, reinscribed or transgressed in varying operations of power?'

This project has inevitably involved borrowing conceptual tools and analytical insights from different subject disciplines, theoretical paradigms and political movements. In the previous chapter, I described this type of confluence – among analytical frameworks, political projects, and the traffic between them – as creolised theory or creolised envisioning. In my view, creolised envisioning is essential to understanding all forms of intersectionality: between the social and the psychic; of politics and intellectual production; as well as that between economic, political, and cultural fields of articulation.

But creolisation can take many forms, not least in terms of political orientation. Hence it is important to spell out, as far as possible, the specificity of a given creolised complex. In this chapter I wish to do just this by revisiting some of the key themes addressed in this book and bringing them together in order to make explicit the relationship of my analysis to some of the major post-war debates which have informed my thinking. My emphasis is not so much on the detailed content of the debates but rather on the theoretical and political frames they inscribe, the intellectual impulse and trends they codify, and the social and cultural context in which they are embedded. I wish to convey where my current thinking 'comes from', but the idea is not to lay out its 'antecedents'. Rather, I hope to clarify how the various intellectual and political debates and practices influenced my under-standing of major issues of the time, what I learned from these debates and political practices, and how my engagement with them helped me to further my own analysis. To undertake this is also, in part, a way of re-emphasising the contribution of the collective struggles of which I have been a part – feminism, especially through membership of black women's groups; activism against racism; and involvement with socialist and other democratic movements for social justice – to the intellectual ferment of our time. It is a means of evaluating the impact of these interventions on fashioning conceptual maps and political agendas with which we are likely to approach the forthcoming *fin de siècle* and the dawn of the third millennium of the Christian calendar.

The problematic of 'difference' and 'commonalty' as relational concepts is at the heart of this text. I have addressed it by thinking of 'difference' across four main modalities: experience, subjectivity, identity and social relation. In Chapter Eight I have tried to analyse difference/commonalty in terms of the contemporary discourse of 'diaspora'. Here, I have sought to distinguish diaspora as an analytical term from its usage in describing diasporic 'experiences' and 'diaspora discourses'. I have also explored the relationship of the concept of diaspora to that of 'border' and the 'politics of location', and suggested a new concept of 'diaspora space' as the point of their intersectionality. It is my hope that this relationship will become further clarified in the present chapter.

In working through these ideas, I – along with the many others embarked on similar projects – have grappled with political projects of the Left and, in the process, with the powerful insights as well as the critiques of Marxism. Whatever the shortcomings of this particular 'grand narrative of modernity' – and there are certainly some major problems which have been the subject of both internal and external critique – some of its theoretical constructs remain indispensable guides to understanding the workings of global capitalism as it is in the process of becoming even further entrenched, albeit in changed forms, at the end of the twentieth century. There can be no analysis of capitalism that does not have some relationship to Marxism, even if it takes the form of a point of departure, a disavowal or – where its self-confessed detractors are concerned – a spirited dismissal. Derrida (1994) is surely right when he suggests that, in this sense, we are all indebted to Marx without whom there would have been no Marxism, although of course one should not conflate Marx's work with the different varieties of Marxism that it generated. Some of us were, and remain, deeply moved by the compassion of Marx's political vision of a more equal and just society. At the same time, however, someone like me who wished to think about issues of equality and justice, not only along the axis of 'class' but also in terms of other forms of inequalities and injustices, began quite early on to develop some serious reservations about this paradigm's limitations in helping with this wider task. We thought class analysis was important, but could not accord it 'primacy' at the expense of treating other axes of differentiation such as gender or racism as epiphenomena.

Given this, the first part of the chapter outlines features of the contestation around the idea of 'primacy' which helped me clarify my own position in the debate. The political movements of the Left in post-war Europe were, of course, always ostensibly 'international' in their orientation. But those of us who encountered them as persons 'from out there' – from the social *and* psychic landscapes of Europe's Others – often experienced them as Eurocentric, heterocentric and patriarchal. The second part of the chapter offers a brief critical commentary upon the 'marginalising' imperatives of Eurocentricism which the framework I suggest in this book explicitly refutes. Ironically, such 'marginalising' tendencies are not confined to the 'grand narratives of modernity' but can all too readily permeate scholarship across the so-called 'modern/postmodern' divide. For example, the critique of the humanist subject cannot be understood only, even primarily, in terms of post-structuralist analyses, for it has simultaneously emerged as part of the global movement against colonialism and imperialism, as well as in feminist, anti-racist and other post-war social movements. To say this is not to deny the achievements of post-structuralism. Indeed, I have learnt much from the theoretical developments summed up by this term, and this book clearly bears its traces. However, I wish to record its indebtedness and relation to these movements for democratic politics. In this part of the chapter I also caution against the *possibility* of 'marginalisation' of a similar kind via the idea of 'postcolonial theory', although of course this is a relatively new construct and its effects are as yet not fully known, and are likely to be contradictory.

The interconnecting theme of this chapter is a critique of the construct 'multi'. Used as a prefix, 'multi' figures prominently amongst some of the most critical intellectual currents of the present moment. To invoke 'multi' is to render salient the variety of different meanings it assumes in different discourses. 'Multi-national' can refer to the operations of multi-national firms whose assets now outstrip the GDP of some nation states. When used to refer to the UN Multi-National Peace-Keeping Force, it foregrounds global politics whereby the non-democratic constitution of the UN, giving rights of veto to a tiny club of powerful nations, ensures that the changing world order is consolidated and strengthened primarily in their interest. On the other hand, the discourse of diversity and multiplicity figures equally prominently in much of feminist, anti-racist, and 'postmodernist' discourse and politics. The idea of 'multi' is also at the heart of the debate about 'multi-culturalism'. This debate continues to play a major role in marking shifting boundaries between 'them' and 'us' in post-war Britain and continental Europe, no less than in the USA, Canada, Australia and New Zealand. At the same time, some of the other highly contested themes of the present moment – difference, pluralism, hybridity, heterogeneity – are also underpinned by a notion of 'multiplicity'.

Earlier chapters have already addressed some key issues surrounding the discourse of the 'multi'. In this chapter I undertake further deconstruction in order to map the broad contours of *a re-figured 'Multi' as a sign for power dynamics of intersectionality which the concept of 'diaspora space' interrogates.* In the process, the chapter *inter alia* addresses certain relevant concerns from the debate about 'modernism/postmodernism', 'multi-culturalism/anti-racism'; 'cultural diversity/difference'; 'new ethnicities'; and 'universalism'.

THE PROBLEMATICS OF 'PRIMACY': MULTIPLE CONTESTATIONS

It is now widely accepted that the creation of 'European Man' as the universal subject in Western social and political thought was realised by defining 'him' against a plethora of 'Others' – women, gays and lesbians, 'natives', 'coloured people', the 'lower orders', and so on. This centring around the figure of European Man constructed these various 'Others' in complex hierarchical relations *vis-à-vis* one another. One far reaching, though not altogether surprising, effect of these differential positionings has been that oppositional discourses and politics have also often converged around the privileging of a single axis of differentiation. In the period since World War II this has led to much dissension, conflict, and factionalisation among social movements of the Left. Such contestation, both within and across these post-war social movements – socialist, feminist, anti-racist, gay liberation, ecology movements, peace movements, the Civil Rights and Black Power movements – marks the complexity of power dynamics in and through which social life is constituted and experienced.

The 'New Left' movements of the 1950s and 1960s ushered a politics of anti-Stalinism that nurtured a variety of discrete neo-Marxist tendencies. The New Left was also energised by the political struggles against colonialism in Africa, Asia and elsewhere. The politics of decolonisation posed a serious challenge to the authority of the 'Western' political subject, highlighting its complicity with colonial racisms. At the same time the horror of Nazi genocide galvanised attention to forms of racism for which colonial genealogies could not provide an adequate answer. This concern about fascism and anti-semitism was to prove central to important strands of critical theory. The effects of colonisation, decolonisation and the Holocaust generated powerful critiques of the unified, unitary, rationalist sovereign subject of humanism.

Also critical in this regard has been the role of solidarity movements in the Third World, such as the Non-Aligned Movement, which resisted the Cold War polarisation of global politics between the socialist bloc and the capitalist powers. These alliances exercised a profound influence on protest movements in the West where the economic boom had created the conditions for labour migrations to advanced capitalist countries from Africa, Asia, the Caribbean and other 'underdeveloped' regions. The formation of these post-war diasporas in the heart of metropolitan centres, and the relationship of these communities with their older established counterparts, marked a new politics of transnationality. For example, the interconnections between the Indian Independence movement, the Irish Home Rule politics, the Civil Rights and the Black Power movements, the struggles against Apartheid, and the politics of the 'black' in Britain, provide important insight into circuits of identifications across differential realms of coloniality and post-coloniality. Their impact upon student politics, mobilisation against the war in Vietnam, the Campaign for Nuclear Disarmament, and the Women's Liberation Movement of the 1960s and 1970s, signal an even wider network of influence.

Yet, despite such precedents – and these by no means exhaust the range – the *intersectionality* they underscored did not, until quite recently, readily find its way into social and cultural analysis, although one would not wish to minimise the growing effort in this direction, and the work of certain feminist scholars is exemplary. But, even today, the residual tendency to assert the primacy of one set of social relations as against another has far from disappeared, and this means that the contestation continues. It demands ongoing attention and vigilance. This comment may be met with impatience and disbelief by those who believe that this debate is now 'old hat', that 'things have moved on'. Indeed, they have. But in what ways? Sometimes one only has to move an inch from certain circles to realise that what is often *presumed* as having been accepted as the norm in one arena of discourse is far from the case in other fields.

It is not out of place, therefore, to revisit certain main features of the 'primacy' debate which have a direct bearing in constituting the analytical terrain from which forms of analysis like mine spring.

The primacy of . . . ?

In the aftermath of the 1989 crumbling of the Berlin Wall and the break-up of the former Soviet Union, together with the events in Eastern Europe, there has been a chorus of rather hasty and categorical dismissals of Marxism. *Inter alia*, this has resulted in the Marxist debate on class having become rather noticeably muted, albeit not silenced, while the discourse of 'underclass' has achieved a renewed lease of life. Such discursive shifts have tended to mask the centrality of Marxist debate on class to social theory. Indeed, the long-standing differences between Marxist and non-Marxist social theory remained the subject of controversy right up to the late 1980s.

The significant influence of socialist visions upon a variety of post-war independence movements, and the installation of 'communist' regimes in China, Cuba, Eastern Europe and elsewhere, gave a renewed vigour to Marxism. On the other hand, the almost parallel disclosures in the Krushchev era about the oppressive practices of Stalinism generated a major reassessment and auto-critique within Marxism. In the process, a variety of neo-Marxist tendencies took shape and flourished.

One issue that became the subject of major controversy among neo-Marxists was that about the relationship between 'economy' and other features of the social formation. Generally known as 'the base and superstructure' debate, it involved an in-depth interrogation of the concept of 'economic determinism'. Economic reductionism had already come under serious scrutiny from Gramsci, and this trend was continued in the post-World War II years in the work of intellectuals ranging from Althusser to Poulantzas and Lacan. The Althusserian critique of reductionist readings of Marx, as if all elements of a social formation could be pared down to an 'expression' of the economic, proved attractive to many. Althusser's idea of historical moment or conjuncture as the outcome of *articulation* of contradictions that defy simplistic reductionism served to problematise teleological notions of history, and portended the demise of monocausality. Social formations could now be conceived of as made up of a number of instances or 'levels', each with its 'relatively autonomous' sphere of effectivity.

Soon, however, the Althusserian project itself came under severe pressure for its inability to live up to its promise by insisting upon the *primacy* of the economic in the 'last instance'. For instance, Laclau and Mouffe (1985) had initially found the psychoanalytic underpinnings to Althusser's concept of 'over-determination' suggestive of a very useful point of departure. The idea of 'over-determination' encapsulated no ordinary fusion or merger, but rather referred to modes of articulation incorporating a symbolic dimension and a plurality of meaning. Consequently, the Althusserian claim that 'everything in the social was overdetermined' was profound in its implications, not least because it defied literality by asserting that the social constitutes itself as a symbolic order. But the possibility that this opened up for a new conception of articulation was, according to Laclau and Mouffe, foreclosed by the efforts to make the concept of 'over-determination' compatible with economic determination in the 'last instance'.

Gramsci's earlier elaboration of the concept of hegemony and his formulation of a non-deterministic theory of ideology was a watershed in neo-Marxist theorisation. These ideas became decisively influential within a newly emerging field now known to us as 'cultural studies'. Some critics argued that, for all its very significant innovatory contribution, Althusser's reworking of the notion of ideology – through the linked concepts of 'interpellation' and the 'Ideological State Apparatuses' – remained embedded within the problematic of 'dominant ideologies'. Gramsci's concept of ideology as everyday processes and practices of 'making sense of the world' with a variable degree of systematicity and coherence, on the other hand, seemed to open up avenues for analysing a variety of discursive formations from commonsense and folklore to philosophy and religion. The enabling potential of the Gramscian paradigm for understanding 'experience' and the 'experiencing subject' as both a conceptual category and lived contradiction was enormous. As Stuart Hall has argued, Gramsci provided 'very much the "limit case" of Marxist structuralism' (Hall 1980: 35)

Some of us witnessed this debate from a cautionary distance, excited by the new conceptual and political vistas it called to view, but critical of its continued class-centricism. It bears emphasising that critique of 'economic reductionism' is not the same as that of 'class reductionism' – although the two may overlap, and sometimes did, although not often. In other words, 'mainstream' neo-Marxist thinking sought to distance itself from 'economic reductionism' but retained 'class' as the privileged subject of 'history'.

The most sustained criticism of this tendency emerged from within projects concerned with questions of gender, racism, ethnicity and sexuality. Paradigms of class reductionism were taken to task for either ignoring these social divisions altogether or, at best, treating them as epiphenomena of class. I was a PhD student at the time, struggling to find concepts and the language to map issues of racism, culture and identity as they were played out in the lives of 'white' and 'Asian' young people and their parents in west London. Surrounded by the then prominent academic discourse of 'race relations' or 'ethnic relations', I felt that my study called out for other ways of thinking about the issues. Radical scholarship into the analysis of colonial formations and the political economy of migration, new developments within Marxist thought, together with emergent feminist work, were singularly influential at this point in setting me off on my own fraught journey. Stuart Hall, for instance, attempted to combine Althusserian and Gramscian insights in the analysis of racism:

> One must start, then, from the concrete historical 'work' which race accomplishes under specific historical conditions – as a set of economic, political and ideological practices, of a distinctive kind, concretely articulated with other practices in a social forma-tion.... In short, they are practices, which secure the hegemony of a dominant group over a series of subordinate ones.... Though the economic aspects are critical, as a way of beginning, this form of hegemony cannot be understood as operating purely through economic coercion. Racism, so active at the level – 'the economic nucleus' – where Gramsci insists hegemony must first be secured, will have or contract elaborate relations at other instances – in the political, cultural and ideological levels.
>
> (Hall 1980: 338)

Soon, a variety of other neo-Marxist studies of racism, gender or sexuality entered the field of debate (cf. Mitchell 1975; CCCS 1978; Kuhn and Wolpe 1979; Eisenstein 1979; Rowbothom *et al.* 1979; Barrett 1980; Aronowitz 1982; CCCS 1982; Miles 1982). These texts constituted very significant advances. But the limitations of trying to bring into the orbit of Marxist analysis elements that were essentially extraneous to its central concerns were soon becoming apparent. The leaps of imagination warranted by this project could proceed largely at the expense of treating racism or gender as 'ideology' in contra-diction to 'structure'; or as 'surface phenomenon' in contrast to the 'essential relations' of class. Hence it is not surprising that feminist attempts, for example, to theorise patriarchal relations in terms of Marxist concepts encountered serious difficulties, of which the cul-de-sac reached by the 'domestic labour debate' was but one example (Mies 1986; Ramazanoglu 1989; Walby 1990).

Academic subject disciplines such as anthropology, sociology, psychology, politics, philosophy and linguistics were similarly dis-rupted by critique and re-visioning. These ruptures were symptomatic of what is now widely accepted as the crisis surrounding the dominant theoretical paradigms of 'modernity'. This crisis inaugurated a new phase of questioning and rethinking.

Of course, the problem of 'primacy' was not confined to class. For years, there was contestation surrounding: the absence of gender in the field of 'race and ethnic relations'; the amnesia about 'race', ethnicity and class in canonical feminist works of the early phase of second wave feminism; and a lack of sufficient attention to gay and lesbian studies in these and other arenas of scholarship. It is not that such marginalising tendencies are no longer around. Indeed, as I said before, there is little room for complacency when we consider the academy as a whole. Nonetheless, if we find ourselves able today to assert with some confidence that 'the politics of primacy' are untenable, it is only because of the arduous efforts already undertaken by many scholars and political activists on many different fronts. It is from this collective space – of refusal, resistance, challenge and alternative discourses – that it has been possible to begin to theorise *intersectionality*. The 'refigured Multi' of which I speak, then, by definition, signifies the confluence and excess from these projects; it traverses through, and across, many different conceptual, disciplinary and political 'borders'. In the process, it also centrally interrogates another form of 'primacy', namely 'Eurocentricity', to which I now turn.

MARGIN OR CENTRE? THE PROBLEM OF EUROCENTRICITY

The question of 'Eurocentricity' has been the subject of much controversy. It is beyond the scope of this chapter to address the many different facets of this controversy. I have a much more modest aim here, and that is to register certain concerns about the possible shoring up of Eurocentric moves in supposedly progressive fields of scholarship where one should least expect to find these. In so doing, I hope to signal the implications of this tendency for the issues with which this book is concerned.

A great deal has been written recently about the debate over 'modernity/postmodernity'. Whichever way the debate unfolds, however, it remains firmly focused around the 'West' as its pivotal icon. The 'West' is often fully centred in discourses which, ostensibly, resolutely seek to decentre it. Of course, to an extent this particular 'centricism' was inevitable in so far as the debate emerged primarily as a critique of the self-referencing subject of certain forms of Western philosophy. Hence, 'West' was precisely what had to be deconstructed. But a somewhat different point is also at issue here, and that is to do with how the debate generally continued to pan out in canonical texts without significantly shifting or dislodging the 'West and the rest' binary.

The binary itself has clearly been long in the making. Over the last five hundred years or more a wide variety of diverse, disparate, and contesting categories of people, economic and political interests, modes of governance, forms of aesthetics, and cultural practices have gradually assumed 'Europe/West' as the masquerade of 'identity'. It is in the interstices of this field of contestation that formations of 'modernity' acquire distinctive shape and gain hegemony as a synonym for Europe (cf. Hall *et al*. 1992; Coley 1992). The consolidation of a certain view of rationality, in particular through discourses of philosophy and science, has a special bearing on understanding the 'rise of the West' and gendered relations of class, sexuality, racism, nationalism and ethnicity. Of major significance here is the myriad of political, cultural, and economic processes through which 'science' became the privileged icon of 'modernity' as against others such as religion, and acquired its authority to establish presumed 'rational truths'.

This hegemonic project confidently stalked the world identifying, categorising and classifying fauna, flora and peoples; asserting its 'scientific neutrality' while marking hierarchies of 'race', class and gender. In time this 'modern' notion of rationality came to stand for a kind of *Western sensibility* at the same time as it came to inscribe the class-inflected gendered discourse of *Man*. Hence, gendered racialisation of class has been a constitutive moment in the rise of Europe.

I have no wish to caricature the multifaceted, complex and disparate formations of 'modernity'. Undoubtedly, 'modernity' is characterised by many contradictory tendencies: e.g. egalitarian principles alongside class, gender and other forms of privilege; internationalism alongside slavery, colonialism and imperialism; visions of cosmopolitanism and global solidarities in parallel with the narrowest of parochialisms, ethnocentricisms and racisms. Such contradictions often defy uniformity implied by the binary opposition of 'progressive' and 'reactionary'. If some Enlightenment thinkers welcomed the maelstrom of change in the belief that it would break the stronghold of what they regarded as religious obscurantism, and outmoded customs and institutions inimical to their professed ideals of equality and liberty, it is also the case that some of the discourses which they themselves elaborated resulted in dire consequences for certain groups of people.

It is worth noting in this regard that colonies often served as sites for the generation, application, confirmation or critique of all kinds of ideas associated with European social and political theory. For example, all the major political currents in Britain since the eighteenth century – Toryism, Whiggism, Liberalism, Utilitarianism, Labourism, Communism – found their British proponents in India. The luminaries of British political and philosophical theory such as Edmund Burke and John Stuart Mill, historians such as James Mill, literary figures such as Scott and Thackeray, and feminists such as Annie Besant, all had some entanglement with the governance of colonial India. John Stuart Mill, for instance, worked as a senior official in the India Office in London. He never directly wrote about India, although his father, James Mill, did indeed produce a highly controversial 'history' of India without having set foot on its soil. But what is relevant for our discussion here is that this weighty icon of nineteenth-century liberal political theory could wax lyrical about representative government yet oppose self-government for the colonies. His political theory speaks justification for his political position:

> Under a native despotism, a good despot is a rare and transitory accident: but when the dominion they are under is that of a more civilised people, that people ought to be able to supply it constantly. The ruling country ought to be able to do for its subjects all that could be done by a succession of absolute monarchs, guaranteed by irresistible force against the precariousness of tenure attendant on barbarous despotism, and qualified by their genius to anticipate all that experience has taught to the more advanced nation. *Such is the ideal rule of a free people over a barbarous or semi-barbarous one.*
>   (Mill 1910 [1861]: 257, emphasis added)

The conflicts between the various political discourses and practices which figures like Mill articulated were often played out in their full intricacy in the colonies. Policies based on European economic and political theory were put into practice in the colonies, often with scant regard to the local circumstances and governed primarily by the interests of the imperial power – interests which, in the Indian case and elsewhere, were thoroughly imbricated with emerging capitalist relations. These policies resulted in contradictory outcomes in India, leaving lasting marks on its socio-political structure. Yet few 'mainstream' courses of study on political theory in Britain address the governance of Empire as an internal dynamic of European social and political thought. This subject is treated as a 'specialism', to be taught on 'specialist courses'.

Indeed, overall, there is no denying the complicity of 'modernity's' scientificity, its progressivist utopias, and the linearity of some of its visions of social and cultural development, in inscribing global inequalities. Its grand narratives of 'development' produced classificatory hierarchies centred on Europe as the norm for plotting the 'achievements' of different peoples of the globe. Such theories generated ways of thinking about tradition, religion, ethnicity and nationalism which increasingly viewed these phenomena as archaic and anachronistic, likely to be swept away by the processes of modernisation. Indeed, the very concepts of tradition, religiosity, ethnicity, and so on, became instruments for measuring the levels of 'modernisation' of the so-called 'developing world'. Such modernisation strategies have proved quite disastrous, bringing in their wake poverty, starvation and the destruction of economies, environments, and indeed peoples.

The dismal failure of these 'prophecies of progress' in the late twentieth century underscores many current critiques and reassessments of the legacies of 'modernity'. Faced with growing retrenchment of global poverty and the resurgence of various racisms, nationalisms and the horrors of 'ethnic cleansing' within its own borders, Europe is forced to confront a renewed crisis of legitimacy, especially in relation to its own claim to 'civilised' status, a claim it has deployed as centrepiece of many of its hegemonic projects. In this context, it is as well to remember that 'modernity' has had its critics from an early stage. It is widely recognised that European thinkers of a variety of political persuasion – from Burke, Nietzsche and Kafka to Horkheimer, Adorno and Weber – have taken part in its critique. What is far less readily acknowledged is the centrality of intellectual currents embedded in anti-slavery and anti-colonial political movements the world over to the challenges which collectively put the grand narratives of 'modernity' seriously into question.

A similar kind of forgetfulness is also discernible in discussions about 'postmodernity'. I use this term advisedly, mindful of the considerable debate over it and the related notions of postmodernism and post-structualism (Lyotard 1991 [1984]; Harvey 1989; Boyne and Rattansi 1990; Jameson 1991; Butler and Scott 1992; Hall et al. 1992). As I understand and use the term here, the discourse of 'postmodernity' is a general code for the economic, political and cultural configurations characteristic of the emerging global formations of the late twentieth century. Theorists of 'postmodernity' argue that these formations assume quite new forms in the period since World

War II. According to some commentators, the 'postmodern' marks 'a noticeable shift in sensibility, practices and discourse formations which distinguish a postmodern set of assumptions, experiences and propositions from that of a preceding period' (Huyssen 1986: 181). Others, such as Jameson, emphasise how ' . . . in postmodern culture, "culture" has become a product in its own right; the market has become a substitute for itself and fully as much a commodity as any of the items it includes within itself: modernism was still minimally and tendentially the critique of the commodity and the effort to make it transcend itself' (Jameson 1991: ix–x). On the other hand, scholars such as Anthony Giddens (1990) continue to maintain that what we are in the process of witnessing at the end of the twentieth century is a rearticulation of the formations of 'modernity' as opposed to a complete rehaul and substitution. Hence it is far from settled in what sense, if at all, we can periodise change by the use of seemingly coherent and overarching concepts of 'modernity' and 'postmodern-ity' as if they signalled a final, even break – which they patently do not.

But it is not this debate *per se* that is central to my concerns here. Rather, I am interested in the Eurocentricity of the parameters within which this debate has generally been conducted. That 'postmoder-nity', however defined, is a global phenomenon is indisputable. Yet discussions about 'postmodernity' rarely foreground the confluence of globally initiated oppositional movements and ideas as a consti-tutive element in the intellectual history underpinning the critique and deconstruction of the 'totalising' tendencies of 'the West'. Nor, on the whole, has much attention been paid to anti-racist theories and struggles in the metropolises as a crucial *internal* feature of 'post-modernist' theoretical and political projects. Indeed, the study of racism is often hived off to 'specialist' courses in 'race relations'. There is nothing wrong, of course, in mounting programmes of study with a particular focus: they are essential to in-depth exploration of a specific subject. But the problem arises when this becomes a mechanism for disavowing centrality of the discourse of 'race' to the constitution of Western annals of knowledge, ethics and aes-thetics. The problem centres on the ways in which the so-called 'mainstream' is constructed and understood.

Despite their regular invocation of the 'crisis of the West', few canonical texts in the study of 'postmodernity' address colonialism, decolonisation or racism in any systematic way. Robert Young (1990) suggests that the Algerian War of Independence should be taken as a far more formative influence in French poststructuralism than the events of May 1968, and notes that a number of key figures in this canon – Althusser, Derrida, Lyotard and Cixous, for example, – were either born in Algeria or personally involved with the events of the war. Yet it is significant that the problematic of the racialised subject, while alluded to, remains largely untheorised in this body of work. On the whole, the 'West' remains the primary focus of attention as both subject and object of this discourse. For these and other intellectuals, such as Foucault, the politics surrounding anti-imperialist struggles in Algeria, Vietnam, Palestine and elsewhere, are said to have provided their deepest engagement in radical movements of the period. Nonetheless, the colonised remains largely elusive as Subject in much of this body of radical criticism. As Gayatri Chakravorty Spivak has argued, such criticism, in effect, tends to:

> conserve the subject of the West, or the West as Subject. The theory of pluralised 'subject-effects' gives an illusion of undermining subjective sovereignty while often providing a cover for this subject of knowledge. Although the history of Europe as Subject is narrativised by the law, political economy and ideology of the West, this concealed Subject pretends it has 'no geo-political determinations'. The much-publicised critique of the sovereign subject thus actually inaugurates a Subject.
>
> (Spivak 1993 [1988]: 66)

She examines how the works of a 'brilliant thinker of power-in-spacing' like Foucault demonstrate a remarkable amnesia about the intertwining of the colonial and imperial projects in the inscription of historical processes which he explores. For example, when he analyses the emergence in seventeenth- and eighteenth-century Europe of a new mechanism of power that did not need to rely upon direct coercion, he fails to acknowledge that this new mechanism was 'secured by *means* of territorial imperialism' (ibid.: 85). In similar vein Edward Said underlines a curious repression in such works about the 'absent present non-Western' subject:

> Yet, in the main, the breach between these consequential metropolitan theorists and either the ongoing or the historical imperial experience is vast. The contributions of empire to the arts of observation, description, disciplinary formation and theoretical discourse have been ignored; and with fastidious discretion, perhaps squeamishness, these new theoretical discoveries have

routinely bypassed the confluence between their findings and the liberationist energies released by resistance cultures in the Third World.

(Said 1993: 304)

In other words, such elisions within highly influential contemporary theoretical paradigms may inadvertently serve to consolidate effects of the imperial gaze in a supposedly 'post-colonial' phase. It is not simply that such works should have historicised imperialism as an internal element of modernity, critical though this is. It is far more centrally about addressing the social, cultural and psychic operations of power which make such 'forgetfulness' *possible* in precisely those texts where one would least expect to find it. *Why the surreptitious presence of an ethnocentrism in the high citadels of radical criticism so resolutely committed to eradicate ethnocentrism?*

The point is that if the idea of 'postmodernity' is to serve as a shorthand for the present historical moment, it cannot remain a Eurocentric vision of global change. It must address worldwide effects – of the legacies of slavery, imperialism, colonialism, decolonisation, the Cold War and its aftermath, and the recent neo-imperial adventures for which the UN seems to have become a ventriloquist (Chomsky 1993) – as esential inscribing moments of this global social condition. It is necessary for it to become axiomatic that what is *represented* as the 'margin' is not marginal but is a *constitutive effect of the representation itself*. The 'centre' is no more a centre than is the 'margin'.

It follows that the signifier 'postmodern' must re-figure in oppositional discourse in such a way as to render the margin/centre opposition unviable. It is only then that discourses of the 'postmodern' become a possible site for progressive politics. That is to say that if, in their barest form, oppositional discourses of the 'postmodern' could articulate a form of interrogation of the rapidly changing cultural, aesthetic and political ambiance with which we are confronted today; if they could serve as registers for the numerous political struggles for democratic voices against late twentieth-century forms of injustice, inequity and oppression; if they could function as the sign for the myriad of challenges to the 'totalising' and silencing tendencies wherever and from whichever part of the political spectrum they arise; if they could address and challenge the exploitative effects of contemporary 'regimes of accumulation'; it is then that 'postmodernist' thought becomes a potential site for envisioning more enabling presents and futures. In practice, proliferating discourses of the 'postmodern' encompass various contradictory tendencies, including some that nurture a 'flight from politics'. Nonetheless, they do all foreground heterogeneity, pluralism, difference and power. And this *re-valorisation of the 'multi'* can be made to work in the service of effecting politics which fosters solidarity without erasing difference.

MULTICULTURALISMS?

If there is one discursive formation which is centred on the 'multi' as its core signifier *par excellence*, it has to be that of multiculturalism. It is a strongly contested discourse with different, though sometimes related, histories in Britain, continental Europe, North America, Australia and New Zealand. In the USA, for example, the current debate over multiculturalism underscores the fraught history of the '*Un*melting Pot', as it is currently brewed, with the arrival of 'new immigrants' in the period since World War II. As elsewhere, the discourse of multiculturalism in the USA is singularly contradictory. In part, it consists of a challenge to the hegemonic moves of Eurocentricism at the heart of the state apparatus, politics and culture. Not that the challenge itself is new. Native Americans, black Americans, Chicanos, Chinese and Japanese Americans, as well as other constituencies, have long contested the dominating imperatives of European influence in the USA. But the present moment has its unique features, with the debate over 'multiculturalism' marked by changing racialised formations which have already undergone significant transformation in the post-war period (Omi and Winant 1986).

That this particular discourse of 'multiculturalism' has come under severe assault from the New Right is perhaps testimony to some of its strengths. Multiculturalism is indicted by its detractors as an untenable attack upon European 'heritage' in the USA; it is ridiculed as caricaturing and dismissing this heritage as 'the outmoded works of white dead males (WDM)'. On the contrary, while 'WDM' might well have served as an ironic code for Eurocentric processes of exclusion, the advocacy of multiculturalism as a politics of resistance can be seen as a wide-ranging critique seeking to decentre rather than displace 'Europe'. On the other hand, the discourse of multiculturalism has also attracted criticism from the left of the political spectrum. For example, Hazel Carby (1992) argues that 'multiculturalism' works to conceal the effects of racism and exploitation in the USA.

A similar debate has occurred in Britain over the last twenty years. I wish to explore some of the main points of this debate because its legacy weighs heavy every time one wants to discuss cultural thematics. One of the most pernicious effects of this debate has been that people mistook its *culturalist* leanings for a discussion of *culture*, and this has seriously inhibited attention to questions of culture outside of racialised parameters. I wish to try and re-figure this 'multi' so as to be able to address the problematic of 'cultural difference' without evacuating concern about racism and economic exploitation.

The post-war British discourse of multiculturalism emerged following the labour migrations which brought workers from the former colonies to perform low-waged work in a period of economic boom and severe labour shortages. Although these shortages were in part also met through the recruitment of British women into the labour market, as well as of persons displaced during the war or workers from the less 'developed' economies of Europe, it was the presence of African-Caribbean and South Asian immigrants that generated the most anxiety in Britain. From as early as 1945 both Labour and, later, Conservative administrations debated the possible consequences of African-Caribbean and Asian immigration on the 'racial character' of the British (Carter *et al.* 1987; Solomos 1989). In contrast to the white immigrants, these groups were constructed as 'racially' different. As I have already noted in earlier chapters, studies of discrimination carried out during the 1960s demonstrated that, while all immigrants experienced some degree of discrimination, colour acted as a significant additional barrier.

This is not to suggest, however, that the form of racism that African-Caribbean and South Asian groups experienced was identical. While discussions about both groups relied on 'culturalist' explanations, the discourses they articulated varied quite considerably. State racism, too, impacted somewhat differently upon them, with some policies such as those on immigration and policing targeting one group far more specifically than the other, although over a period of time there was growing convergence in their experiences of different institutions of the state (Brah and Deem 1986).

Under the signs of 'colour' and 'culture' these communities were *differentially racialised*, and represented simultaneously as similar and different. These discourses and practices emerged initially in the context of an ascendancy of assimilationist perspectives expecting 'immigrants' to submerge into some imagined and imaginary British national culture. Special funding was to be provided to assist those 'whose language and customs differ from those of the British community' so that they may be 'absorbed into British society'. British 'society' was generally conceived as a hermetically sealed homogeneous whole into which the 'immigrant' was expected to integrate, leaving behind the baggage of 'inferior and archaic' cultures incommensurate with the 'British way of life'. In schools, quota systems were introduced following agitation by white parents who believed that the presence of African-Caribbean and Asian children would lower educational standards: henceforth these children were to be bussed out of local schools if their numbers rose above a certain level (see Chapter One). In some local authority areas, bussing was not fully discontinued until the early 1980s – a reminder that the assimilationist impulse far from disappeared with the emergence of 'multiculturalism'.

Although the 1966 speech of Roy Jenkins, the then Home Secretary, is often cited as inaugurating a new, officially sanctioned, politics of multiculturalism, it was not until the 1970s that this discourse assumed significant credibility. Arguing against policies of assimilation, Jenkins advocated 'integration', defining it as: 'not a flattening process of assimilation but as equal opportunity, accompanied by cultural diversity, in an atmosphere of mutual tolerance' (see Chapter One; Jenkins 1966). Couched in the liberal rhetoric of the period, this speech acknowledged the scarcity of equal opportunity and tolerance – something that was difficult to ignore in the face of growing racist violence, discrimination and the persistence of social inequalities. However, racism was constructed in this discourse mainly as a human failing, with its structured forms in institutions, state practices, politics and culture frequently ignored. The language of 'integration' was, in any case, difficult to dissociate from connotations of 'assimilation' when the debate was still couched in terms of the 'cultural integration of minorities'. What this discourse manifestly concealed was that 'immigrant' workers were already integrated as replacement labour at the lowest rungs of the economy. As Street-Porter (1978) argued, 'immigrant' cultures continued to be seen in terms of posing a hindrance to integration, and the Jenkins homily was accepted at best as 'modest tokenism'.

British 'multiculturalism' carries the distinctly problematic baggage of being part of a 'minoritising impulse', discussed in the previous chapter; the term has been used as a synonym for 'minority cultures'. It is essentially a discourse about the 'Ethnic Other' – one which *ethnicises* ethnicity. It conceals 'othering' processes around class, gender, and so on. On the other hand, it is also the case that 'multiculturalism' caught the imagination of many as a means of confronting the policy and practice of assimilation, even if some versions of multiculturalism might themselves have represented an assimilationist tendency. Hence the discourse encompassed a wide variety of contradictory practices that cannot be easily subsumed under the simplistic 'samosa, sari and steel band' formula with which it was often tarnished.

One of the main arenas in which the idea of multiculturalism was translated into state policy was that of education. It was here that multiculturalism first came under systematic scrutiny and critique (see, for instance: Stone 1981; Mullard 1982; Carby 1982; Hatcher and Shallice 1984; Troyna and Williams 1986). Critics argued that, although the pluralism implied within the multicultural model acknowledged 'cultural difference', it patently ignored the power relations within which such 'difference' was inscribed. Multicultural education was criticised for its failure to take account of what was described as 'institutional racism'. Some discourses of anti-racism, notably those influenced by Marxism, emphasised the link between racism and class. Advocates of feminist anti-racism drew attention to gender as a crucial feature of racialised inequalities, in addition to class (cf. Brittan and Maynard 1984; Brah and Minhas 1985; Weiner and Arnot 1987).

By the 1980s the debate was seriously polarised between proponents of 'multiculturalism' and 'anti-racism'. The confrontation was generally perceived as an opposition between the woolly liberalism of multiculturalism and the Left radicalism of anti-racism. This polarisation was rather unfortunate for it compelled people to take sides at the expense of engaging in productive exchange. In practice, the two projects held more in common than most protagonists in the debate would care to admit. Moreover, institutional policy frequently drew upon both strands, using them selectively in varying combinations. Suffice it to say that both tendencies were internally heterogeneous, embodied many contradictions, and chalked up some credible achievements, as well as suffering some spectacular failures. The virulence of the attacks from the New Right on 'multiculturalism', as much as on 'anti-racism', is some measure of the important ground gained by work on the terrain subsumed under both categories.

During the 1980s, both 'multicultural' and 'anti-racist' projects came under criticism from the Right as well as the Left of the political spectrum (Palmer 1986; Macdonald Inquiry 1989; Anthias and Yuval-Davis 1992; Rattansi 1992). For the New Right these projects, together with the policies towards gender equality and gay and lesbian rights, constituted an assault upon 'the British way of life'. For example, the 'Committee of Inquiry into the Education of Children from Ethnic Minority Groups', set up by the Education Secretary and chaired by Lord Swann, reported to Parliament in 1985. Written in measured tones with the weight of specially commisioned research behind it, this lengthy report disputed the 'IQ explanation' of educational under/achievement. Instead, it drew attention to a variety of other contributory factors, notably the effects of racism and class inequality. One of its main conclusions was that:

> The fundamental change that is necessary is the recognition that the problem facing the education system is not how to educate children of ethnic minorities, but how to educate all children. Britain is a multi-racial and multi-cultural society and all pupils must be enabled to understand what this means.
>
> (Swann Report 1985: 769)

Widely known as the Swann Report, and dismissed by some sections of the Left as empty official rhetoric, this document was also subjected to a stinging attack from the Right, who saw this committee as pandering to the 'multicultural lobby'. Ironically, the report contains a foreword by Keith Joseph, himself a doyen of the Right within the Conservative Party. As such it is interesting to see his colleague Simon Pearce, the then Deputy Chairman of the Conservative Monday Club's Immigration and Race Relations Committee, condemn this document as 'profoundly dangerous', 'incipiently totalitarian', 'contemptuous of the rights of the native inhabitants of the UK' and one which 'throbs with all the ugly passions and inhumane ideals of the twentieth century' (Pearce, quoted in Palmer 1986:136–48).

Critique from the Left may be exemplified by the report of the Macdonald Inquiry Panel, set up by the Manchester City Council in 1987, in order to investigate the circumstances surrounding the fatal stabbing of 13-year-old Ahmed Iqbal Ullah by a 13-year-old white student, Darren Coulburn, at Burnage High School. The incident occurred when Ahmed was stabbed by Darren while trying to stop Darren bullying smaller Asian boys in the school. Members of the

Macdonald Panel were described by the press as having 'impeccable anti-racist credentials'. The implication was that, whatever the verdict of the Inquiry about Ahmed Ullah's death, its members were unlikely to challenge the anti-racist policies adopted by Burnage. In the event, the media had a field day when the Panel claimed the 'anti-racist' policy of the school to be seriously flawed. The Inquiry report argues that the way in which the policy was put into practice produced the opposite effects to what had been intended.

Newspapers, television, radio reports, editorial comments and discussion programmes either directly claimed or indirectly suggested that 'anti-racism' or 'anti-racists' at the school were to blame for Ahmed Ullah's death. The Panel had been careful to point out that they considered the task of challenging racism within educational institutions of paramount importance. What they really condemned was a form of anti-racism which was 'symbolic, moral and doctrinaire' (Macdonald *et al.* 1989: xxiii). Of course, one may question the use of 'symbolic' and 'moral' as undesirable characteristics in this context, but that would be 'nit-picking'. The point is that a long-standing record of advocacy of anti-racism by members of the Inquiry was now taken as giving an added weight to their conclusions about Burnage. Moreover, Burnage was no longer seen as a specific case but became a symbol of the failure of anti-racism writ large. The report came to stand as proof that anti-racist policies stood for what the Right had already categorised as an extremist platform of the 'loony Left'.

It is the height of irony that, in the eyes of many, the Right seemed to have been shown to be right by a report produced by individuals with Left credentials. Indeed, during this period, all types of 'Equal Opportunity Policy' concerning racism, gender, or gay and lesbian rights, were castigated as examples of extremist nonsense which all 'sensible people' should reject. This specific construction of 'commonsense' proved a distinctively successful element within politics. Even those who were previously vociferous critics of racism, heterosexism, gender or class inequality became curiously silent. The Burnage incident is one of the watershed cases whose fallout can still be felt today. I do not believe that the anti-racist project has yet recovered from this setback, its impact within education having been multiplied by the imperatives of the National Curriculum, introduced in 1990, and the effects of massive educational cuts (cf. Minhas and Weiner 1991).

It is beyond the scope of this chapter to undertake a fuller evaluation of the 'multicultural/anti-racist' debate and its aftermath which, at minimum, would necessitate making distinctions about 'multiculturalism' or 'anti-racism' as: *sets of discourses; modes of analysis; state policy and practices; and political identities*. However, it may be stated in brief that one of the issues which any reassessment must confront is the manner in which the debate set up an intractable opposition between 'multiculturalism' and 'anti-racism', and between structure and culture. Another crucial point which must be taken on board is the very significant limitations of conceptualising *agency* in voluntarist terms.

Burnage High School had a formal anti-racist policy, but the account produced by the Inquiry Panel shows that the task of examining complex questions of racialised *subjectivity* had hardly begun. The psychologism of some 'multicultural' approaches with their focus upon 'prejudice' and 'attitude' and an abiding faith in rationalist strategies for combating racism by 'teaching about other cultures' was certainly misleading. But this did not mean that the anti-racist project did not have to concern itself with questions of subjectivity: about the contradictory ways in which deep-seated psychic investments in particular subject positions can, in many subtle ways, disrupt the espousal of specific political positions. It is simply not possible to dismiss by sheer political fiat the myriad ways in which we can all become subjectively implicated in practices that sustain hierarchies of power. One might proclaim to be feminist, anti-racist or egalitarian, and yet experience deep-seated ambivalence when the security of one's own position of status and power is threatened by the same practices one might politically espouse. Social transformation demands much more than the reconstruction of 'structural' relations. Change must also occur in the realm of subjectivity.

The strongly 'culturalist' ethos of 'multiculturalism' was a serious problem but, as I have already argued in previous chapters, 'culturalism' cannot be equated or conflated with 'culture'. Racism can scarcely be understood as existing outside culture. How, after all, are racialised discursive formations constituted if not, in a major way, through cultural processes? Indeed, what are structures if not the changing configurations of power relations that we heuristically define as economic, political or cultural? The debate reached a stasis because it failed to deal with the relationality between these different modalities of power.

CULTURAL DIFFERENCE AND ETHNICITY

A major consequence of this hiatus has been to inhibit meaningful and open discussion about 'cultural difference' by those committed to a politics of equality and justice. It is not surprising, therefore, that the idea of 'cultural difference' is often hijacked within racialised discourses and practices. But the question of 'cultural difference' cannot be banished into oblivion, since it is at the heart of issues of belonging, identity and politics. Throughout this book I have attempted to address questions of culture on the assumption that culture cannot be understood independently of processes of commodification (including those which produce culture itself as a commodity) and the effects of global regimes of accumulation on regions, localities, households and individuals. I have stressed the importance of studying the articulation between different forms of social differentiation empirically and historically, as contingent relationships with multiple determinations.

Culture is the play of signifying practices; the idiom in which social meaning is constituted, appropriated, contested and transformed; the space where the entanglement of subjectivity, identity and politics is performed. Culture is essentially process, but this does not mean that we cannot talk about cultural artifacts, such as those understood in terms of customs, traditions and values. Rather, the emphasis on process draws attention to the *reiterative performance* constitutive of that which is constructed as 'custom', 'tradition' or 'value'. What is at issue is how *this* cultural practice and not *that* one comes to be represented as 'custom'? Why is it that one set of ethics and not another achieves emblematic significance as embodying the 'values' *par excellence* of a given cultural formation? What is it that renders certain inherited narratives, and not others, the privileged icons of 'tradition'? Why is it that, under given circumstances, this and not that 'tradition' is invoked and valorised?

Cultural difference, then, is *the movement of reiterative perform-ance* that marks historically variable, fluid, internally differentiated, contested and contingent *specificities*. To say that they are contingent does not imply that they do not take identifiable form or that there are no continuities, if by continuity we mean the ongoing everyday *re-assemblage* of the familiar; a re-enactment that performatively changes as it repeats. In other words, cultural specificity and cultural syncretism are linked and interdependent categories. Cultural syncretism presupposes the articulation of distinctive cultural elements.

But the *distinctiveness* of a specific cultural element is itself an *historical product* of previous syncretisms, not a primordial principle, although essentialist discourses might represent it as such. As Talal Asad (1993) rightly points out, one does not have to invoke teleology or resort to essentialism in order to address cultural particularities.

Processes which produce and regulate 'cultural difference' are the site of profound contradictions. The idea of cultural difference can and does, of course, form the basis of inferiorising imperatives inscribing hierarchies within and across cultural formations. On the other hand, if understood as specificity, cultural difference is also the site of identificatory processes figuring narratives of belonging and community. It can make possible a politics of solidarity. Cultural specificities do not in and of themselves constitute social division. It is the meaning attributed to them, and how this meaning is played out in the economic, cultural and political domains, that marks whether or not specificity emerges as a basis of social division.

If culture is the play of signifying practices, what is its significance for the production of subjectivity and identity? What kind of subjective and psychic investment do we unconsciously make in particular cultural representations, practices and positionalities that, under certain socio-economic conditions and political circumstances, we are willing to love, hate, kill or die for something? Indeed, what is the power – symbolic and material – of this something? Or, to put it another way, what is the purpose of the symbolism of materiality, and the materiality of the symbol on our social and psychic imaginations? In Chapter Five, I argue at some length that the production of subjectivity is at once social and psychic, and that the relationship between the social and the psychic is one of non-reductive interruption (indeed, disruption), undermining both rationalist and empiricist conceptualisations of mind and knowledge. How is *'cultural difference'* figured and played out in the flux of this non-reductive interjection?

In this regard, Gananath Obeyesekere's (1990) notion of the 'work of culture' which is analogous to, but distinctive from, Freud's concept of 'dream work' can serve as one useful point of departure. Obeyesekere argues that Freudian insights are useful for *trans*cultural analysis provided that the idea of universal symbolisation is jettisoned. No symbol can be understood outside its context. Indeed, contexualisation of symbols, Obeyesekere emphasises, is a key part of the 'dream work' no less than that of the 'work of culture'. The idea of the 'work of culture' would seem to refer to the process of the formation and transformation of symbolic forms through an irreducible entanglement of the psychic and the cultural. As such, the concept may be mobilised to address not only the symbolic transformation of the images of the unconscious into public culture, but also how culture itself 'works' in marking the particularity of different universes of meaning.

Psychoanalysis is attractive to Obeyesekere, and indeed to many others, as an interrogation of the 'logocentric' tendency within certain elements of Western philosophy to construct all symbolic forms as if they were consciously accessible configuration of signs within presumed synchronic matrices of meaning. However, Obeyesekere's own work is valuable for its innovative reading of psychoanalysis as a means of analysing cultural formations that are *not necessarily embedded in logocentricism*. It brings into the orbit of debate different ways of imagining and imaging psychic and social forces in cultures across the globe.

Drucilla Cornell (1993) describes Obeyesekere's psychoanalytic study of culture as a fruitful approach representing what she describes as 'nonlogocentric ethnography'. She reworks and extends Obeyesekere's framework, by way of Lacanian understanding of the constitution and working of the unconscious. Alive to feminist and other critiques of Lacanian psychoanalysis, Cornell makes a convincing case for, at minimum, twofold significance of Lacan to Obeyesekere's understanding of the 'work of culture'. As she observes:

> First, Lacan allows us to understand how the unconscious is continually generated as the isolation of usually imagistic signifiers and their corresponding relegation to the position of signified. . . . The unconscious, in other words, *is not*, it is always 'coming to be'. . . . But secondly, because the analysis of the unconscious through the principles of metonymy and metaphor allows us to trace the repressed trajectory or passageway through which the congelation of meaning took place, it also protects the possibility of change. . . . Lacan, in other words, gives us a way of thinking about the very principles of condensation and displacement so as to understand both the establishment and change in the work of culture. Such an understanding of the work of culture, since it does not just skim along the surface, by its very process of analysis does not just leave things as they were.
>
> (Cornell 1993: 186)

Cornell's re-working of Obeyesekere foregrounds the Lacanian refiguration of Saussure's insight that the sign is not a referent for a pre-given concept but is constitutive of the relation between the signifier and the signified. Lacan rejects Saussureian reversibility of the signifier and the signified, suggesting instead that it is the relation between the signifiers that generates the signified, and not the other way round. For Lacan, meaning may be pinned down, but as constituted within a chain of signifiers so that it can slide, yielding new meaning. Identity, then, is invariably established through difference, posing a continual challenge to moves of self-enclosure through metaphoric substitution and metonymic displacement. I find the combined Cornellian/Obeyesekereian framework illuminating. But my interest in it should not be taken to suggest that I endorse post-Lacanian psychoanalytics to the exclusion of other approaches. The point really is that analysis of the formations of subjectivity within cultures which do not privilege logocentricism is not only valuable for the richness of insight it can offer or the possibility it creates for facilitating understanding about different ways of constructing life worlds (cf. Taussig 1986; Morrison 1988; Appaiah 1992). Rather, it is central to rendering discussions of the 'global' manifestly global.

In the light of the above, how might we reconsider the relationship between culture and ethnicity? In previous chapters I have highlighted Fredrik Barth's attempt to distinguish between ethnicity and culture as conceptual categories. As we saw in Chapter Seven, Barth treats ethnicity primarily as the process of boundary formation between groups. What is central to the concept of ethnicity, according to Barth, is not some objective criterion of cultural difference. Ethnicity is not about communicating a pre-given, already existing cultural difference. Rather, it is the process whereby one group seeks to distinguish itself and mark its own distinctiveness from another, drawing upon a variety of historically variable criteria. The process of boundary formation is grounded in the socio-economic and political circumstances of the moment.

Some of the strengths of the Barthian approach were demonstrated in British studies of the late 1970s. Yet, at the time, this type of work came under considerable criticism. Since I endorse a Barthian understanding of the concept of ethnicity, it is worth revisiting, albeit briefly, a decade or so later, the main thrust of the major criticisms in order to identify what may be learned from this debate, and also to specify my own position on the subject.

Robert Miles (1982) found the 'ethnicity' project seriously flawed, despite its radical promise, for two main reasons. First, by using ethnicity to refer to the 'perception of group difference' in these studies, the term was made to refer to any criteria by which a group might distinguish itself from another. Could 'Mods', Miles percep- tively observed, be treated as an ethnic group? The question remains pertinent. It is clearly important and necessary to specify how one conceptual category might be distinguished from another. In re- sponse, I would venture to suggest that the criteria by which ethnic boundaries tend to be marked (see Chapters Six and Seven), such as a belief in shared history, or membership of a particular religion – while likely to be invoked in contextually contingent forms – do, never- theless, act to delimit the category. Yet a mere listing of criteria seems to miss the Barthian insight that it is not the criterion *per se* that is central to understanding ethnicity, but rather, the *processes whereby it comes into play and constitutes the 'difference'* by which a group distinguishes itself from another.

The 'Mods' did, indeed, assert a particular cultural style as a signifier of their distinctiveness. But this 'style' served as a marker of *intra-group*, generation-specific, class difference. The category 'ethnic group', on the other hand, subsumes such intra-group differences even as it remains differentiated along such axes. Ethnicity emerges out of shared socio-economic, cultural and political conditions and is played out in the construction of *cultural narratives* about these conditions which invoke notions of distinctive genealogies and particularities of historical experience. To call ethnicity a cultural narrative is not, however, the same thing as saying that such narratives are invariably about *cultural difference*. Studies from various parts of the globe show that two groups sharing a broadly similar cultural space may construct themselves as ethnically distinct; conversely, culturally distinct groups may assert a common ethnicity (Eriksen 1993). Indeed, 'class difference' can also be so narrativised and transmuted into 'cultural credentials'.

Second, Miles argues that an exclusive emphasis upon 'phenom- enal' relations in the work of the 'ethnicity school' serves to conceal the 'economic, political and ideological conditions that allow the attribu- tion of meaning to take place' (Miles 1982: 64). Miles's critique is grounded in the Marxist distinction between 'phenomenal' form – that is, the world of appearance – and 'essential relations' as referring to the conditions of existence of the phenomenal forms. However, it is not necessary to subscribe to this dichotomy between 'phenomenal' and 'real' relations in order to appreciate what Miles's critique demonstrates, namely, that this body of work made only a partial use of the Barthian framework, paying inadequate attention to the emphasis he places on the changing economic and political context in which ethnicity is constituted and mobilised.

The other strident critique of such work came from a research collective at the Birmingham-based Centre for Contemporary Cultural Studies (CCCS 1982). The collective argued that these studies examined the relationship between black communities (the term 'black' was used here in its political sense to refer to British settlers of Caribbean and South Asian descent) and the white 'majority', primarily in *culturalist* terms. This culturalist emphasis was seen as erasing the histories of slavery, indenture, colonialism and neo-colonialism, and deflecting attention away from the shifting economic and political terrain of advanced capitalism, all of which provided the context in which black community life took shape in post-World War II Britain. It was not only the omission of these legacies that was problematic, but also how they were represented, as when slavery was presumed to have stripped people of African descent of any agency, so that African diasporic cultural formations were refused any independent identity, and were seen as a mimicry of 'European cultures'. Culture was understood as an autonomous sphere that 'merely interacted' with other similarly constituted spheres. As a result, the effects of class and gender in the formation of racialised social relations were reduced to a problem of 'cultural misunderstanding'. With their primary focus upon the social organisation of family and kinship, child care practices, marriage systems, forms of cohabitation, and so on, these studies implicitly or explicitly constructed the 'white family' as the norm, and, as such, they served to pathologise the specificity of black community life. The critical issues of racism and its effects, the CCCS collective argued, are often elided, with little or no attention paid either to the 'structural' features of the British social formation or to state racism.

The overall force of these important arguments retains its relevance and resonance today. Together these critiques comprise a systematic and thorough deconstruction of a variety of academic discourses of the period, laying bare their underlying assumptions and internal contradictions. They interrogate what, at the time, had become *de rigueur* in certain academic and other professional circles. That is, they challenged the prevailing academic 'commonsense'. These critiques made a major impact and generated considerable intellectual debate. They also produced some considerable degree of political polarisation. It is as well to remember that at least some of the authority of these critiques derived from the ascendancy of Marxist thought in British academia during the 1970s and early 1980s. Eschewing the emphasis placed by the 'ethnicity school' on the 'customs and traditions of black communities', these critiques were concerned to show how these groups were *reproduced as a specific class category*. Although self-consciously seeking to reject economic reductionism and place racism and, in the case of the CCCS, additionally gender at the centre of analysis, overall these texts, nevertheless, ended up reproducing a framework that emphasised the primacy of class.

Some critics have suggested that these critiques of 'ethnicity studies' so emphasised the centrality of state racism that they inhibited work on issues that could not always be wholly reduced to the effects of racism, such as the question of 'domestic violence'. The acrimony ensuing from the debate, these critics maintain, also had the, perhaps unintended, effect of hindering instead of facilitating political mobilisation (cf. Southall Black Sisters 1989). How far this was indeed the case is not, of course, easy to judge. But what is undoubtedly true is that, for a period, there was a hiatus on how to take forward analyses of culture, ethnicity and identity without reproducing the problems highlighted by this debate.

A shift occurred in 1988 when, in a lecture presented at the Institute of Contemporary Arts, London, Stuart Hall described a rupture in the discourse of ethnicity which he argued heralded a 'new politics of representation'. He pointed out that to speak of this shift did not mean that there was a substitution of one kind of politics for another. The conditions that had precipitated the earlier struggles were still very much around. These struggles were 'predicated on a critique of the fetishisation, objectification and negative figuration... of the black subject' (Hall 1992a [1988]: 252). What he had in mind was 'a new phase in cultural politics that did not so much replace as *displace*, reorganise and reposition the different cultural strategies in relation to one another' (ibid.). He was speaking specifically about the inscription of these new politics in expressive cultural forms, most notably in cinematic practices.

In previous chapters I have discussed other parallel attempts to re-cast the political subject – in feminist debates, and in the contestations around the sign 'black' as a political colour. I suggested there that, while Hall's emphasis on the need for de-coupling ethnicity from *essentialist* discourses of 'race', 'nation' or 'culture' is vital, the process of doing so is replete with enormous contradictions. I have indicated above that *ethnicity is best understood as a mode of narrativising the everyday life world in and through processes of boundary formation.* If ethnicity, following Barth, is not about communicating an already existing 'difference', the political project, then, is crucially about identifying how narratives of 'commonalty' and 'difference' are constituted and contested, and how these are marked by the conjuncture of specific socio-economic and political circumstances. What ethnicity narrativises is the everyday lived experience of social and cultural relations, however they are constituted. The point is that 'ethnicity' is no less or more 'real' than class or gender, or any other marker of differentiation. What is at issue is the specificity of power that configures and is exercised in a given articulation of these differentiations.

My own reflections about these articulations have led me to emphasise relationality across multiple modalities of power – class, gender, 'race' and racism, ethnicity, nationalism, generation and sexuality. I have analysed 'difference' and 'commonalty' as relational concepts, thinking of 'difference' across four main modalities: experience, subjectivity, identity and social relation. This particular conceptualisation of 'difference' is integral to my subsequent discussion of 'diaspora' and 'diaspora space'. In the final section of the chapter I attempt to clarify these relationships with reference to discourses of 'particularity', 'multiplicity' and 'universalism'.

DIFFERENCE, DIASPORA SPACE AND THE REFIGURATION OF 'MULTI'

In the last chapter I proposed that the *concept* of diaspora – as distinct from the trajectory of specific historical or contemporary diasporas such as African, Jewish or Asian – should be understood as an ensemble of investigative technologies for genealogical analysis of the relationality within and between different diasporic formations. The potential usefulness of the concept of diaspora today rests largely upon the degree to which it can deal with the problematics of the late twentieth-century transnational movements of people, capital, commodities, technologies, information and cultural forms. I have also suggested that the concept of 'diaspora' articulates with that of 'borders'. The latter is concerned with the construction and meta-phorisation of territorial, political, cultural, economic and psychic borders. In these various forms, borders are social constructions with everyday effects in real lives. I have argued that the concepts of 'diaspora', 'border' and the 'politics of location' are immanent. I define this site of immanence as *diaspora space*.

The concept of diaspora space is central to the framework I am proposing. It marks the *intersectionality* of contemporary conditions of transmigrancy of people, capital, commodities and culture. It addresses the realm where economic, cultural and political effects of crossing/transgressing different 'borders' are experienced; where contemporary forms of transcultural identities are constituted; and where belonging and otherness is appropriated and contested. My point is that *diaspora space*, as distinct from diaspora, foregrounds what I have called the *'entanglement of the genealogies of dispersal'* with those of 'staying *put*'. Here, politics of location, of being situated and positioned, derive from a simultaneity of diasporisation and rootedness. The concept of diaspora space decentres the subject position of 'native', 'immigrant', 'migrant', the in/outsider, in such a way that the diasporian is as much a native as the native now becomes a diasporian through this entanglement. However, I do not mean to suggest by this that these positionalities are identical or unproblematically equivalent. Far from it.

Of central importance to understanding the concept of diaspora space are the various configurations of power that differentiate empirical diasporas internally as well as situate them in relation to one another. The concept of diaspora space relies on a multi-axial performative notion of power. This idea of power holds that individuals and collectivities are simultaneously positioned in social relations constituted and performed across multiple dimensions of differentiation; that these categories always operate in articulation. Multi-axiality foregrounds the intersectionality of economic, political and cultural facets of power. It highlights that power does not inhabit the realm of macro structures alone, but is thoroughly implicated in the everyday of lived experience. Multi-axiality draws attention to how power is exercised across global institutions – such as the International Monetary Fund, the World Bank and the World Trade Organisation; through the operations of multinational, national or local capital; and via the policies and practices of the local, national and supra-national state. On the other hand, it also emphasises the flow of power within the inter- and intra-subjective space. That is, it is equally firmly tuned to the unexpected disruptions of psychic processes to the complacency of rationality.

In other words, power is not always already constituted but is produced, and reiterated or challenged, through its exercise in multiple sites. Its effects may be oppressive, repressive, or suppressive, serving to control, discipline, inferiorise and install hierarchies of domination. Yet on the other hand, power is also at the heart of cultural creativity, of pleasure and desire, of subversion and resistance. Power is the very means for challenging, contesting and dismantling the structures of injustice. Either way, its operations are rarely disinterested or neutral. But power does not incite resistance in and of itself as if we were looking at an automatic chemical reaction. Power is exercised in/through/by human discursively constituted subjects, and such operations of power are the very basis of agency. But agency, as we now well know, is not voluntaristic but marked by the contradictions of subjectivity.

The social topography of late twentieth-century diasporas marks a tension between legitimation and interrogation of boundaries of the nation state. Dispersed across nation states, diasporic collectivities figure at the heart of the debate about national identity. These collectivities may be demonified as a threat to the integrity of the 'nation'. Alternatively, the condition of diasporisation may be celebrated either as the very basis of the identity of 'plural societies' or as a sign of the interdependency of the 'global village'. The social effects of such discursive practices will, of course, vary according to circumstances. This is especially the case since the relationship of transnational collectivities to the nation state is circumscribed by their socio-economic and political position. *But during the late twentieth century diasporisation is an offer nation states can scarcely refuse.* Contemporary forms of transnational migrancy of capital, commodities, peoples and cultures is the very condition of both the persistence and erosion of the nation state.

The ways in which diasporic collectivities themselves mobilise collective resources and identities is also crucial to the construction of diaspora space. With modern means of transport and communication, regular contact across transnational boundaries may be maintained with comparative ease through travel, telephone, fax machine, video, computer and satellite. Cultural travel through mass media – television, film, the electronic super-highway, etc. – may facilitate the creation or consolidation of 'imagined communities'. The resources of the larger diaspora may be called upon in order to achieve specific goals. Members of a diaspora may either support or oppose practices within countries they regard as their 'historical homes'. Black Americans, for instance, played no small part in generating support in American political circles for the economic boycott against the

Apartheid regime in South Africa. Similarly, support by East European immigrants and exiles abroad for dissident movements in Eastern Europe was an important feature of global politics which helped bring about the recent changes in that region.

In such instances, discourses of ethnicity centring variously on notions of shared language, religion, common culture, place of 'origin', or historical experiences of great significance, such as slavery or expulsion, may come into play as the means of eliciting support for a cause. The precise outcomes, however, would depend crucially upon the articulation of constructions of ethnicity with other discourses such as class. In the case of the USA, the process of ethnicity around the signifier 'black experience' – a narrative of the history of slavery, racism and class exploitation – would articulate with other iconography destined to appeal to different constituencies in the USA in securing support against Apartheid: for example, the discourse about liberty, the right to self-determination, the injustice of Apartheid, and the wealth of economic opportunities on offer to American capital in South Africa. Through appeals to a variety of political positions, economic and political interests, cultural norms and values, and presumed commitment to 'universal' human rights, a political 'commonsense' sympathetic to the aims of the campaign is created out of some significant contradictions. The point is that diasporas play a very important part today within regimes of accumulation and geo-politics.

We noted earlier that the concept of 'diaspora space' is a mode of genealogical analysis of different kinds of 'borders'. It addresses the transmigration across these 'borders' of people, cultures, capital and commodities, marking a space where new forms of belonging and otherness are appropriated and contested. It charts the contours of a heterogeneous and differentiated site where cultural narratives of 'difference' articulate specific formations of power. I elaborated my own view of how 'difference' might be addressed in Chapter Five, and I do not wish to rehearse again the arguments presented there. Suffice it to say that the four modalities of 'difference' are an integral element within the heterogeneity of 'diaspora space'. I believe that thinking about difference in the way I have suggested goes some way towards distinguishing constructions of 'difference' that are essentialist – as, for instance, the inherent and immutable 'difference' invoked by racism – from those that inscribe 'difference' as historically produced particularities.

The problematic of 'difference' is inseparable from the production, representation and contestation of meaning. It is crucial that we address the processes whereby a category is invested with particular meanings *without* ourselves taking recourse to discursive strategies that take meaning as pre-given. The post-structuralist insight that meaning is not intrinsic but relational is useful for this purpose. The Derridean concept of *différence* highlights a simultaneous process of difference and deferral in the production of meaning. Derrida (1976, 1982) argues that there can be no fixed signifiers or signifieds, that meaning is subject to the 'infinite' and 'limitless' play of differences, and hence is perennially deferred. This emphasis on an endless process of deferral has caused some considerable consternation. The concept of *différence* would certainly be problematic if the emphasis on 'indefinite play' is understood as a permanent dissolution of meaning; in other words, if the *process* (in the sense of a mechanism) of meaning construction is not distinguished from *specific operations of signification*. The two cannot be conflated. I believe that the concept of *différence* is a powerful tool for understanding the former. But the latter is precisely about dynamics of power that invest representations with *particular*, rather than arbitrary, meaning. For example, patriarchal signifying practices may not constitute *one fixed set* of meaning, in so far as the process of signification is contingent and relational. But they cannot be assumed perpetually to defer meaning, for their power resides precisely in constituting particular meanings in given situations and trying to pass them off as if these meanings were natural, substantive, definitive, self-evident and fixed.

Thinking of meaning production as being continuously in process, but recognising that a given set of strategies of representation might be implicated precisely in producing signs as if they embodied fixed meanings, has major political import, because it highlights that a specific mode of representation is a construction which can be politically challenged and contested. The power of a given set of already constituted constructions, stereotypes if you will, passing off as though they asserted a 'truth' can thus be confronted in its current discursive, institutional and political articulation. The paradox is that deferral is possible precisely because the implosion among historically coded multiple universes of meanings prevents closure. *In other words, meaning can be deferred, can remain in process – that is, there can be change in meanings – only because there are 'meanings' already in circulation.* This reading of *différence* relies on re-figuring 'textuality', via an emphasis on discursive formations as thoroughly enmeshed within institutional power dynamics. That is to say, not 'world as text' so much as multiple modalities of meanings and practices articulating in and across economic, political and cultural fields in relations of mutual constitution and dissolution.

Re-thinking the 'multi', then, demands attention to how differences, multiplicities and commonalties are played out; how these are constituted, contested, reproduced or re-signified in many and varied discourses, institutions and practices. It involves eschewing marginalising impulses of the kind discussed at the beginning of this chapter. It means that we must not only interrogate but go beyond claims which assert the 'primacy of' this or that axis of differentiation over all others. In other words, refiguring the 'multi' calls for forms of analysis and political practice that take the paradigm of *articulation* very seriously indeed. This is not to suggest, however, that one cannot prioritise a particular axis of differentiation as a focus of study or politics. I hope that my discussion of the politics of 'primacy' will have clarified the distinction between 'primacy' and 'priority'. What we prioritise in a specific context is contingent, but whatever has been prioritised, be it gender, racism or class, it cannot be understood as if it were an autonomous category, even though it can certainly have independent effects. If, for instance, we focus on processes of economic exploitation and inequities, this project means that these cannot be addressed purely as 'economic' or 'class' issues without reference to other modalities of differentiation. Indeed, there are serious questions as to how class is to be understood in an age where knowledge and information are the key dynamic of economic growth as well as means of social control, and where there is an intensification of the processes of gender segmentation of the labour market in and through constructions of 'race' and ethnicity. The implications of these changes for reconceptualising class are far reaching (cf. Derrida 1994; Magnus and Cullenberg 1995; Žižek 1995).

Similarly, thinking through multiplicity requires reconceptualisation of 'cultural difference'. Culture, as I understand it, is a semiotic space with infinite class, caste, gender, ethnic or other inflections. I have suggested that it is possible to hold non-essentialist and non-reductive understandings of 'cultural difference' which would defy and undermine 'minoritising' impulses. There is a sense in which no culture is fully translatable; translation is not a transparent transfer of meaning; it is always an interpretation and, as such, operates as a mode of resignification. But the act of translation-as-a-resignifying-practice is the very condition of communicative practice between individuals and collectivities. The borders of 'other cultures' begin in our every communicative practice with another. What is at issue then is the kind of shared political and cultural values these everyday social actions and practices cumulatively help generate, endorse or repudiate.

Thinking about 'multi' in the way I have done helps me to approach the question of agency from a different angle. I understand the subject, as constituted in the interstices of the articulation of 'difference' (and 'commonalty'), as inherently relational processes of identification and differentiation marking experience, subjectivity, identity and social relation. To envision subject formation in this way is to understand agency shorn of its voluntarist connotations. As I discussed in Chapter Five, what disappears is not the 'I' but merely the idea of subject as unified, stable and pre-given. In other words, agency is the irreducible continuing psycho-social interpellations of 'I'. These interjections simultaneously partially erase even as they carry traces of other identities. Since identity is process, what we have is a field of discourses, matrices of meanings, narratives of self and others, and configuration of memories, which, once in circulation, provide a basis for identification. Every enunciation of identity, whether individual or collective, in this field of identifications represents a reconstruction. Since there is no necessary direct correspondence between individual and collective identity, the proclamation of a particular collective identity could well entail considerable psychic and emotional disjunction. Political mobilisation needs to be sensitive to these processes.

Finally, the question of 'universalism' has been an underlying concern of the previous chapters. No one committed to the principles of freedom from poverty, exploitation, oppression and domination can remain indifferent to the importance of analysing 'commonalty of conditions'. But given the plethora of critiques of the humanist subject, do we continue to rely on the discourse of 'universalism' in order to do this? The issues raised by such questions seem far from settled, as the recent controversy among four feminist philosophers – Seyla Benhabib, Judith Butler, Drucilla Cornell and Nancy Fraser in the USA – testifies (Benhabib 1992; Benhabib *et al.* 1995).

Is 'difference' incompatible with 'universalism'? This query was implicit in my discussion of 'cultural difference' in Chapter Four. In a sense, much of what I have explored in subsequent chapters is an attempt to address this concern. In Chapter Four I proposed the idea of recasting 'universalism' in terms of a situated and historically variable commonalty. The problem remains, however, whether or not to continue using the term 'universal' with its fraught history in recent years. Foucault deployed 'transversal' as a way of decentring the 'uni'. Transversalism has also been used as a political emblem by which a group of Italian feminists (from the movement Women in Black) have attempted to construct dialogue among women from groups who are in serious political conflict, including war (Yuval-Davis 1994). On the other hand, Gayatri Chakravorty Spivak (1995) speaks of 'globe-girdling movements' (such as 'the non-Eurocentric ecological movement') in order to signal transnational politics which seem – to use Donna Haraway's phrase – to figure 'humanity outside the narrative of humanism' (Haraway 1992). I have tried to suggest in this book that one possible way of thinking this through is with the aid of the concept of 'diaspora space', where difference and commonalty are figured in non-reductive relationality. Here, axes of differentiation and division such as class, gender and sexuality articulate a myriad of economic, political and cultural practices through which power is exercised. Each axis signifies a *specific modality of power relation*. What is of interest is how these fields of power collide, enmesh and configure; and with *what effects*. What kinds of inclusions or exclusions does a *specific articulation of power* produce? That is, what patterns of equity or inequality are inscribed; what modes of domination or subordination are facilitated; what forms of pleasure are produced; what fantasies, desires, ambivalence and contradictions are sanctioned; or what types of political subject positions are generated by the operations of given configurations of power?

In other words, the project which I hope my refiguration of the 'multi', in and through processes of 'diaspora space', enables us to address is one which takes cultural, economic, political, psychic and social intersectionality fully on board. A project where analysis – of the effects of changing political orders, global regimes of accumulation, and cultural formations of the late twentieth century – can lead to the formulation of appropriate forms of political strategies and action. What I am arguing for is a project in which the 'uni' is transfigured through the 'multi' so as to enable the constitution of new political subjects and new collective politics.

Bibliography

Acker, J.(1989) 'The problem with patriarchy', *Sociology*, 23(2).

Adams, M. L. (1989) 'Identity politics', *Feminist Review*, 31.

Afshar, H. (1989) 'Gender Roles and the "Moral Economy of Kin" among Pakistani Women in West Yorkshire', *New Community*,15(2): 211–24.

Aldrich, H. E., Cater, C. J., Jones, T. P. and McEvoy, D. (1981) 'Business development and Self Segregation: Asian Enterprise in Three British Cities', in C. Peach, V. Robinson and S. Smith (eds) *Ethnic Segregation in Cities*, London: Croom Helm.

Allen, J. and Massey, D. (1988) *The Economy in Question*, London: Sage.

Allen, S. and Wolkowitz, C. (1987) *Homeworking: Myths and Realities*, Basingstoke: Macmillan Education.

Allen, S., Bentley, S. and Bornat, J. (1977) *Work, Race, and Immigration*, University of Bradford, School of Studies in Social Sciences.

Alloula, M. (1986) 'The Colonial Harem', *Theory and History of Literature*, Minneapolis: University of Minnesota Press.

Anderson, B. (1983) *Imagined Communities*, London: Verso.

Anthias, F. and Yuval-Davis, N. (1982) 'Contextualising feminism', *Feminist Review*, 15.

—— (1992) *Racialized Boundaries*, London: Routledge.

Anwar, M. (1979) *The Myth of Return*, London: Heinemann.

—— (1982) *Young People and the Job Market*, London: Commission for Racial Equality.

Anzaldua, G. (1987) *Borderlands/La Frontera: The New Mestiza*, San Francisco: Spinsters/Aunt Lute.

Appaiah, K. A. (1992) *In My Father's House: Africa in the Philosophy of Culture*, New York and Oxford: Oxford University Press.

Ardill, S. and O'Sullivan, S. (1986) 'Upsetting an applecart: difference, desire and lesbian sadomasochism', *Feminist Review*, 23.

Aronowitz, S. (1982) *The Crisis in Historical Materialism*, New York: Praeger.

Asad, T. (1993) *Genealogies of Religion: Discipline, and Reasons of Power in Christianity and Islam*, Baltimore and London: Johns Hopkins University Press.

Ashton, D. and Maguire, M. (1982) *Youth in the Labour Market*, London: Department of Employment, Research Paper No. 34.

Bagchi, A. K. (1973) 'Foreign capital and economic development in India', in K. Gough and H. Sharma (eds) *Imperialism and Revolution in South Asia*, London: Monthly Review Press.

Balibar, E. (1991) 'Is there a "Neo Racism"?' in E. Balibar and I. Wallerstein *Race, Nation, Class: Ambiguous Identities*, London and New York: Verso.

—— (1991) 'Migrants and racism', *New Left Review*, 186.

—— (1982) *The New Racism*, London: Junction Books.

Barrett, M. (1980), *Women's Oppression Today: Problems in Marxist Feminist Analysis*, London: Verso.

—— (1987) 'The concept of difference', *Feminist Review*, 26.

—— (1992) *The Politics of Truth: from Marx to Foucault*, Cambridge: Polity Press.

Barrett, M. and McIntosh, M. (1985) 'Ethnocentrism and socialist-feminist theory', *Feminist Review*, 20.

Barrett, M. and Phillips, A. (eds) (1992) *Destabilizing Theory: Contemporary Feminist Debates*, Cambridge: Polity Press.

Barth, F. (1969) *Ethnic Groups and Boundaries*, London: George Allen & Unwin.

Baumann, Z. (1989) *Modernity and the Holocaust*, Ithaca, NY: Cornell University Press.

Beechey, V. (1986) 'Women's Employment in Contemporary Britain', in V. Beechey and E. Whitelegg (eds) *Women in Britain Today*, Milton Keynes: Open University Press.

—— (1988) 'Rethinking the Definition of Work: Gender and Work', in J. Jensen, E. Hagen and G. Redd (eds) *Feminisation of Labour Force*, London: Polity Press.

Beechey, V. and Whitelegg, E. (eds) (1986) *Women in Britain Today*, Milton Keynes: Open University Press.

Beetham, D. (1970) *Transport and Turbans: A Comparative Study in Local Politics*, London: Oxford University Press for the Institute of Race Relations.

bell hooks (1981) *Ain't I a Woman?*, Boston: South End.

—— (1984) *Feminist Theory: From Margin to Center*, Boston: South End.

—— (1992) *Black Looks: Race and Representation*, London: Turnaround.

—— (1994) *Outlaw Culture*, London and New York: Routledge.

Beneria, L. and Sen, G. (1981) 'Accumulation, Reproduction and Women's Role in Economic development: Boserup Revisited', *Signs*, 7(2).

Benhabib, S. (1992) *Situating the Self: Gender, Community and Postmodernism in Contemporary Ethics*, Cambridge: Polity Press.

Benhabib, S., Butler, J., Cornell, D. and Fraser, N. (1995) *Feminist Contentions: A Philosophical Exchange*, New York and London: Routledge. This book has an introduction by Linda Gordon.

Berger, P. L. and Luckman, T. (1971) *The Social Construction of Reality*, Harmondsworth: Penguin.

Bethnal Green and Stepney Trades Council (1978) *Blood on the Streets*, London: BGSTC.

Bhabha, H. K. (1986a) 'Signs taken for Wonders: Questions of Ambivalence and Authority under a tree outside Delhi, May 1817', in H. L. Gates jr. *'Race', Writing and Difference*, Chicago: Chicago University Press.

—— (1986b) 'The Other Question: difference, discourse and differentiation', in F. Barker, P. Hulme, M. Iversen and D. Loxley (eds) *Literature, Politics and Theory*, London: Methuen.

—— (ed.) (1991) *Nation and Narration*, London: Routledge.

Bhavnani, K. K. (1991) *Talking Politics*, Cambridge: Cambridge University Press.

Bhavnani, K. K. and Coulson, M. (1986) 'Transforming socialist feminism: the challenge of racism', *Feminist Review*, 23.

Birmingham City Council (1988) *Homeworking in Birmingham*, report by Birmingham City Council.

Bisset, L. and Huws, U. (1984) *Sweated Labour: Homeworking in Britain Today*, Pamphlet No. 33, London: Low Pay Unit.

Bourne, J. (1983) 'Towards an anti-racist feminism', *Race and Class*, 25(1).

Boyne, B. and Rattansi, A. (eds) (1990) *Postmodernism and Society*, London: Macmillan.

Bradley, H. (1986) 'Work, Home and the Restructuring of Jobs', in S. Allen *et al.* (eds) *The Changing Experience of Employment: Restructuring and Recession*, London: Macmillan.

Brah, A. (1978) 'South Asian teenagers in Southall: their perceptions of marriage, family and ethnic identity', *New Community*, VI: 197–206.

—— (1979) 'Inter-generational and Inter-ethnic Perceptions: a comparative study of South Asian and English adolescents and their parents in Southall, West London', PhD thesis, University of Bristol.

—— (1987) 'Journey to Nairobi', in S. Grewal *et al.* (eds) *Charting the Journey: Writings by Black and Third World Women*, London: Sheba Press.

—— (1988) 'Race, class and gender: which way the trinity?', *British Journal of Sociology of Education*, 9(1).

Brah, A. and Deem, R. (1986) 'Towards anti-sexist and anti-racist schooling', *Critical Social Policy*, 16.

Brah, A. and Minhas, R. (1985) 'Structural racism or cultural difference: schooling for Asian girls', in G. Weiner (ed.) *Just a Bunch of Girls*, Milton Keynes: Open University Press.

Brah, A. and Shaw, S. (1992) *Working Choices: South Asian Young Muslim Women and the Labour Market*, London: Department of Employment, Research Paper No. 91.

Breines, W. (1992) *Young, White, and Miserable: Growing Up Female in the Fifties*, Boston: Beacon Press.

Brittan, A. and Maynard, M. (1984) *Sexism, Racism, and Oppression*, Oxford: Blackwell.

Brixton Black Women's Group (1984) 'Black women organising autonomously', *Feminist Review*, 17.

Brooks, D. (1983) 'Young Blacks and Asians in the Labour Market: A critical Overview', in B. Troyna (ed.) *Racism, School, and the Labour Market*, Leicester: National Youth Bureau.

Brooks, D. and Singh, K. (1978) *Aspirations versus Opportunities: Asian and*

White School Leavers in the Midlands, London: Commission for Racial Equality.

Brown, C. (1984) *Black and White Britain*, London: Heinemann.

Bruegel, I. (1989) 'Sex and Race in the Labour Market', *Feminist Review*, 32.

Bryan, B., Dadsie, S. and Scafe, S. (1985) *Heart of the Race*, London: Virago Press.

Butler, J. (1990) *Gender Trouble: Feminism and the Subversion of Identity*, New York: Routledge.

—— (1992) 'Contingent Foundations: Feminism and the Question of Postmodernism', in J. Butler and J. W. Scott (eds) *Feminists Theorize the Political*, New York: Routledge.

—— (1993) *Bodies That Matter*, London: Routledge.

Butler, J. and Scott, J. W. (eds) (1992) *Feminists Theorize the Political*, New York: Routledge.

Cain, H. and Yuval-Davis, N. (1990) 'The "Equal Opportunity Community" and the antiracist struggle', *Critical Social Policy*, 29, 10(2).

Calderon, H. and Salvidar, H. (1991) *Criticism in the Borderlands: Studies in Chicano Literature, Culture and Ideology*, Durham, NC: Duke University.

Campaign against Racism and Fascism/Southall Rights (1981) *Southall: Birth of a Black Community*, London: Institute of Race Relations and Southall Rights.

Campbell, M. and Jones, D. (1981) *Asian Youth in the Labour Market*, Bradford College.

Carby, H. (1982) 'Schooling in Babylon', in Centre for Contemporary Cultural Studies, *The Empire Strikes Back*, London: Hutchinson.

—— (1982) 'White women listen! Black feminism and boundaries of sisterhood', in Centre for Contemporary Cultural Studies, *The Empire Strikes Back*, London: Hutchinson.

—— (1992) 'Multiculturalisms', in G. Dent (ed.) *Black Popular Culture*, Seattle: Bay Press.

Carter, B., Harris, C. and Joshi, S. (1987) 'The 1951–55 Conservative Government and the racialisation of black immigration', *Policy Papers in Ethnic Relations, No 11*, University of Warwick, Centre for Research in Ethnic Relations.

Castles, S. and Miller, M. J. (1993) *The Age of Migration: International Population Movements*, London: Macmillan.

Cavendish, R (1982) *On the Line*, London: Routledge & Kegan Paul.

CCCS (Centre for Contemporary Cultural Studies) (1978) *Women Take Issue*, London: Hutchinson.

—— (1982) *The Empire Strikes Back*, London: Hutchinson.

Chand, T. (1970) *History of the Freedom Movement in India, Vol. 1*, Ministry of Information and Broadcasting, Government of India, Publication Division.

Chatterjee, P. (1993) *Nationalist Thought and the Colonial World: A Derivative Discourse*, Minneapolis: Minnesota University Press [1986].

Chomsky, N. (1993) *Year 501: The Conquest Continues*, London: Verso.

Clarke, J., Hall, S., Jefferson, T. and Roberts, B. (1977) 'Subcultures, cultures and class', in S. Hall and T. Jefferson (eds) *Resistance through Rituals*, London: Hutchinson.

Clifford, J. (1988) *The Predicament of Culture*, Cambridge: Harvard University Press.
—— (1992) 'Travelling Cultures', in L. Grossberg, C. Nelson and P. Treichler (eds) *Cultural Studies*, New York: Routledge.
—— (1994) 'Diasporas', *Cultural Anthropology*, 9(3): 302–38.
Cohen, P. (1988) 'The perversions of inheritance: studies in the making of multi-racist Britain', in P. Cohen and H. Bains (eds) *Multi-Racist Britain*, London: Macmillan.
—— (1992) *Home Rules: Some Reflections on Racism and Nationalism in Everyday Life*, London: The New Ethnicities Unit, University of East London.
Cohen, R. (1987) *The New Helots: Migrants in the International Division of Labour*, Aldershot: Gower Press.
Coley, L. (1992) *Forging the Nation:1707–1837*, Yale University Press.
Commission for Racial Equality (1978) *Looking for Work: Black and White School Leavers in Lewisham*, London: CRE.
Coombes, A. E. (1992) 'Inventing the Postcolonial: Hybridity and Constituency in Contemporary Curating', *New Formations*, 18.
—— (1994) *Re-Inventing Africa*, Yale University Press.
Cornell, D. (1991) *Beyond Accommodation: Ethical Feminism, Deconstruction, and the Law*, New York: Routledge, Chapman & Hall.
—— (1993) *Transformations: Recollective Imagination and Sexual Difference*, New York and London: Routledge.
Cross, M., Wrench, J. and Barnett, S. (1990) *Ethnic Minorities and the Careers Service: Investigation into Processes of Assessment and Placement*, London: Department of Employment, Research Paper No. 73.
Crowley, H. and Himmelweit, S. (eds) (1992) *Knowing Women*, Cambridge: Polity Press.
Dalal, F. (1988) 'The racism of Jung', *Race and Class*, 24(3).
Daniel, W. W. (1968) *Racial Discrimination in England*, Harmondsworth: Penguin.
David, M. (1983) 'Sexual morality and the New Right', *Critical Social Policy*, 2, 3.
Davin, A. (1978) 'Imperialism and motherhood', *History Workshop*, 5.
Davis, A. (1981) *Women, Race and Class*, London: The Women's Press.
—— (1990) *Angela Davis: An Autobiography*, first published 1974, London: The Women's Press.
de Lauretis, T. (1984) *Alice Doesn't: Feminism, Semiotics, Cinema*, Bloomington: Indiana University Press.
—— (ed.) (1986) *Feminist Studies/Critical Studies*, Bloomington: Indiana University Press.
Deem, R. (1980) *Schooling for Women's Work*, London: Routledge & Kegan Paul.
—— (1983) 'Leisure, Women, and Inequality', *Leisure Studies*, 1.
Deleuze, G. and Guattari, F. (1986) 'What is a Minor Literature?', in *Kafka: Towards a Minor Literature*, trans. Diana Polan, Minneapolis: University of Minnesota Press [1975].
Department of Education and Science (1965) Circular 7/65, London: HMSO.

Derrida, J. (1976) *Of Grammatology*, trans. Gayatri Chakravorty Spivak, Baltimore: Johns Hopkins University Press.
—— (1982) 'Différence', in *Margins of Philosophy*, trans. Allan Bass, Chicago: University of Chicago Press.
—— (1994) *Specters of Marx: The State of the Debt, the Work of Mourning, and the New International*, New York and London: Routledge.
Dhaya, B. (1974) 'The Nature of Pakistani Ethnicity in Industrial Cities in Britain', in A. Cohen (ed.) *Urban Ethnicity*, A.S.A. Monograph (12), London: Tavistock Publications.
Donald, J. and Rattansi, A. (eds) (1992) *'Race', Culture and Difference*, London: Sage.
Drew, D., Gray, J. and Sime, N. (1991) *Against the Odds: The Educational and Labour Market Experiences of Black Young People*, Sheffield: Department of Employment Training, Research and Development Series.
Dutt, R. (1901) *The Economic History of India*, London: Routledge & Kegan Paul.
Ealing International Friendship Council (1968) *A Report of the Education Committee*, unpublished.
Eisenstadt, S. (1971) *From Generation to Generation*, New York: The Free Press.
Eisenstein, Z. R. (1979) *Capitalist Patriarchy*, New York: Monthly Review Press.
El Sadawi, N. (1980) *The Hidden Face of Eve*, London: Zed Press.
Enloe, C. (1989) *Bananas, Beaches and Bases: Making Feminist Sense of International Politics*, London: Pandora Press.
Epstein, A. L. (1978) *Ethos and Identity*, London: Tavistock Publications.
Eriksen, T. H. (1993) *Ethnicity and Nationalism: Anthropological Perspectives*, London: Pluto Press.
Erikson, E. H. (1968) *Identity: Youth and Crisis*, London: Faber & Faber.
Fanon, F. (1967) *The Wretched of the Earth*, London: Penguin.
Feminist Review (1984) 'Many voices, one chant: black feminist perspectives', *Feminist Review*, 17.
—— (1986) 'Feedback: feminism and racism', *Feminist Review*, 22.
Finn, D. (1984) 'Britain's Misspent Youth', *Marxism Today*, 28: 20–4.
Flax, J. (1990) *Thinking Fragments: Psychoanalysis, Feminism and Post-modernism in the Contemporary West*, Oxford: University of California Press.
Foucault, M. (1984) *A History of Sexuality: An Introduction*, Harmondsworth: Peregrine.
Frankenberg, R. (1993) *White Women, Race Matters: The Social Construction of Whiteness*, London: Routledge.
Frankenberg, R. and Mani, L. (1993) 'Crosscurrents, Crosstalk: Race, "postcoloniality", and the politics of Location', *Cultural Studies*, 7(2): 292–310.
Frobel, F., Heinrichs, J. and Kreye, O. (1980) *The New International Division of Labour*, Cambridge: Cambridge University Press.
Fuss, D. (1989) *Essentially Speaking*, London, Routledge.
—— (1992) *Inside/out: Lesbian Theories, Gay Theories*, London: Routledge.

Ghai, D. P. and Ghai, Y. P. (1970) *Portrait of a Minority*, London, Oxford University Press.

Giddens, A. (1990) *The Consequences of Modernity*, Cambridge: Polity Press.

—— (1991) *Modernity and Self-Identity*, Cambridge: Polity Press.

—— (1994) 'Living in a post-traditional society', in U. Beck, A. Giddens and S. Lash (eds) *Reflexibility and Its Doubles: Structures, Aesthetics and Community*, Cambridge: Polity Press.

Gilroy, P. (1987) *There Ain't No Black in the Union Jack*, London: Hutchinson.

—— (1993) *The Black Atlantic: Double Consciousness and Modernity*, Cambridge, Mass.: Harvard University Press.

Ginsburg, N. (1992) *Divisions of Welfare: A Critical Introduction to Comparative Social Policy*, London: Sage.

Glazer, N. and Moynihan, D. A. (1975) *Ethnicity: Theory and Experience*, Cambridge, Mass.: Harvard University Press.

Goldstein, N. (1984) 'The Training Initiative: A Great Leap Backwards', *Capital and Class*, 23: 83–106.

Gopal, R. (1963) *British Rule in India*, London and Delhi: Asia Publishing House.

Gordon, P. (1985) *Policing Immigration: Britain's Internal Controls*, London: Pluto.

—— (1986) 'Racism and Social Security', *Critical Social Policy*, 17.

Green, A. (1983) 'Education and Training under New Masters', in A. M. Wolpe and J. Donald (eds) *Is There Anyone Here From Education?*, London: Pluto Press.

Greenberger, A. J. (1969) *The British Image of India: A Study in the Literature of Imperialism 1880–1960*, London: Oxford University Press.

Grewal, S., Kay, J., Landor, L., Lewis, G. and Parmar, P. (1988) *Charting the Journey: Writings by Black and Third World Women*, London: Sheba.

Hall, C. (1992) *White, Male and Middle Class: Explorations in Feminism and History*, London: Verso.

Hall, S. (1978) 'Racism and Reaction', in *Five Views of Multiracial Britain*, London: British Broadcasting Corporation/Commission for Racial Equality.

—— (1980) 'Race, articulation and societies structured in dominance', in *Sociological Theories: Race and Colonialism*, Paris: UNESCO.

—— (1990) 'Cultural Identity and Diaspora', in J. Rutherford (ed.) *Identity: Community, Culture, Difference*, London: Lawrence & Wishart.

—— (1992a) 'New Ethnicities', in J. Donald and A. Rattansi (eds) *'Race', Culture and Difference*, London: Sage.

—— (1992b) 'What is this "Black" in Black Popular Culture?', in G. Dent (ed.) *Black Popular Culture*, a project by Michelle Wallace, Seattle: Bay Press.

Hall, S., Critcher, C., Jefferson, T., Clarke, J. and Roberts, B. (1978) *Policing the Crisis: Mugging, the State, and Law and Order*, London and Basingstoke: Macmillan.

Hall, S. and Gieben, B. (eds) (1992) *Formations of Modernity*, Cambridge: Polity Press.

Hall, S., Held, D. and McGrew, A. (eds) (1992) *Modernity and its Futures*, Cambridge: Polity Press.

Hall, S. and Jacques, M. (eds) (1983) *The Politics of Thatcherism*, London: Lawrence & Wishart.

—— (1989) *News Times*, London: Lawrence & Wishart.

Haraway, D. J. (1989) *Primate Visions: Gender, Race, and Nature in the World of Modern Science*, New York and London: Routledge.

—— (1991) *Simians, Cyborgs, and Women: The Reinvention of Nature*, London: Free Association Books.

—— (1992) 'Ecce Homo, Ain't (Ar'n't) I a Woman, and Inappropriate/d Others: The Human in a Post-Humanist Landscape', in J. Butler and J. W. Scott (eds) *Feminists Theorize the Political*, New York: Routledge.

Harding, S. (1990) 'If I should die before I wake up: Jerry Falwell's pro-life gospel', in F. Ginsburg and Lowenhaupt Tsing (eds) *Uncertain Terms*, Boston: Beacon Press.

Hartman, P. and Husband, C. (1974) *Racism and the Mass Media*, London: Davis-Poynter.

Harvey, D. (1989) *The Condition of Postmodernity: An Inquiry into the Origins of Cultural Change*, Oxford: Blackwell.

Hatcher, R. and Shallice, J. (1984) 'The Politics of Anti-racist Education', *Multi-Racial Education*, 12, 1.

Hazareesingh, S. (1986) 'Racism and cultural identity: an Indian perspective', *Dragon's Teeth*, 24.

Henriques, J., Holloway, W., Urwin, C., Venn, C. and Walkerdine, V. (1984) *Changing the Subject: Psychology, Social Regulation and Subjectivity*, London: Methuen.

Hesse, B. (1993) 'Black to front and black again: racialization through contested times and spaces', in M. Keith and S. Piles (eds) *Place and the Politics of Identity*, London: Routledge.

Hicks, E. (1991) *Border Writing: The Multidimensional Text*, Minneapolis: University of Minnesota Press.

Hiro, D. (1971) *Black British, White British*, London: Eyre & Spottiswoode.

Hirst, P. (1989) *After Thatcher*, London: Collins.

Hobsbawm, E. (1990) *Nations and Nationalisms Since 1780: Programme, Myth, Reality*, Cambridge: Cambridge University Press.

Hobsbawm, E. and Ranger, T. (1983) *The Invention of Tradition*, Cambridge: Cambridge University Press.

Home Office (1981) *Racial Attacks*, London: HMSO.

Hubbuck, J. and Carter, S. (1980) *Half a Chance: A Report on Job Discrimination Against Young Blacks in Nottingham*, London: Commission for Racial Equality.

Husband, C. (ed.) (1975) *White Media & Black Britain*, London: Arrow Books.

Hutchins, F. G. (1967) *The Illusion of Permanence: British Imperialism in India*, London: Princeton University Press.

Huyssen, A. (1986) *After the Great Divide: Modernism, Mass Culture, and Postmodernity*, London: Macmillan.

Jameson, F. (1991) *Postmodernism and the Cultural Logic of Late Capitalism*, London: Verso.

JanMohammed, A. (1995) 'Refiguring values, power, knowledge, or Foucault's disavowal of Marx', in B. Magnus and S. Cullenberg (eds) *Whither Marxism?: Global Crisis in International Perspective*, New York and London: Routledge.

JanMohammed, A. and Lloyd, D. (1990) *The Nature and Context of Minority Discourse*, New York: Oxford University Press.

Jeffreys, P. (1976) *Migrants and Refugees*, Cambridge: Cambridge University Press.

—— (1979) *Frogs in a Well: Indian Women in Purdah*, London: Zed Press.

Jenkins, R. (1966) Address given on 23 May 1966 to a meeting of the Voluntary Liaison Committees, London: National Council for Civil Liberties.

Jenks, L. H. (1963) *The Migration of British Capital to 1875*, London: Nelson.

Jensen, J., Hagen, E. and Redd, G. (eds) (1988) *Feminization of the Labour Force*, London: Polity Press.

Jessop, B., Bonnet, K., Bromley, S. and Ling, T. (1988) *Thatcherism: A Tale of Two Nations*, Cambridge: Polity Press.

Kiernan, V. G. (1969) *The Lords of Human Kind*, London: Weidenfeld & Nicolson.

Knowles, C. and Mercer, S. (1992) 'Feminism and Anti-Racism', in J. Donald and A. Rattansi (eds) *'Race', Culture and Difference*, London: Sage.

Kroeber, A. L. and Kluckhohn, C. (1952) 'Cultures: a critical review of concepts and definitions', Cambridge, Mass.: Peabody Museum Papers, 47(1).

Kuhn, A. and Wolpe, A. M. (eds) (1979) *Feminism and Materialism*, London: Routledge & Kegan Paul.

Laclau, E. and Mouffe, C. (1985) *Hegemony and Socialist Strategy: Towards a Radical Democratic Politics*, London: Verso.

Layton-Henry, Z. (1980) 'Immigration', in Z. Layton-Henry (ed.) *Conservative Party Politics*, London: Macmillan.

Lee, G. and Wrench, J. (1983) *Skill Seekers*, Leicester: National Youth Bureau.

Lees, S. (1986) *Losing Out: Sexuality and Adolescent Girls*, London: Hutchinson.

Leicester City and County Councils (1984) *Survey of Leicester 1983*, Leicester: LCCC.

Leonard, D. and Speakman, M. A. (1986) 'Women in the Family: companions or caretakers?', in V. Beechey and E. Whitelegg (eds) *Women in Britain Today*, Milton Keynes: Open University Press.

Lewis, G. (1990) 'Audre Lorde: vignettes and mental conversations', *Feminist Review*, 34.

Liddle, J. and Joshi, R. (1985) 'Gender and Imperialism in British India', *South Asia Research* 5(2), School of Oriental and African Studies, University of London.

Lloyd, D. (1990) 'Genet's Geneaology: European Minorities and the Ends of the Canon', in A. JanMohammed and D. Lloyd (eds) *The Nature and Context of Minority Discourse*, New York: Oxford University Press.

Lowe, L. (1991a) *Critical Terrains: British and French Orientalisms*, Ithaca, NY: Cornell University Press.
—— (1991b) 'Heterogeneity, Hybridity, Multiplicity: Marking Asian American Differences', *Diaspora*, 1(1): 24–44.
Lutz, H. (1991) *Migrant Women of 'Islamic Background': Images and Self Images*, Amsterdam: Middle East Research Associates, Occasional Paper (11).
Lyotard, J. F. (1991) *The Postmodern Condition: A Report on Knowledge*, Minneapolis: University of Minnesota Press [1984].
Macdonald Inquiry (1989) *Murder in the Playground: The Report of the Macdonald Inquiry into Racism and Racial Violence in Manchester Schools*, London: Longsight Press.
Mackenzie, J. (1984) *Propaganda and Empire*, Manchester: Manchester University Press.
Magnus, B. and Cullenberg, S. (eds) (1995) *Whither Marxism?: Global Crisis in International Perspective*, New York and London: Routledge.
Mama, A. (1986) 'Black Women and the Economic Crisis', in *Feminist Review* (ed.) *Waged Work: A Reader*, London: Virago.
—— (1989) 'Violence against black women: gender, race, and state responses', *Feminist Review*, 32.
Mamdani, M. (1976) *Politics and Class Formation in Uganda*, Monthly Review Press.
Mani, L. (1987) 'Contentious traditions: the debate on Sati in colonial India', *Cultural Critique*, Fall.
Manneheim, K. (1952) 'The Problem of Generations', in P. Kecskemeti (ed.) *Essays on the Sociology of Knowledge*, London: Routledge & Kegan Paul.
Marsh, P. (1967) *The Anatomy of a Strike*, London: Institute of Race Relations.
Martin, B. and Mohanty, C. T. (1986) 'Feminist Politics: What's Home Got to Do with It?', in T. de Lauretis (ed.) *Feminist Studies/Critical Studies*, Bloomington: Indiana University Press.
McRae, S. (1989) *Flexible Working Time and Family Life*, London: Policy Studies Institute.
Mercer, K. (1994) *Welcome to the Jungle*, London: Routledge.
Mies, M. (1986) *Patriarchy and Accumulation on a World Scale*, London: Zed Press.
Miles, R. (1982) *Racism and Migrant Labour*, London: Routledge & Kegan Paul.
—— (1989) *Racism*, London: Routledge.
—— (1993) *Racism after 'Race Relations'*, London and New York: Routledge.
Mill, J. S. (1910) 'Representative Government', in *Utilitarianism, Liberty, and Representative Government*, London: Dent [1861].
Minh-ha, T. T. (1989) *Woman, Native, Other: Writing Post Coloniality and Feminism*, Indianapolis: Indiana University Press.
Minhas, R. and Weiner, G. (1991) 'Resources and Funding for State Education', in C. Chitty (ed.) *Changing the Future*, London: Tufnell Press.

Minsky, R. (1990) '"The trouble is it's ahistorical": the problem of the unconscious in modern feminist theory', *Feminist Review*, 36.

Mitchell, J. (1975) *Psychoanalysis and Feminism*, Harmondsworth: Penguin.

Mitter, S. (1986) *Common Fate, Common Bond: Women in the Global Economy*, London: Pluto Press.

Modood, T. (1988) '"Black" racial equality and Asian identity', *New Community*, 14(3).

Mohanty, C. T. (1988) 'Under Western eyes: feminist scholarships and colonial discourses', *Feminist Review*, 30.

Mohanty, S. P. (1989) 'Kipling's Children and the colour line', *Race and Class*, 31.

Moore, R. (1975) *Racism and Black Resistance in Britain*, London: Pluto Press.

Morris, M. D. *et al.* (1969) *Indian Economy in the Nineteenth Century: A Symposium*, Delhi: School of Economics Press.

Morrison, T. (1988) *Beloved*, London: Pan Books in association with Chatto & Windus.

Mukherjee, R. (1974) *The Rise and Fall of the East India Company*, London: Monthly Review Press.

Mullard, C. (1982) 'Multi-racial Education in Britain: From Assimilation to Cultural Pluralism', in J. Tierney (ed.) *Race, Migration, and Schooling*, New York: Holt, Rinehart & Winston.

Nairn, T. (1988) *The Enchanted Glass: Britain and Its Monarchy*, London: Radius.

—— (1990) *The Break-Up of Britain*, London: New Left Books [1977].

National Council for Civil Liberties (NCCL) (1980) *The Death of Blair Peach: The Supplementary Report of the Unofficial Committee of Enquiry*, London: NCCL.

Nazir, P. (1981) 'Transformation of Property Relations in the Punjab', *Economic and Political Weekly*, xvi(8), Bombay.

—— (1986a) *The Life and Work of Rajni Palme Dutt*, London: Greater London Council.

—— (1986b) 'Marxism and the national question', *Journal of Contemporary Asia*, 16, 4.

—— (1991) *Local Development in the Global Economy: The Case of Pakistan*, Aldershot: Avebury Press.

New Community (1991) Special issue on European Integration, 18, 1.

Nugent, N. and King, R. (1979) 'Ethnic Minorities, scapegoating and the extreme right', in R. Miles and A. Phizacklea (eds) *Racism and Political Action in Britain*, London: Routledge & Kegan Paul.

Obeyesekere, G. (1990) *The Work of Culture: Symbolic Transformation in Psychoanalysis and Anthropology*, Chicago: University of Chicago Press.

Omi, M. and Winant, H. (1986) *Racial Formations in the United States from the 1960s to the 1980s*, New York and London: Routledge & Kegan Paul.

Pahl, R. E. (1988) *On Work*, Oxford: Basil Blackwell.

Palme Dutt, R. (1940) *India To-day*, London: Victor Gollancz.

Palmer, F. (1986) *Anti-Racism: An Assault on Education and Value*, London: The Sherwood Press.

Papaneck, H. (1971) 'Purdah in Pakistan', *Journal of Marriage and Family*, August.

Parker, A., Russo, M., Sommer, D. and Yaeger, P. (1992) *Nationalisms and Sexualities*, New York and London: Routledge.

Parmar, P. (1982) 'Gender, race and class: Asian women in resistance', in Centre for Contemporary Cultural Studies, University of Birmingham, *The Empire Strikes Back*, London: Hutchinson.

—— (1989) 'Other Kinds of Dreams', in *Feminist Review*, 31.

Parmar, P. and Mirza, N. (1983) 'Stepping forward: work with Asian young women', *Gen*, 1.

Patnaik, P. (1975) 'Imperialism and the growth of Indian Capitalism', in R. Blackburn (ed.) *Explosion in a Subcontinent*, Harmondsworth: Penguin.

Penley, C. (1989) *The Future of an Illusion: Film, Feminism and Psychoanalysis*, London: Routledge.

Phillips, A. (1991) *Engendering Democracy*, Cambridge: Polity Press.

Phizacklea, A. (1990) *Unpacking the Fashion Industry*, London: Routledge.

Phizacklea, A. and Miles, R. (1980) *Labour and Racism*, London: Routledge & Kegan Paul.

Phoenix, A. (1987) 'Theories of gender and black families', in G. Weiner and M. Arnot (eds) *Gender under Scrutiny*, Milton Keynes: Open University Press.

—— (1990) 'Black Women and the maternity services', in J. Garcia, R. Kilpatrick and M. Richards (eds) *The Politics of Maternity Care*, Oxford: Clarendon.

Pollert, A. (1981) *Girls, Wives, Factory Lives*, Basingstoke: Macmillan.

Pratt, M. B. (1984) 'Identity: Skin, Blood, Heart', in E. Bulkin, M. B. Pratt and B. Smith (eds) *Yours in Struggle: Feminist Perspectives on Racism and Anti-Semitism*, New York: Long Haul.

Pratt, M. L. (1992) *Imperial Eyes: Travel Writing and Transculturation*, London and New York: Routledge.

Probyn, E. (1993) *Sexing the Self: Gendered Positions in Cultural Studies*, New York: Routledge.

Race and Class (1991) *Europe: Variations on a Theme of Racism*, 32, 3.

Ramazanoglu, C. (1989) *Feminism and the Contradictions of Oppression*, London: Routledge.

Ransom, D. (1980) *License to Kill: The Blair Peach Case*, Friends of Blair Peach Committee, Box 353, London NW5.

Rattansi, A. (1992) 'Changing the Subject? Racism, Culture and Education', in J. Donald and A. Rattansi (eds) *'Race', Culture and Difference*, London: Sage.

Redclift, N. (1985) 'The Contested Domain: Gender Accumulation and the Labour Process', in N. Redclift and E. Mingion (eds) *Beyond Unemployment*, Oxford: Blackwell.

Rex, J. and Mason, D. (eds) (1986) *Theories of Race and Ethnic Relations*, Cambridge: Cambridge University Press.

Rose, J. (1986) *Sexuality in the Field of Vision*, London: Verso.

Rose, S., Kamin, J. and Lewontin, R. C. (1984) *Not in Our Genes*, Harmondsworth: Pelican.

Rouse, R. (1991) 'Mexican Migration and the Social Space of Postmodernism', *Diaspora*, 1(1): 8–23.

Rowbothom, S., Segal, L. and Wainwright, S. (1979) *Beyond the Fragments: Feminism and the Making of Socialism*, London: Merlin.

Runnymede Trust (1983) *Employment, Unemployment, and the Black Population*, London: Runnymede Trust.

Safran, W. (1991) 'Diasporas in Modern Societies: Myths of Homeland and Return', *Diaspora*, 1(1): 83–99.

Said, E. (1978) *Orientalism*, New York: Pantheon Books.

—— (1993) *Culture and Imperialism*, New York: Alfred A. Knopf.

Saifullah-Khan, V. (1974) *Pakistani Villagers in a British City*, unpublished PhD thesis, University of Bradford.

Sassen, S. (1988) *The Mobility of Labour and Capital: A Study in International Investment and Labour Flow*, Cambridge: Cambridge University Press.

Scott, J. W. (1992) 'Experience', in J. Butler and J. W. Scott (eds) *Feminists Theorize the Political*, New York: Routledge.

Segal, L. (1987) *Is the Future Female?*, London: Virago.

—— (1990) *Slow Motion: Changing Masculinities, Changing Men*, London: Virago.

Seton-Watson, J. (1977) *Nations and States: An Inquiry into the Origins of Nations and the Politics of Nationalism*, Boulder, Col.: Westview Press.

Sharma, U. (1980) *Women, Work and Property in North India*, London: Tavistock Publications.

Sharpe, J. (1993) *Allegories of Empire: The Figure of Woman in the Colonial Text*, Minneapolis and London: University of Minnesota Press.

Shaw, A. (1988) *A Pakistani Community in Britain*, Oxford: Basil Blackwell.

Sherridan, P. (1981) *Career Aspirations and Prospects of Asian and Indigenous Students in Suburban and Inner City Leicester*, B.Ed. dissertation, Leicester Polytechnic.

Sills, A., Tarpey, M. and Golding, P. (1982) *Asians in the Inner City*, Inner Area Research Project Social Survey, Centre for Mass Communication Research, University of Leicester.

Sivanandan, A. (1976) *Race, Class and the State: The Black Experience in Britain*, London: Institute of Race Relations.

—— (1979) 'Imperialism and Disorganic Development in the Silicon Age', *Race and Class*, xxi: 11–26.

—— (1982) *A Different Hunger*, London: Pluto.

—— (1990) *Communities of Resistance: Writings on Black Struggles for Socialism*, London: Verso.

Smith, A. D. (1991) *National Identity*, Harmondsworth: Penguin.

Smith, D. J. (1974) *Racial Disadvantage in Employment*, London: Political and Economic Planning.

—— (1981) *Unemployment and Racial Minorities*, London: Policy Studies Institute.

Solomos, J. (1989) *Race and Racism in Contemporary Britain*, London: Macmillan.

Sondhi, R. (1987) *Divided Families*, London: Runnymede Trust.

Southall Black Sisters (1989) *Against the Tide*, London: SBS.

Spelman, E. V. (1988) *Inessential Woman: Problems of Exclusion in Feminist Thought*, London: The Women's Press.

Spender, D. (1982) *Invisible Women: The Schooling Scandal*, London: The Women's Press.

Spillers, H. J. (1987) 'Mama's Baby, Papa's May Be: An American Grammar Book', *Diacritics*, Summer 1987.

—— (1989) 'The Permanent Obliquity of an In(pha)llibly Straight: In the Time of the Daughters and Fathers', in C. A. Wall (ed.) *Changing Our Own Words: Essays on Criticism, Theory, and Writing by Black Women*, Rutgers University Press.

Spivak, G. C. (1987) *In Other Worlds: Essays in Cultural Politics*, London: Methuen.

—— (1993) 'Can the Subaltern Speak?', in P. Williams and L. Chrisman (eds) *Colonial Discourse and Postcolonial Theory*, Harvester Wheatsheaf.

—— (1995) 'Supplementing Marxism', in B. Magnus and S. Cullenberg (eds) *Whither Marxism?: Global Crisis in International Perspective*, New York and London: Routledge.

State Research (1981) *State Research Bulletin*, 4(25), London: State Research.

Stone, M. (1981) *The Education of the Black Child: The Myth of Multiracial Education*, London: Fontana.

Street-Porter, R. (1978) 'Race, Children, and Cities', Open University Course E361, *Education and the Urban Environment*, Milton Keynes: Open University Press.

Supplementary Report of the Unofficial Committee of Enquiry (1980) *The Death of Blair Peach* (chaired by Prof. Michael Dummett), London: Council for Civil Liberties.

Swann Report (1985) *Education for All: Report of the Committee of Enquiry into the Education of Children from Ethnic Minority Groups*, Cmnd 9453, London: HMSO.

Tang Main, G. (1990) 'Black women, sexism and racism: black or anti-racist?', *Feminist Review*, 37.

Taussig, M. (1986) *Shamanism, Colonialism, and the Wild Man: A Study in Terror and Healing*, Chicago: Chicago University Press.

Taylor, S. (1979) 'The National Front: anatomy of a political movement', in R. Miles and A. Phizacklea (eds) *Racism and Political Action in Britain*, London: Routledge & Kegan Paul.

Tinker, H. (1977) *The Banyan Tree: Overseas Emigrants from India, Pakistan and Bangladesh*, London: Oxford University Press.

Tizzard, B. and Phoenix, A. (1993) *Black, White, or Mixed Race?: Race and Racism in the Lives of Young People of Mixed Parentage*, London and New York: Routledge.

Tölölian, Khachig (1991) 'The Nation State and its Others: In lieu of a Preface', *Diaspora*, 1(1): 3–7.

Trivedi, P. (1984) 'To deny our fullness: Asian women in the making of history', *Feminist Review*, 17.

Troyna, B. (1982) 'Reporting the National Front: British values observed', in C. Husband (ed.) *'Race' in Britain: Continuity and Change*, London: Hutchinson.

Troyna, B. and Smith, D. I. (eds) (1983) *Racism, School, and the Labour Market*, Leicester: National Youth Bureau .

Troyna, B. and Williams, J. (1986) *Racism, Education and the State*, London: Croom Helm.

Van Den Berghe, P. (1979) *The Ethnic Phenomenon*, New York: Wiley.

Visram, R. (1986) *Ayahs, Lascars and Princes*, London: Pluto Press.

Walby, S. (1990) *Theorizing Patriarchy*, Oxford: Basil Blackwell.

Ware, V. (1992) *Beyond the Pale: White Women, Racism, and History*, London: Verso.

Weedon, C. (1987) *Feminist Practice and Poststructuralist Theory*, Oxford: Basil Blackwell.

Weiner, G. and Arnot, M. (eds) (1987) *Gender Under Scrutiny*, London: Hutchinson.

West, C. (1990) 'The New Cultural Politics of Difference', in R. Ferguson *et al.* (eds) *Out There: Marginalization and Contemporary Cultures*, Cambridge, Mass.: MIT Press.

Westwood, S. (1984) *All Day Every Day,* London: Pluto Press.

Westwood, S. and Bachu, P. (eds) (1989) *Enterprising Women*, London: Routledge.

Williams, F. (1987) *Social Policy: A Critical Introduction*, Cambridge: Polity Press.

Willis, P. (1984) 'Youth Unemployment', *New Society*, 67: 475–77.

Young, K. and Wolkowitz, C. (eds) (1981) *Of Marriage and the Market: Women's Subordination in International Perspective*, London: CSE Books.

Young, R. J. (1990) *White Mythologies: Writing, History, and the West*, London: Routledge.

——(1994) *Colonial Desire: Hybridity in Theory, Culture, and Race*, London: Routledge.

Yuval H. Davis, N. (1994) 'Women, Ethnicity and Empowerment', in K. K. Bhavnani and A. Phoenix (eds) *Shifting Identities, Shifting Racism*, London: Sage.

Yuval-Davis, N. and Anthias, F. (1989) *Women-Nation-State*, Basingstoke: Macmillan.

Yuval-Davis, N. and Saghal, G. (1992) *Refusing Holy Orders*, London: Virago.

Žižek, S. (1995) *Mapping Ideology*, London: Verso.

Zubaida, S. (ed.) (1970) *Race and Racialism,* London: Tavistock Publications.

Index

and labour market in Birmingham
    129–51
Palestinians 86, 182
Palmer, F. 231
Panjab 1, 2
Panjabi cultures 138
Pannel, Norman 23
Papaneck, H. 139
Parker, A. 164
Parmar, P. 70, 80, 108, 136
particuliarity 244–5
Patel, Jaya Ben 8
patriarchal 67, 108–9; Left political
    movements 213
patriarchal discourses/practices 44,
    140, 157, 245
patriarchal power 104, 155
patriarchal racism 69, 72–5
patriarchal relations 4–5, 158, 219;
    neo-Marxist feminism 219
patriarchal values and norms 76,
    143–4, 149
patriarchy 67, 169; critique of concept
    108–9
peace movements 120, 215
Peach, Blair 45
Pearce, Simon 231
Penley, C. 122
people 166
Peoples Unite Education and Creative
    Arts Centre 46
Persian Gulf, crisis in 86–7
Phillips, A. 187
philosophy 219
Phizacklea, A. 128, 134, 147
Phoenix, A. 108, 166, 193
Plamenatz, John 159
pluralism 95, 214, 227
police 44–6, 57, 174, 228; struggles
    against harassment by 8–9, 106
Policy Studies Institute 49, 54
political agency, Muslim women
    149–50
political economy, international 152,
    179
political religious movements 114
politics 67, 219; *see also under
    individual subjects, e.g.* location,
    politics of
Pollert, A. 59, 141
popular culture, East Africa 32

post-industrialism 154
post-structuralism 119, 120, 121, 213,
    214, 223, 225, 245
postcolonial theory 210, 214
postcolonialism 186; Uganda 1–2
postmodernism 214, 223, 224–7
postmodernity 154, 223–7
Poulantzas, N. 217
poverty: Asian 50, 54; East Africa 31;
    global 223; USA 6, 7
Powellism 27, 37, 106, 165, 166
power 125, 176, 179, 227, 241; and
    diasporas 185–6, 189, 197;
    multiaxiality of 16, 181, 189, 197,
    209, 242–3; and subjectivity 93
power dynamics 215, 245
power hierarchies 233; women and 82,
    87, 90
power regimes 3, 155, 156; and
    diaspora 183
power relations 67, 90, 100, 112, 181,
    185, 186, 207–8, 211,
248; and culture 18–20; gender and
    102–4; global 87, 102, 242;
    international 108; and minority
    187, 188, 189; multiculturalism 230,
    233; Muslim women 138, 150
practice 125
Pratt, Minnie Bruce 180, 205–6
Prevention of Terrorism Act 9
primacy 213, 215–20, 246
priority, distinguished from primacy
    246
protest movements 98, 215
psychoanalysis 121–3, 217
psychoanalytic study of culture 235–7
psychology 219
purdah 137, 143, 144, 169

race 95, 156, 164, 165; class and 28–9;
    concept of 154–5; and female
    workplace cultures 59; ideologies of
    73; and immigration control 23, 37,
    172; media and 27; and minorities
    188; young South Asian Muslim
    women and labour market 128–51
Race and Class 97, 173, 174
race relations 23, 218, 220, 224
Race Relations Act 1976 26
Race Relations Board 26
race relations industry 26, 29
Race Today 97